GLOBALIZA
AND THE

NEW REGIONALISM

WITHDRAWN

GLOBALIZATION AND THE NEW REGIONALISM

GLOBAL MARKETS, DOMESTIC POLITICS AND REGIONAL COOPERATION

STEFAN A. SCHIRM

polity

First published in 2002 by Polity Press in association with Blackwell Publishers Ltd

Editorial office:
Polity Press
65 Bridge Street
Cambridge CB2 1UR, UK

Marketing and production:
Blackwell Publishers Ltd
108 Cowley Road
Oxford OX4 1JF, UK

Published in the USA by
Blackwell Publishers Inc.
350 Main Street
Malden, MA 02148, USA

ISBN 0 7456 2969 5
ISBN 0 7456 2970 9 (pb)

A catalogue record for this book is available from the British Library.

Library of Congress Cataloging-in-Publication Data

Schirm, Stefan A., 1963
   Globalization and the new regionalism : global markets, domestic politics and regional co-operation / Stefan A. Schirm.
       p. cm.
   ISBN 0-7456-2969-5 (hb) ISBN 0-7456-2970-9 (pb)
   1. International economic relations. 2. International economic integration. 3. Globalization. I. Title.
   HF1359 .S354 2002
   382'.9 dc21

                                                                    2002001670

Typeset in 10 on 12.5pt Times New Roman
by Kolam Information Services Pvt. Ltd., Pondicherry, India
Printed in Great Britain by T. J. International, Padstow, Cornwall

This book is printed on acid-free paper.

CONTENTS

PREFACE

Starting this project in 1996, I intended to explain the new wave of regional cooperation in Europe and the Americas by using and integrating the different approaches to integration theory. Soon I discovered that neither neofunctionalist institutionalism nor liberal intergovernmentalism was able to explain the analytical 'puzzle' – that is, the timing of the preference for cooperation and the shift in economic strategy towards market liberalization. In looking for a plausible driving force I opted for the most important novel feature of the international economy, the development of global markets. Thus, the theoretical conceptualization and the empirical testing of the impact of globalization on domestic politics became the analytical focus of this book. As a consequence, the global markets approach (GMA) developed here is essentially about the transnational economic sources of national and international political preferences. Therefore, the book is a contribution not only to regional integration studies, but primarily to the debate on the impact of globalization on industrialized as well as newly industrializing countries.

This book was originally written as a post-doc thesis, the German *Habilitation*, at the Faculty for Social Sciences of the University of Munich. I would like to thank Peter J. Opitz for his enduring support. During the conceptual phase of this project I received indispensable intellectual inspiration as a J. F. Kennedy Memorial Fellow at the Center for European Studies at Harvard University in 1995–6. I would like to thank Peter A. Hall, Andrew Moravcsik, Elmar Rieger and Ronald Rogowski for valuable debates and Abby Collins for caring for the foreign scholars at CES. I am indebted to the Deutsche Forschungsgemeinschaft (DFG – German Research Community) for generous financial support in 1997–8. The Institute for International Relations of the Stiftung Wissenschaft und Politik (SWP) provided the infrastructure for this project in 1996–9. I am grateful to my former colleagues for their comments on the work in progress.

The empirical foundation of this book is based on previous research in Argentina, Brazil, Mexico, the USA, France, the UK and Germany throughout the 1990s. In these countries I spoke to numerous experts from government, academia and business, whom I would like to thank for valuable insights. Special thanks go to Jeffrey Kopstein whose comments on contents and style clearly improved this book. None of the above, of course, should be blamed for the result of my research.

Stefan A. Schirm
Munich

ABBREVIATIONS

AFTA	ASEAN Free Trade Association
ALADI	Asociación Latino-Americana de Integración (Latin American Integration Association)
ALALC	Asociación Latino-Americana de Libre Comercio (Latin American Free Trade Association)
ASM	Arbeitsgemeinschaft Soziale Marktwirtschaft
BDA	Bundesvereinigung der Deutschen Arbeitgeberverbände (Federal Association of German Employers)
BDI	Bundesverband der Deutschen Industrie (Federal Association of German Industry)
BID	Banco Interamericano de Desarrollo (Inter-American Development Bank)
BIS	Bank for International Settlements
CAP	Common Agricultural Policy
CBI	Confederation of British Industry
CDU	Christlich Demokratische Union (Christian Democratic Union)
CEI	Centro de Economia Internacional
CEN	Centre Européen de Normalisation (European Norm Organization)
CEPAL	Comisión Economica para America Latina y el Caribe (UN Economic Commission for Latin America)
CES	Center for European Studies
CET	Common External Tariff
CFDT	Confédération Française Démocratique du Travail
CGT	Confédération Générale du Travail

CMC	Consejo del Mercado Común (Council of the Common Market)
COHA	Council on Hemispheric Affairs
CNPF	Conseil National du Patronat Français (French Employers' Association)
CRS	Congressional Research Service
CSU	Christlich Soziale Union (Christian Social Union)
CTM	Confederacion de Trabajadores Mexicanos (Mexican Trade Union Confederation)
CUSFTA	US–Canada Free Trade Agreement
DESEP	Departamento de Estudos Sócio-Econômicos e Políticos da CUT
DFG	Deutsche Forschungsgemeinschaft (German Research Community)
DGB	Deutscher Gewerkschaftsbund (German Association of Trade Unions)
ECU	European Currency Unit
EEA	Einheitliche Europäische Akte
EMS	European Monetary System
EMU	European Monetary Union
EN	European Norms
EP	European Parliament
FDI	foreign direct investment
FDP	Freie Demokratische Partei (Liberal Party)
FGV	Fundaçao Getúlio Vargas
FIEL	Fundación de Investigaciones Económicas Latinoamericanas
FRG	Federal Republic of Germany
FUNCEX	Fundaçao Comercio Exterior
GATT	General Agreement on Tariffs and Trade
GMA	global markets approach
GMC	Grupo Mercado Común (Group of the Common Market)
HWWA	Hamburgisches Welt-Wirtschafts-Archiv
IAD	Inter-American Dialogue
IBRD	International Bank for Reconstruction and Development (World Bank)
IDB	Inter-American Development Bank
IIE	Institute for International Economics
ILAM	Instituto Latino Americano

ILET	Instituto Latinoamericano de Estudios Transnacionales
IMF	International Monetary Fund
IRELA	Instituto de Relaciones Europeo-Latinoamericanas
ISI	import substitution industrialization
ITC	International Trade Commission
KNO	Kritische Nederlandse Ondernemers
LIBOR	London Interbank Offered Rate
MERCOSUL	Mercado Comum do Sul (Common Market of the South: Portuguese)
MERCOSUR	Mercado Común del Sur (Common Market of the South: Spanish)
NAFTA	North American Free Trade Agreement
NIC	newly industrializing country
ODC	Overseas Development Council
OECD	Organization for Economic Cooperation and Development
OPEC	Organization of Petroleum Exporting Countries
PAN	Partido Acción Nacional (Party of National Action)
PICAB	Programma de Integración y Cooperación Argentina–Brasil
PMI	Philip Morris Institute for Public Policy Research
PRD	Partido de la Revolución Democrática (Party of the Democratic Revolution)
PRI	Partido Revolucionario Institucional (Party of the Institutionalized Revolution)
PS	Parti Socialiste (French Socialist Party)
REI	Round Table of European Industrialists
SAM	Secretaría Administrativa del Mercosur (Mercosur's Administrative Secretariat)
SEA	Single European Act
SECOFI	Secretaría de Comercio y Formento Industrial
SELA	Sistema Economico Latinoamericano (Latin American Economic System)
SHCP	Secretaría de Hacienda y Credito Publico
SMP	Single Market Project
SPD	Sozialdemokratische Partei Deutschlands (German Social Democratic Party)
SRE	Secretaría de Relaciones Exteriores
SWP	Stiftung Wissenschaft und Politik

TLC	Tratado de Libre Comercio (NAFTA)
TNC	transnational corporation
TUC	Trades Union Congress
UNCTAD	United Nations Conference on Trade and Development
UNCTC	United Nations Center on Transnational Corporations
UNICE	Union of Industrial and Employers' Confederations in Europe
UNO	United Nations Organization
USIA	US Information Agency
USTR	US Trade Representative
VWD	*Vereinigter Wirtschaftsdienst*
WTO	World Trade Organization

1

EMPIRICAL PUZZLE AND THEORETICAL APPROACH

1.1 Introduction: Relevance and Focus of Research

New treaties on economic cooperation among states at a regional scale have become central features of international relations since the end of the 1980s. European integration was revitalized by the Single European Act (SEA) and the Treaty of Maastricht. The North American Free Trade Agreement (NAFTA) formally established the second-largest economic area in the world. The Common Market of the South (MERCOSUR) symbolizes the end of traditional rivalry and the new attractiveness of free market policies in South America. Other initiatives, like the ASEAN Free Trade Association (AFTA), are still in a nascent stage. These regional economic frameworks increasingly influence political and private actors and structure the process of international relations. Government decision-makers and political scientists assume that policies and economies will increasingly be shaped by regional frameworks. The former French foreign minister Jean François-Poncet sees regional agreements as the 'centers for the political and economic development' of a new world order (Wörl 1994: 21). Peter Katzenstein (1995: 14) observes the emergence of a 'world of regions' and stresses the need for more research on this subject by political scientists. The question that guides this book is a simple one: why do states decide to restrict their freedom of action by signing regional treaties with other states?

Theoretical understanding and empirical analysis of the reasons for these new agreements are important prerequisites for an explanation of regional cooperation. The reasons and motivations behind cooperation are in need of explanation, especially because the recent initiatives represent two fundamental political changes. First, the new regionalism is market and competition oriented. Growth is to be achieved by deregulating and leaving the allocation of production and capital to the market. This strategy represents a distinct change of course for many members of regional agreements and a weakening of formerly dominant models of domestically focused interventionism, such as neo-Keynesianism in Europe and the import substitution industrialization (ISI) in Latin America. Second, recent historical developments and specific circumstances in the 1980s made a resurgence of regionalism appear unlikely: existing cooperation seemed to have either stalled ('Euro-sclerosis') or failed altogether (Latin America, Africa) and the end of the cold war led some observers to expect a new wave of nationalism and conflict, even in Western Europe (Mearsheimer 1990: 5–56). In addition, the globalization of economy and communication made worldwide integration, the 'global village' scenario, seem more plausible than new regionalism. In the light of these developments, the new agreements suggest a puzzle. Why did regional cooperation among states gain new momentum in the 1980s and 1990s? *Which factors led governments to agree on new market-oriented, liberalizing regional cooperation?*

In the pages that follow I specify the empirical 'puzzle' more thoroughly. Which cases of new regionalism are to be considered, and why do they require explanation? Political science offers diverging theories on cooperation. The explanatory power of these theories will be discussed in section 1.2. Given the fact that these approaches fall short of explaining why governments formed a preference for new cooperation, I develop a new approach in section 1.3. I argue that the simultaneous convergence of national preferences for cooperation was stimulated by the influence of global markets on domestic policies and national economies. In the final section of this introductory chapter I discuss methodological questions and the operationalization of the approach for the following case studies (chapters 3, 4 and 5).

Regional cooperation in Europe and the Americas

Since the 1980s initiatives for new cooperation have been introduced in nearly all regions of the world. If one defines regional cooperation as a partial devolution of a member's unilateral capacity to act in specific economic policy areas and towards specific regional partners, however, only a few cases remain: the EC single market of 1992, the Monetary Union envisioned in the Maastricht Treaty, NAFTA and

MERCOSUR.[1] In addition to global trends, the specific regional characteristics, the timing and the strategies pursued also contribute to the unexpected nature of the new regionalism and underscore the empirical puzzle.

In Europe, the completion of the Single Market and the ratification of the Maastricht Treaty raise the question as to why these projects became possible now, although they had been discussed since the 1960s without ever passing the planning stage. The paralysis of European integration in the 1970s, the increasing heterogeneity of national interests following the various enlargements, and the disappearance of the cold war's unifying force did not make the development towards '1992' and Maastricht appear self-evident (Anderson 1995; Rosamond 1995). It is also puzzling that European economic policy turned away from its previous neo-Keynesian paradigm to push through the liberalization of the single market, which weakened government demand management and interventionism and strengthened supply-side liberalism. What caused EC members to depart from existing cooperative regimes and to introduce substantial changes in their economic policies? Why did national interests converge in the 1980s and not before?

With MERCOSUR, the *rapprochement* of its two leading members, Argentina and Brazil, reached an unexpected peak.[2] Until the beginning of the 1980s, relations between these two countries were shaped by their traditional rivalry for dominance on the South American continent. Bilateral trade was practically non-existent. Moreover, attempts at regional integration encompassing all Latin American countries failed in the 1970s and 1980s mainly because of the then dominant protectionist import substitution policies. MERCOSUR adheres to the opposite strategy by trying to promote competitiveness on world markets (Schirm 1997a: 79–112). Since the creation of MERCOSUR in 1991, nearly all the measures for a full customs union have been implemented and intraregional trade has quadrupled. Why did member countries agree on liberal economic rules in MERCOSUR that contradict long-standing development strategies? What stimulated the MERCOSUR states to create a cooperative approach, whose binding character and regulatory scope is second only to European integration?

NAFTA formalizes a North American economic area encompassing Canada, Mexico and the USA.[3] In signing NAFTA, Mexico basically agreed to adapt to the US economic model and merge further into the economy of its larger neighbour. The binding commitments of the agreement were undertaken after decade-long political conflicts between Mexico and the USA and after Mexico's attempts to 'free' itself from economic dependence on the USA (Weintraub 1990: 16ff). In order to join NAFTA, Mexico had to put an end to its traditional development model of ISI and to strengthen the free-market reforms of the 1980s. In this case, as in the others, regional cooperation represents a departure from former traditions and policies and thus raises questions about the causes of change.

1.2   The Weaknesses of Regional Integration Theory

Prior to any discussion of current theories in this area, it should be said that regional integration theory is only partially concerned with the *reasons* for cooperation – in other words, with preferences that lead to cooperation at a specific time. Instead, most theories focus on *how* cooperation works (decision making, institutions) and *which* characteristics it demonstrates (supranational, intergovernmental, regime-specific).[4] In addition, theories concentrate almost exclusively on the *European* case (an exception is Nye 1971/1987). By offering an analysis and a theoretical conceptualization of regional cooperation in Europe *and the Americas*, this book also attempts to overcome eurocentrism. This approach is based on the assumption that social interaction, and therefore international relations, follow generally applicable rules. Powerful theories should be able to explain regional cooperation in Europe and other areas of the world. Thus, it is assumed that European integration is not *per se* a unique case, but can be compared to other examples of regional cooperation (see Mols 1993).

Neofunctionalist institutionalism

Until the theoretical debate on regional integration broke off in the mid-1970s, functionalism (Mitrany 1943/1966), neofunctionalism (Haas 1958) and the various corollary theories (Lindberg and Scheingold 1971; Nye 1971/1987) formed the dominant paradigm. Cooperation occurs where it is functionally efficient – that is, where specific government functions can be exercised more efficiently by means of regional cooperation than by an individual nation. All variations of functionalism focus on explaining how the process of integration, once begun, builds on factors that are inherent in the cooperation itself. It is assumed that cooperation in areas of technical-economic issues necessarily (functionalism) or probably (neofunctionalism) leads to cooperation in new political issue areas through spillover effects. Because different versions of functionalism were unable to explain the de facto development of the EC, even through an inflation of variables (Nye 1971 / 1987), one of functionalism's intellectual fathers, Ernst B. Haas, proclaimed the 'Obsolescence of Regional Integration Theory' (1975). The continued decisiveness of the nation-states' role in determining the progress of integration rather than the functional overcoming of the nation-state shaped the EC, thus weakening the validity of functionalist assumptions.

But recent works on functionalism show that it is relevant in interpreting the effect of regional non-national dynamics on the deepening of cooperation. Common policy areas, supranational institutions (Commission, European Court of Justice, European Parliament) and regional interest groups have been identified as driving forces for recent developments (Pierson 1996; Sandholtz and Zysman 1989). 'New institutionalism' follows the functionalist tradition of assuming that common regional institutions decisively influence the integration process. As Pierson (1996) argues, institutions shape member states' expectations and possess a certain independence in specific situations (on institutionalism, see Keohane 1989). According to this line of thought, European integration can be explained primarily by the influence of the European Court of Justice and the Commission. The latter acts as a supranational political *entrepreneur*, which conducts regional policies in its own ('European') interest while enjoying relative autonomy from member states.

But neofunctionalist institutionalism does not suffice to explain regional cooperation in the 1980s and 1990s. First, it cannot explain the central role of the nation-states in the creation of the new regionalism. Second, while the EC Commission may have played an important part in the formation of the single market, NAFTA and MERCOSUR cannot be traced back to the activities of a supranational institution because no comparable institutions existed in those cases. In the European case, the Commission served as a catalyst rather than a cause (Moravcsik 1991: 66ff; Cameron 1992: 51ff). Most importantly, neofunctional institutionalism cannot explain why the Commission was possibly able to promote cooperation in the mid-1980s but not in the previous decades, and why integration was suddenly accompanied by a liberalizing and deregulative economic strategy. Finally, the hypothesis of 'functional efficiency' as a driving force for cooperation offers only a theoretical scaffold without specifying those factors that could make functional efficiency a necessary or viable force. Which developments led a liberalizing regional cooperation to be perceived as 'functionally efficient' in the 1980s?

Neorealist liberal intergovernmentalism

The functional-institutionalist approach has been criticized since the 1960s with arguments drawn from a general theory of international relations, neorealism. This gave rise to a second school of thought on regional cooperation. It focused on the continuing centrality of the nation-state to the integration process in Europe. Starting with the dominant role of the member states, which became obvious in the EC crisis of the 1960s, this school argued that national activities, more than other factors, initiate and shape cooperation (S. Hoffmann 1966). The convergence or divergence of national interests was held to be the decisive factor for the progress or paralysis of cooperation. According to the neorealist paradigm, states are the decisive *driving force* in international relations and act as power-seekers in line with their national interests (primarily security interests) in an anarchic international system, in which non-state actors, domestic politics, international organizations and economic issues matter only at a secondary level. Sovereign nation-states 'decide' on regional cooperation when their 'national interests' prove to be compatible (on neorealism, see Keohane 1986).

In the 1970s, this view of nation-states in international relations was critically modified by adding the concept of interdependence among states and by introducing non-state actors and international interconnectedness as central elements of international relations (Keohane and Nye 1977). The interdependence of states, together with the assumption of their basic willingness to cooperate, is an underlying feature of the concept of 'international regimes' for regulating specific policy issues (Rittberger 1993). Transferred to regional cooperation, this view explains cooperation as a function of management requirements between states. Regional cooperation is thus considered an 'intergovernmental regime designed to manage economic interdependence' (Moravcsik 1993: 474).

While the traditional literature on interdependence and regimes took 'national interests' largely as given, recent works have propagated more differentiated views. In publications *inter alia* by Evans et al.

(1993), Moravcsik (1991, 1993), Sorensen (1995) and Zürn (1993), domestic politics (societal coalitions, political institutions, etc.) are used to explain governments' foreign policy behaviour. It is assumed that regional cooperation is a consequence of domestic coalition building and the desire of governments to strengthen their power vis-à-vis domestic interest groups (Moravcsik 1993: 485). Governments' international actions are seen as a reaction to endogenous influences – as instruments that either accede to or resist domestic pressures. National interests are thus delineated in accordance with domestic policy requirements and subsequently introduced into the intergovernmental bargaining process at a regional level (e.g. the EC Council). According to neorealist assumptions, this bargaining process then reflects the distribution of national power (Moravcsik 1991: 75). State sovereignty is therefore not weakened. Instead it is conjoined in order to establish regional regulations through a 'pooling of sovereignty' (Keohane and Hoffmann 1990: 277).

The neorealist-intergovernmental approach, expanded by the dimension of domestic politics and thus 'liberal'-intergovernmental, is considered the dominant explanatory model for the study of the European Union by some authors (Rosamond 1995: 396). Nonetheless, it would be problematic to use this approach because it cannot adequately explain the empirical developments. Why did domestic coalitions and national governments favour cooperation in the 1980s and 1990s but not before? Moreover, this line of thought does not explain why new cooperative moves were undertaken with liberal economic strategies, thus changing longstanding economic policy paradigms. The formation of 'national interests' occurs in an analytical vacuum: there are explanations of *how* interests are articulated and shape foreign policy behaviour, but none of *why* interests emerge and *which* interests succeed in becoming driving forces. For example, Moravcsik (1991: 42, 67) mentions the 'convergence of the economic policy prescriptions' in the major EC countries as an 'essential precondition' for the Single Market Project (SMP), but does not sufficiently investigate whether there is a common explanatory factor for this simultaneous convergence of national preferences, for the dominance of neoliberal domestic coalitions and the 'failure' (Moravcsik 1991: 73) of neo-Keynesian politics. The frequent reference to 'interdependence' (Moravcsik 1993: 474) as a reason for cooperation is a static description of a certain situation that does not delineate clear causalities. The neorealist, 'liberal' intergovernmental approach thus fails to offer a full explanation of the simultaneous preference for cooperation in several states. If government preferences are shaped by domestic coalitions, what led domestic interests to develop in a way that stimulated governments to favour liberalizing regional cooperation in the 1980s?

The gap in research   The conclusion of this short analysis of regional integration theories is that, while they do explain how convergent interests can induce cooperation (through 'functional efficiency', 'institutional dynamics', 'domestic coalitions' and 'intergovernmental bargains'), their explanation for the causes of convergence is insufficient.

   Which specific driving forces encourage the perception of regional cooperation as a desirable option to further 'functional efficiency' and 'national interests'? The research community agrees on the decisive role of liberal economic reforms in major EC countries in the mid-1980s for the decision on the SMP (Keohane and Hoffmann 1991: 24; Moravcsik 1991: 42, 67). However, the question of whether there is a factor that brought about the alignment of national preferences around liberalizing reforms and for the functional efficiency of regional cooperation has not been investigated. What remains to be explained, therefore, is the simultaneous convergence of national preferences for new cooperation in liberalizing markets and enhancing global competitiveness.

The global economic context as a complementary factor

The target of the new agreements and their liberalizing strategies offer a possible explanation: the agreements were created specifically in order to enhance their members' competitiveness on the world market. This global economic context is neglected by both liberal intergovernmentalism and neofunctional institutionalism. Neither approach has taken account of the fact that globalization has dramatically increased the transborder mobility of economic factors, thus modifying states' power to shape policy. Owing to the increase in private actors' transborder activities, developments in the domestic economy can be influenced more easily by transnational processes. This has lowered the efficiency of governments' ability to regulate the domestic economy because governmental outreach is territorial in scope. However, if economic interaction increasingly transcends state structures and relies to a growing extent on transnational private networks, then those theories that focus on national and supranational 'statehood' reflect a diminishing proportion of the government's decision-making environment and thus of the causes of government preferences. Therefore, any explanation of government action must take into account the transnational, non-state environment in which decisions on regional cooperation are made. Since cooperation was conceived as an instrument to enhance competitiveness on the world market, we can presume that the global economy was a driving force.

Such a supposition also seems plausible when considering the specific developments in the regions at stake here. In the case of regional cooperation in the Americas, focusing on states and domestic politics seems insufficient given the thorough integration of Mexico, Brazil and Argentina into the world economy. This became obvious during the debt crisis of the 1980s and in view of the dominance of foreign direct investment (FDI) in industrialization (Schirm 1990: 74–99). Moreover, NAFTA and MERCOSUR were explicitly created as 'springboards to the world market' (Schirm 1997a: 52, 83).

Europe's SMP was a product of the fear that Europe was falling behind in global competition and therefore reflects the expectation that a better position in the global economy could be achieved through cooperation (Checchini 1988: xix; Keohane and Hoffmann 1991: 22ff). As Zürn (1995: 159) has pointed out, with regard to Western Europe, intergovernmental approaches and neorealist structuralism have to be augmented. Because of the increasing permeability of territory, the erosion of sovereignty and the denationalization of the economy, the analytical focus on domestic politics is increasingly inadequate as the separation of 'internal' and 'external' becomes more difficult to sustain. Analysing 'domestic politics', regional institutions and intergovernmental bargains without including the global economy weakens the explanatory power of these theoretical approaches. Although they mention international interconnectedness, they fail to answer the question: *which* developments have *what* repercussions on government preferences?

Furthermore, we need an explanation of why the participating governments developed new preferences for cooperation *simultaneously*. Causal factors that could have provoked a simultaneous and strategically convergent formation of interests need to be identified. Such causal links must be valid for all the states involved and therefore need to reach beyond single states and regions. The global context meets these criteria.

1.3   The Global Markets Approach in Explaining Cooperation

In the following, I will conceptualize the global economic context in order to explain specific cases of regional cooperation. The approach does not invalidate existing theories; it complements and encompasses them. The aim is to explain national governments' preferences for new liberalizing and world-market-oriented cooperation in Europe and the Americas.

   For this purpose, I am developing a new approach, which will attempt to explain these preferences as a function of the influence of global economic actors and processes on national economies and economic policies. The first part formulates two hypotheses on the cross-section 'global context–governmental preferences–regional co-operation'. The second step provides an empirical and theoretical foundation of the first hypothesis on the impact of global markets on states. The third part offers a foundation of the second hypothesis on why governments perceive regional cooperation as an adequate answer to the impact of global markets. Finally, I discuss the extent of the new approach's applicability.

Hypotheses

In accordance with the theories discussed previously, the following assumptions are taken as a point of departure: regional cooperation results from new challenges, which governments believe can be better met by means of new regional regulations than by adhering to present national or regional strategies. Such new challenges make regional cooperation seem 'functionally efficient' and compatible with the 'national interest'. By engaging in new regional cooperation, states create or strengthen a policy domain in which they receive new instruments for dealing with specific actors, situations and processes. The attractiveness of a common regional capacity to act is due to the inadequacy – or the perceived inadequacy – of purely national means to face new challenges. Thus, it is necessary to discover which new challenges increased the benefits of new (or further) cooperation to such a degree that participating governments developed a preference for cooperation. Therefore, the premise is that regional cooperation gains attractiveness if several governments see themselves exposed to new challenges that they believe can be better met by a regional approach than by national strategies.

Hypothesis I: the impact of global markets on states   Challenges that meet the criteria of the premise have to influence a group of states at the same time in order to explain *simultaneous* government preferences for cooperation. In addition, national means must be less efficient than regional policies in dealing with these challenges. Alternatively, the challenges may overwhelm or weaken national policy instruments. Developments with these characteristics have to transcend national structures and affect several states, in this case several continents (Europe, North and South America) at the same time. These criteria are fulfilled by *global* processes. As the purpose is to explain economic cooperation among states, this study will focus on the global economic phenomena identified in the previous section and subsumed here under the term 'global markets'.

Although I have referred to the term 'globalization' in earlier works (Schirm 1996, 1997b), I will refrain from doing so here because the term's varying definitions in the academic literature increase the probability of misunderstandings (see Germann et al. 1996: 18ff; Schirm 1999a: 24). In addition, the term 'globalization' is increasingly used as a tool for special interests in the public debate. The term 'global markets' is more precise because it is restricted to the economic dimension. Most importantly, it provides the definitional distinction between 'market' and 'state' necessary for any theoretical conceptualization of the interaction between the two. Global markets function in accordance with the logic of profit maximization of private, transnational and potentially globally operating actors. Therefore, global markets are clearly distinguishable from the allocation of public goods as undertaken by governments, which are restricted by the confines of the nation-state and aim in principle at the common weal.

The development of 'global markets' is characterized by the increasing cross-border mobility and connectedness of private economic activities. This integration of markets can influence several states simultaneously. While private entities such as markets and actors can be present in a multitude of states, governments remain restricted to 'their' nation-states with regard to their governing capacity. Global markets are shaped by interactions that transcend the boundaries of nations and are not determined by single national frontiers, norms and interests. Therefore, functions and character of global markets clearly differ from those of the state and its government, which are determined by territoriality, sovereignty and community interests.[5]

The following supposition derives from these conceptualizations and definitions: governments find themselves restricted in their autonomy to act[6] and pressured to adapt to the logic of the global economy according to their national economy's level of integration into global markets. To that degree (i.e. the extent of trade, loans, investment), the costs of a policy that does not take the profit expectations of transnational economic actors into account will rise. The decisive cost factors are both the increased mobility, which facilitates the withdrawal of resources by private actors, and the potentially global possibilities for investment, which permits private actors to direct their resources to those locations that offer the most promising conditions for profits. At the same time, increased mobility and the potential for global investment also imply higher incentives for governments to adjust to the expectations of global markets. These incentives take the form of a potential influx of resources to the locations with the most attractive conditions.

For a government's policy to be considered attractive by global markets, it must accommodate this increase in factor mobility by pursuing economic liberalization and entice potentially global resources by increasing the profitability of the national location for global actors, for example, by enhancing free market conditions and implementing supply-side and employer-friendly measures. In this regard, global markets imply a deterritorialization and denationalization of economic activity because their operational logic transcends the functional logic of states. As global markets grow in importance, as they have since the 1970s, they exert pressure on states to align their policies increasingly with the competition-driven logic of transnational private activities (Schmidt 1995; Strange 1996: 3–43).

In the light of the fact that, in the decades prior to the liberalizing regional treaties, economic policies in Europe (neo-Keynesianism) and Latin America (import substitution) were mostly domestically oriented and tended to be interventionist, global markets appear to have the following effects.

1 *Crises*. Inward-looking interventionist policies presumably reach a crisis because they do not take the increasing relevance of global markets' expectations and mechanisms into account. In addition, these policies are based on the states' ability to govern the na-

tional economy – an ability that declines with the denationalization of private economic activities.

2 *Interests.* A shift in the interests of important groups in domestic politics becomes plausible given that the increasing integration of economic sectors into global markets weakens their orientation towards the national arena and strengthens their involvement in competition at the global level.

3 *Instruments.* The denationalization of economic interaction following the integration of national into global markets presumably restricts the efficiency of governmental instruments because transnational activities cannot be influenced as effectively by the state as national activities.

In sum, I suppose that governments develop a preference for world market-oriented liberalization as a result of the impact of global markets. *Hypothesis I: if global markets influence several states by triggering a crisis of inward-looking interventionist policy, by strengthening transnational interest groups, and by weakening the governments' regulatory instruments, then a simultaneous preference for liberal, global competitiveness-enhancing policies will be stimulated.*

Hypothesis II: on the attractiveness of regional cooperation as an answer to the impact of global markets on states   Under which conditions would liberalizing regional cooperation be an adequate means of adjustment to the impact of global markets? As regional economic cooperation falls into the realm of economic policy, we can presume that the basic government task involved is 'wealth' (and not 'security'). The support of a majority of voters and therefore the maintenance of power for governments vitally depends on their economic performance. If the impact of global markets reduces the efficiency of previous policies in providing economic goods, then new instruments allowing for an efficient adjustment to these influences become attractive. To put it differently, if the increasing integration of a national economy into global markets makes the inward-looking interventionist pursuit of growth and wealth unviable or costly and stimulates liberalizing reforms, then instruments that permit the efficient implementation of these reforms will be given priority.

Governments presumably perceive regional cooperation to be a better option than purely national strategies on both the economic and the political level.

1   *Economic efficiency.* The economic impact of liberalizing reforms
    can be enhanced by the economy of scale, the specialization and
    the competition effects of a regional market or a free trade area.
2   *Political acceptability.* The implementation of reforms can be im-
    proved by anchoring the new political approach in a regional
    framework. Regarding domestic opposition, the government will
    gain additional leverage because its new economic course will no
    longer be solely a matter of national responsibility but will be
    part of a binding multilateral commitment.

Therefore, I presume that regional cooperation will offer governments
an attractive instrument for reacting to the challenges of global
markets in a way that is more economically efficient and easier to
implement politically than a purely national approach could have
been. These considerations lead directly to *Hypothesis II*: *regional cooperation gains attractiveness to the degree that it offers a means for an
economically more efficient and politically more acceptable adjustment to
global markets and competitiveness, giving governments a better chance
of staying in power as a result of enhanced economic performance.*

In suggesting 'global markets' as an explanatory approach, I have
chosen a factor that is widely neglected by existing theories but that
does not contradict them. I maintain that regional cooperation is
stimulated indirectly by global markets through a shift in national
interests, domestic coalitions, international interdependence, functional efficiency and supranational institutional dynamics.[7] This
book will attempt to meet Müller's and Risse-Kappen's claim for an
approach that 'incorporates the three levels of analysis – society,
political system, and international relations' (Müller and Risse-Kappen 1990: 379). By cooperating on a regional level, the state does lose
autonomy vis-à-vis its partners (other states), but it hopes to gain
new instruments for dealing with new domestic and transnational
pressures, which derive from the influence of global markets. Therefore, the approach chosen complements existing theories in so far as
it focuses on the relationship between governments' strategic options
and transnational developments. As the latter change states' economic capacities, regional cooperation offers an option not attainable
by any individual state.

Actors in global markets operate transnationally and follow private
economic interests. They are not determined by any *specific* national
context (interests, norms, territory) and therefore differ from state

actors.[8] This applies to transnational firms and banks as well as to the world financial system, to the worldwide division of labour, trade and investment. The 'global markets approach' (GMA) also resembles the transnationalism debate, which has recently experienced a revival (Kaiser 1969; Keohane and Nye 1972; Risse-Kappen 1995). Where it differs, however, is that global markets are not identical with 'transnational actors'. The latter can also be non-economic in nature (e.g. Greenpeace) and be transnational even if they cross only *one* border. Global markets (and transnational actors as defined here) are distinguished by their profit-seeking interest and by their potentially – and increasingly – global reach.[9] The argument that global integration changes national policy options might at first resemble the 'management of international interdependence', but on further consideration goes beyond this. While 'interdependence' denotes interconnectedness *among states* and their mutual vulnerability, this book's central focus is on the interconnectedness *between states and global markets*. The decisive question is not how interdependent states influence each other, but what impact global markets have on government actions and preferences.

On the impact of global markets on states (Hypothesis I)

The explanatory factor 'global markets' is defined as the process of increasing integration of markets and economies, driven by the competition-oriented interaction of private actors in the interest of enhanced competitiveness, by growing factor mobility and shrinking transaction costs (Dunning 1990: 9–58; Germann et al. 1996: 18–55). This interaction differs from international relations because its *modus operandi* is not determined by specific national interests and frontiers. The allocation of resources is driven primarily by the logic of the market and not by politics. Obviously, this is an analytical distinction. To avoid the impression of simplification and reductionism, three caveats must be made.

1 The question of the impact of global markets on states should not lead to the conclusion that states do not influence the world economy. States and global markets mutually influence each other. Without the liberalizing policies of nation-states, global markets would not have emerged (Wade 1996). The impact of markets *on*

    states is the focus of this work because the purpose is to explain government preferences. I do not argue here that states are powerless against global markets, or that regionalism will inevitably occur, as Ohmae (1995) suggests.

2   The development of global markets is – historically speaking – not a new phenomenon. The transborder integration of production and capital flows was very strong at the end of the nineteenth century (Hirst and Thompson 1996: 2). This era of openness lasted until the 1910s. Possible parallels to historical developments, however, are not at stake here. The decisive question in explaining regional cooperation in the 1980s and 1990s is whether global markets gained importance after the 1970s in comparison to the preceding decades (1920s–1960s).

3   The term 'global' does not imply that economic transactions are *predominantly* global. It indicates only that the share of cross-border activities is *increasing* in proportion to global output (measured as the sum of the gross domestic products). 'Global' actors do not necessarily operate in every country or worldwide. Rather, their activities are in the process of global expansion and extension to a growing number of countries. Global markets are characterized by their ability *potentially* to extend to any country, if the respective government offers attractive conditions. States are integrated into global markets to very different degrees. Some are not integrated at all – like most African states.

    Since the 1970s, the relevance of global markets has grown in the areas of production, finance and trade, driven by liberalization, global communication networks, better transportation and the worldwide proliferation of technology. The decisive point is not whether these phenomena are totally new, but whether the transnationally produced portion of GNPs has grown compared to purely domestic production.[10] Because of this progressive development, the tendency towards denationalization of economic activity was strengthened. Entrepreneurial concepts, such as 'strategic alliances', 'private global players' and 'global sourcing', indicate that private actors' activities are increasingly organized according to the opportunities of global planning, competition and allocation of resources (Kohler-Koch 1996: 87).

    Even though production and services are still generated predominantly within national boundaries, the state is losing regulatory capacity because of the relative growth of transborder trade and division of labour (Gereffi 1995: 100–20; Hirst and Thompson 1996: 18–98). Increasingly, the production of goods and components is undertaken wherever the most competitive conditions are offered in global comparison. These conditions include the attractiveness of local markets and – depending on the good at stake – productive factors, such as levels of education, wages and taxation, environmental protection measures and access to technology and capital (Bernard 1994: 216–29; Junne 1996: 516). While companies compete on the world market via their products, states compete with one another as locations for the activities of transnational and potentially global producers, investors and technology developers. Thus, the pressure to dismantle inward-looking interventionist policies mounts, because of the need to establish attractive and competitive conditions for globally mobile economic activities.

Those states that provide the best locational advantages will, in principle, benefit most from investment, credit and technology flows. The internationalization of economic activity, intra-firm trade, the deregulation and liberalization in industrialized countries, especially in the USA and the UK in the 1970s and 1980s, increased the worldwide competition in attracting investment, which has stimulated other states to improve conditions by permanently lowering restrictions and controls. Government authority over economic developments is reduced not only by this competition among states but also by transnational corporations (TNCs), which increasingly exert a 'parallel authority' over the allocation of resources (Strange 1996: 65).

As a result, states are less autonomous in determining their economic policy on the basis of purely domestic considerations without high opportunity costs if they wish to participate in the growing dynamics of the global economy. Therefore, the impact of global markets on states does not imply a weakening of the state *per se*, but rather a modification of the cost–benefit relationship of specific government policies. The costs of policies that do not take the functional logic of global markets into account rise owing to the higher mobility of an increasing proportion of economic factors. At the same time, the benefits of market liberalization rise because this stimulates an influx of resources. Link (1997: 270) argues, therefore, that 'globalization' does not cause the state to wither away but rather ties government decisions more strongly to the conditions of global markets.

The restriction of government autonomy by the costs and benefits of global markets and global locational competition was to a large

extent a result of the expansion of financial markets, which was triggered by the demise of the Bretton Woods System at the beginning of
the 1970s and by subsequent national liberalization. Deregulation, the
rapid growth of financial activities and the increasing interconnectedness of transnational banks through equity swaps and telecommunications led to the emergence of global financial markets, which can
hardly be reregulated by individual states (Helleiner 1994: 101–91).
Every year global financial markets trade amounts that exceed the
value of world trade a hundredfold. These financial flows influence
currency exchange rates (and thereby exports and imports) as well as
national interest rates and inflation levels and thus affect the ability of
governments to stimulate wealth and growth (see chapter 2). Global
markets also affect the efficiency of specific instruments for domestic
economic policy (Cable 1995; Milner and Keohane 1996b: 247–9). For
example, the internationalization of capital markets lowers the impact
of central banks' monetary and currency policies, while in many countries the increasing role of foreign trade leads to the weakening of neo-
Keynesian demand management through import leakages. One-third
of world trade by the 1990s was intra-firm trade (*The Economist*, 7
Dec. 1996: 25), which is difficult for customs and tax authorities to
oversee. The proliferation of subsidiaries and transborder alliances
has created more actors, which operate on several territories and are
thus less controllable by the 'sovereign authority' of *one* territory.

This transnationalization of world trade and stronger competition
leads world-market-oriented domestic groups to pressure their governments for economic policies that would enhance their access to and
competitiveness on world markets – for example, through selective
trade liberalization and monetary stability (Busch and Milner 1994;
Rogowski 1989). Frieden and Rogowski (1996: 26) argue that the development of global markets increases the cost of non-participation
in the global economy (e.g. higher prices, lower productivity and competitiveness) because of the 'exogenous easing of international exchange'. This implies first a loss of wealth in the case of non-
participation and, second, interest-group pressure on the government
to establish competitive conditions by deregulating and opening up the
economy (Frieden and Rogowski 1996: 35). On the other hand, those
domestic groups that are negatively affected will demand protection
from or a slower adjustment to global markets. Therefore, govern-

ments see themselves exposed to new challenges regarding policy instruments and political legitimacy in securing growth and wealth.

Together, these developments stimulate states to adjust to the challenges of global markets by liberalizing and opening up to the world economy because global markets weaken governments' ability to attain a positive economic performance using inward-looking interventionist measures (Biersteker 1992: 113). Wessels argues that citizens in modern industrialized states tend to hold the government responsible for their well-being. In order to meet this demand, the state has to open up the economy to stimulate growth and competition. However, this opening creates a dilemma because, owing to the heightened impact of external forces, the state can no longer compensate for the negative social effects of liberalization by traditional national dirigisme. Therefore, governments tend to seek joint governing capacity on the regional level (Wessels 1992: 42ff). The political liability of governments for the well-being of their citizens is characteristic of all political systems, and the more participatory they are in structure, the stronger this liability is.

In summary, the conceptual and empirical foundation of the hypothesis on the impact of global markets on states (Hypothesis 1) leads to the following conclusion. We can presume that global markets put pressure on states to enhance their attractiveness as economic locations via liberalizing reforms. The discussed effects of global markets can be categorized according to the three pathways introduced previously:

1   *Crises*. Global markets react to the locational disadvantages of inward-looking interventionist measures by withdrawing or withholding capital and production and thus provoke the crisis of such policies.
2   *Interests*. World-market-oriented groups are strengthened by the increasing transnational share in national economies and the exogenous easing of global exchange.
3   *Instruments*. The efficacy of political instruments that are necessary for inward-looking interventionism is weakened.

Why do groups of states develop a preference for a liberalizing regional cooperation as an answer to the impact of global markets?

On regional cooperation as an answer to global markets (Hypothesis II)

The connection between global markets, government preferences and regional cooperation should not be seen as functioning mechanically. States do not have to cooperate regionally. Rather, the costs and benefits of policy options are modified by global markets that produce specific pressures on states and stimulate their preference for regional agreements. The central impact of global markets is the increased competition for trade shares, production locations, stock market capital and investment. The adjustment to this competition requires governments to reorient their sets of regulations, for example, towards more deregulation and opening-up. The argument is that regional cooperation of a *liberalizing, market-oriented type* offers better instruments and leverage than purely national strategies: the adjustments are economically more efficient and politically better acceptable when undertaken in cooperation.

In liberal[11] free trade areas, customs unions and common markets, restrictions on economic activity are lowered, and thus efficiency and specialization gains as well as economies of scale and division of labour effects can be achieved. These benefits also provide new impulses for growth and higher competitiveness outside the region on world markets.[12] The reduction or elimination of national barriers increases the mobility of productive factors and makes a more efficient allocation of these resources possible. The European single market, for example, is working towards the unrestricted mobility of goods, services, capital and labour among the member countries, its 'Four Freedoms'. Thus, the process of the global integration of markets is met by an even deeper integration on the regional scale through a cooperation among states. Because of the enlargement of national markets, larger amounts of goods can be produced by a specific company, which makes capital-intensive production more cost efficient and reduces the price level because the costs per unit decrease and the profit margin per unit becomes less relevant.

Stronger competition in larger markets leads to a more efficient allocation of resources and thus to more specialization and division of labour. Economic cooperation also lowers transaction costs (customs, different norms, etc.) and enhances comparative and competitive advantages over competitors in world markets. Only a worldwide free trade area, a global common market, would have even greater efficiency gains.[13] Through the reduction of barriers and regulations on the regional level, the member states increase the competitiveness of their economies and their chances to benefit from global economic dynamism (Streeck 1996: 306).

Compared to the economically sensible option of a unilateral lowering of barriers, the members of a regional association gain 'politically' from the relative discrimination of third parties that do not benefit from regional free trade, a common external tariff, harmonization or mutual recognition of norms. Therefore, regional cooperation has three functions: it strengthens the competitiveness of its members (1) on the regional market and (2) on world markets, and (3) it discriminates against those competitors from third countries whose comparative advantage could provoke politically unsustainable costs (Junne 1996: 517–19). Regional cooperation offers a custom tailored mix of economically and politically viable measures. According to the political weight of those groups interested in higher world competitiveness or in protection from world markets, regional cooperation can be conceived as globally open or only regionally open. Given the costs of protection (reduced competitiveness, etc.), the mixture of both variations will – among other aspects – be influenced by the dependence of the respective region on world markets.

Besides strengthening their competitiveness, the members create a common regulatory capacity, which can prevent unfair trade, beggar-thy-neighbour policies (e.g. via currency devaluations) and market distortions by different national regulations. The binding agreement on common rules of the game (customs, norms, taxes) reduces interventionist competition among member states and enhances the attractiveness of the region for investors by the increased market size and the stability of multilaterally secured investment and production conditions. In addition, regional cooperation allows for a restriction of transnational activities in certain areas and thus the reduction of their impact on the state. This applies, for example, to the elimination of currency-related trade and speculation through a monetary union with a common currency. Furthermore, regional cooperation can increase the bargaining power of the members vis-à-vis third actors (investors, states) without reducing government power *per se*. Rather, it is modified and transferred partially to the regional level. Regional cooperation in the sense of joint policy-making complements national policy. In addition, the region's influence on transnational actors and international organizations (e.g. GATT / WTO) can be strengthened if it acts from a joint position or with pooled resources.

The enhancement of the political acceptability and implementability of market liberalization follows from the possibility of legitimizing the adjustments to global markets as regional treaty obligations, by arguing that external obligations and the necessity of reaching a regional consensus do not permit the pursuit of purely national goals (Petersmann 1994: 41). In order to 'protect' themselves from demands of domestic opponents of liberalization, governments can 'tie their hands' by means of regional commitments and thus better resist protectionist pressures. Regarding the political costs of the liberalizing reforms (voter dissatisfaction owing to job losses, elimination of subsidies, etc.), regional cooperation offers instruments not attainable at the national level. The options for shifting responsibility reach from regional-level decisions with 'common' responsibility to the establishment of joint institutions (such as the European Commission and Court of Justice), for whose activities national governments are only indirectly accountable. The 'freedom' of national governments from political responsibility can be expanded if the regional commitments are justified on the basis of the coercive power of world market pressures.

The transfer of regulatory power to the regional level without the creation of respective mechanisms for democratic control constitutes an additional instrument with which governments can enlarge their room for manœuvre against domestic opposition (Moravcsik 1993; Rieger 1995: 351ff; Scharpf 1996: 15–25). A *binding* regional definition of government functions and economic rules gives national governments (1) the opportunity to attain greater autonomy from domestic groups by delegating responsibilities, and (2) the possibility of claiming external commitments when legitimizing their policies.

According to Scharpf (1991: 624), political science should not only explain but also judge. Thus, one criticism of regional cooperation is that it can have a negative effect if it leads to an erosion of governments' democratic accountability and to less societal participation. However, it is equally possible that it will have a positive effect by enhancing governments' capacity to stimulate growth and wealth. The ideal would, of course, be a participatory (i.e. encompassing as many segments of society as possible) improvement in the securing of welfare effects. This book concentrates on explaining the causal relationships.

In summary, the empirical and conceptual foundation of the hypothesis on the function of regional cooperation as an answer to the impact of global markets (Hypothesis II) yields two advantages of the regional option over that of individual nations.

1 *Economic efficiency.* A greater improvement of national economies' competitiveness as locations for production, investment
   and innovation can be reached by means of a liberalizing regional
   cooperation – the enlargement of markets, stronger competition,
   specialization and efficiency gains.
2 *Political acceptability.* Through regional cooperation, governments can obtain new possibilities of shifting responsibility for the
   costs of the liberalizing reforms. Its autonomy from domestic pressure groups increases through regionally self-imposed constraints.
   The acceptance and implementation of reforms are enhanced.

Therefore, governments' preference for new or renewed regional cooperation is stimulated to the degree that the cooperation offers an
instrument for realizing an economically more efficient and politically
better implementable adjustment to global markets through liberalizing reforms.

The strengths and weaknesses of the global markets approach (GMA)

The argument outlined here complements integration theories in the
effort to explain why states developed a preference for a liberalizing
regional cooperation in the 1980s and 1990s. The analysis in chapters
3, 4 and 5 will show to what extent this approach is empirically relevant and able to explain the cases. Conceptualizing the impact of
global markets identifies a specific factor in governments' decision-
making environment, which may cause 'functional efficiency' and
'national interest formation' to favour cooperation. The single most
important effect that global markets have on the policy options of
governments is increased global integration, which undermines
inward-looking interventionist models, changes interests and con-
strains government instruments. Thus, states are pressured to adjust
to the logic of global markets if they wish to benefit from global
economic dynamics.

   Since the approach concentrates on a specific driving force for economic policy and international cooperation, it does not claim to explain regional cooperation *per se* (as do the theories discussed earlier).
Economic cooperation in other decades (e.g. in the 1950s and 1960s),
as well as regional cooperation in foreign policy and security matters,
is subject to different causal relations (see Schirm 1998). But even

with regard to the new initiatives for economic cooperation in Europe and the Americas, the GMA attempts to explain only the simultaneous emergence of preferences for liberalizing, world-market-oriented cooperation. The approach does not deal with the question of how parallel interests translate into successful intergovernmental negotiations if distributive conflicts and imbalances of power have to be overcome.[14] Therefore, the hypotheses of this work do not claim to explicate the different levels of cooperation in the various agreements. The differences in the depth of integration between the European Single Market Project, NAFTA and MERCOSUR might be explained by other causes than 'global markets' (Grieco 1994).

Moreover, the approach explains neither the interaction of intergovernmental activities and supranational institutions, nor the domestic distribution of the benefits of liberalization and growth. While liberalizing cooperation can be an adequate answer to the pressures of global markets, it is not necessarily the best strategy for every citizen of a given country. Indeed, there are usually losers. Moreover, more competitive conditions for transnational companies cannot be equated with the governments' task to secure 'the common weal'. But higher growth rates can improve the preconditions for a socially more balanced distribution of economic resources.[15] Obviously, deeper socioeconomic disparities may occur if growth and efficiency gains are not subject to distributive considerations.

The GMA to the *reasons* for preferences predicts that governments' preferences for a liberalizing cooperation will endure as long as the pressures of global markets persist.

Why did global markets not lead to binding regional cooperation in other regions, which are also integrated into the global economy? Testing the hypotheses on the Asian case, where no substantially binding cooperation was agreed upon, reveals some caveats to the explanatory power of the GMA (Schirm 1997b: 95–8):

- if the impact of global markets does not create pressures for economic reforms because a *competitive world market orientation* is already dominant;
- if global markets do not stimulate a regional enlargement of national markets because high growth rates are given;
- if the present market size as well as the *participation in global capital and trade flows is perceived as sufficient*; or
- if strong historical resentments or the danger of *new power asymmetries* exist,

then a binding cooperation due to global markets is *not* to be expected. Other forms of cooperation or no cooperation at all will be more likely.

1.4   Methodology and the Empirical Plausibility of the Hypotheses

How can the hypotheses and causal relations of the GMA be made empirically plausible? Two basic methodological directions seem viable and are to be discussed below.

Quantitative flows and political preferences

One way of testing the hypotheses is to measure the data on the integration of national economies with global markets. First, did the degree of integration rise? Second, did a closer integration create problems for inward-looking interventionist models? In order to test the impact of global markets on 'crises, interests and instruments', we can examine whether states' participation in global transactions had changed before they implemented liberalizing reforms and regional cooperation: did they become less attractive as a site for investment and less competitive versus other states or former times and were thus exposed to pressures to adjust and improve their attractiveness? Examples of indicators are growth in exports, in national share in world trade, in global investment flows and in credit, as well as data on how much production shifted abroad. Indicators for an increasing integration of national economies into global markets, and thus for their dependence on the logic of global markets, are external debt ratios and the growth of foreign trade compared to the growth of GDP. The increasingly transnational orientation of private actors (exports, investment, etc.) can serve as an indicator of growing lobbying in these sectors for better access to world markets, for conditions that enhance the global competitiveness of their location, and against protectionism.

The interests of companies that operate transnationally are particularly relevant because governments have to offer especially attractive conditions to keep these firms in the country or to attract new firms. Because of their transnational method of operation, these companies are affected more strongly by changes in the world economy and can shift their activities to other locations ('exit option') more easily than purely national companies. Such shifts can be prejudicial to government attempts at stimulating growth, and thus endanger the maintenance of power of the respective governing coalitions. The political weight of these world-market-oriented firms can be expressed by their share in GDP. The political influence of pro-liberalization and anti-protectionist groups increases, for example, with a growth in exports' share of GDP. *Domestic pressures on governments to ameliorate conditions for global competitiveness through liberalizing reforms and regional market enlargement increase with a growing share of transnational activities (exports, imports, capital and investment flows) of GDP.*

If these figures change before national and regional liberalization is undertaken, this may indicate that a government's capacity to provide competitive conditions with its former inward-looking policies is either decreasing or increasing. If this capacity diminishes and induces an economic crisis (recession, unemployment, deterioration of the trade and current account balance, etc.), then the decision-making environment stimulates an adjustment to the demands of global markets in order to secure the government's positive contribution to growth. Indicators for domestic pressures deriving from an economic crisis are sinking growth rates, electoral results and public opinion polls.

Testing the hypotheses with these indicators is subject to the caveat that a change in quantitative values does not *necessarily* lead to a change in political preferences – even if rational behaviour would support such a conclusion. Just because it would be rational for a government to change its preferences on account of quantitative changes in its decision-making environment does not mean it is inevitable. Therefore, this book will treat quantitatively measurable flows and data only as plausible indicators for the formation of governments' preferences. I presume only a *plausible* and not a *necessary* causality between the material dimension of global markets and the policy course of governments.

For several reasons it would be problematic to draw conclusions about changes in social interaction solely from the aforementioned quantitative changes. A quantification of social processes, for example, by applying econometric-mathematical methods to social science, would provide only a façade of more scientific precision because the problem of the multiplicity of causalities in social interactions is transferred from the analysis to the premise. That is to say, if one assumes that a larger world market share of GNP necessarily leads to liberalizing policies through mounting pressures from involved groups, then the 'testing' becomes easy and precise: only the measurement of the share of GNP produced transnationally is necessary. But does a higher export share inevitably induce such political pressures? Do these pressures really lead to a change in government preferences? Therefore, the quantitative measurement of data must be complemented by indicators of the actors' perceptions of these developments in order to provide a convincing analysis of the resulting political situation.

Besides the problem of translating quantitative data into political preferences, a second dilemma emerges in using the measurement of material flows as a method to test the hypotheses. How many and which data are relevant? How are they to be weighted against each other? The solution offered by game-theoretical approaches is the reduction of complexity by restricting the number of variables to very few and the adoption of the *ceteris paribus* proviso from economics. But this 'solution' is only of very limited value in explaining complex and continuously changing social interactions. The use of very few variables and *ceteris paribus* would mean that, if governments were not exposed to *any other* influences, the pro-liberalization lobbying of world-market-oriented groups would shape policy preferences.

Taking only very few variables or indicators into account increases the probability that important factors will be overlooked. For example, a government would possibly have pursued reforms without any pressure from world-market-oriented groups. Possibly the weakness of other influences, such as inward-looking interventionist strategies or domestically oriented groups, which could also have been induced by exposure to global markets, was more decisive than the strength of world-market-oriented sectors in causing the government to pursue certain policies. On the other hand, a consideration of *all* possibly relevant indicators can obviously not be operationalized and would not allow the selection necessary for analysis. The GMA already focuses on specific causalities and indicators, but should not be restricted to the measurement of data. Instead, this analysis incorporates all methodological approaches delineated in the following. The critical remarks on the methodological power of numbers, however, should not be taken to imply that this way of testing hypotheses is considered invalid. The plausibility of the hypotheses will *also* be underpinned by quantitative evidence.

Qualitative reasons for political preferences

An additional method for drawing plausible causal connections between global markets, national economies and the preference for regional cooperation is the investigation of the perceptions of involved individuals or groups. What reasons do governments give for implementing liberalizing reforms and regional cooperation? With which arguments do opposition parties, entrepreneurs, unions and the media respond? Did growing global mobility and competition lead to an increasing perception of the costs of inward-looking interventionism? Was this the reason why pressure groups demanded better conditions for global competitiveness? Indicators for the perception of global markets as a reason for national reforms and for the perception of regional cooperation as an instrument for more economic efficiency and political acceptability of liberalizing reforms can be found in governments' arguments in favour and in opposition parties' criticism of reforms.

The contents of the treaties on the European single market (the SEA), NAFTA and MERCOSUR also reflect perceptions. Do the treaties aim at an economically more efficient execution of national reforms? Were the new initiatives explained in the treaties as a response to global competition? The presumed causal relationship is especially evident in the case of political conditionalities. Were governments explicitly asked to enhance competitiveness by liberalizing their markets through a regional agreement? This conditionality could consist of demands by transnational actors for a regionally assured liberalization as a precondition for their engagement (investment, loans, etc.). This indicator refers to new investment as well as to the maintenance of the current level of production and investment – that is, the threat to shift activities abroad. Indicators for the governments' attempts to use the regional level in order to offload political responsibility for domestically controversial reforms can be found in statements to that effect by ruling politicians and in criticism from opposition parties, companies, corporate organizations and unions.

The dilemma of testing the hypotheses with 'perceptions' is similar to the dilemma of 'numbers' – both can provide only plausibility, not 'proof'. A public statement by the government that new cooperation is vital in order to increase the efficiency of the liberalization made imperative by the impact of global markets does not necessarily provide the 'real' reasoning behind the government's preference. Governments may find that the impact of global markets offers a more convincing basis for justifying to the public its preference for a policy that is actually based on other motives. Although public statements of decision-makers do not necessarily reflect their motivations, the political discourse on the consequences of global markets and the reasons for cooperation does create or reflect dominant perceptions and thus shapes the decision-making environment. Therefore, the debates over regional cooperation provide an insight into the attitudes of and information available to those involved and into the reasoning with which they approach the public. Thus, this enquiry is going to operate in a pluralistic way with regard to its methods. Qualitative statements about perceptions will be used in tandem with quantitative indicators in order to test the plausibility of the hypotheses.

Additional methodological elements: historical, comparative and cost–benefit analyses

As the aim of this book is to investigate the change in political preferences, it makes more sense to track the trends of change over a longer period than to undertake an analysis of the moment in which the decision to cooperate was made. Given that global markets began to (re-)emerge in the 1970s, the period most interesting to this investigation starts in the 1970s and culminates with the agreement on the respective treaties: 1986 for the European single market, 1991 for MERCOSUR, and 1992 for NAFTA. Moreover, an evaluation of the agreements' early results is vital. Did they achieve their goals? To what extent did the criticism of the treaties articulate the relationship between global markets and national preferences? In order to encompass these concerns, the period of analysis extends to the end of the 1990s. This longer period of time also takes into account the progressive character of the emergence and the impact of global markets. They did not 'occur' at a specific time, but rather, according to the GMA, have exerted an increasing influence on national economies and policies since the 1970s.

An additional methodological element is the possibility of strengthening the power of the GMA by comparing the results of multiple cases. The comparative element of testing the same hypotheses on several empirical cases can provide a broader and deeper verification of the GMA as well as a clearer definition of its reach and boundaries. Even though the 'preference for world-market-oriented, liberalizing regional cooperation' is given in all seven countries, the presumed causal impact of global markets could manifest itself in different ways, or it might not possess explicatory relevance at all. The hypotheses-based analysis of countries with different levels of development (industrialized, industrializing) and different political as well as economic cultures, institutions and traditions also enables us to make statements on the interaction between politics and economics, between global markets and other determinants of government preference formation. To what extent was the impact of global markets altered by national specificities?

As pointed out before, the approach of this enquiry does not assume that global markets *automatically* lead to a liberalizing cooperation, but rests on the hypothesis that they *stimulate* government preferences in this direction. Therefore, the analysis has to concentrate methodologically on showing plausibly that the *costs* and *benefits* of political options have changed. 'Figures' and 'perceptions' suggest the likelihood that global markets increased the *costs* of inward-looking interventionist policies ('crises, interests and instruments') and the *benefits* of the liberalizing reforms as well as the benefits of regional cooperation ('economic efficiency, political acceptability'). The deduction of new preferences from the altered costs and benefits of political options presupposes rational perceptions and rational actions on the part of those involved. But political action and a priori preference formation derive not only from cost–benefit relations, but also from fundamental goals, cultural legacies, norms and institutional settings. Some underlying factors that must be taken into account are the states' fundamental tasks (such as 'wealth creation'), the basic governmental goal of staying in power and the political acceptability of governments' policies. Incorporating perceptions into the methodology not only permits the consideration of these underlying or prioritized goals, but can also contribute to answering questions concerning the relationship between the perception of global markets and fundamental governmental tasks as well as cultural values. Do global markets lead to an instrumental change of the latter? Are the answers to global markets shaped by the latter?

Regarding the reference to statistics, treaties and perceptions, this work will make use of primary sources, documents and public speeches (articles, memoirs, etc.) of decision-makers. The extent to which data will be used systematically in the case studies is subject to their availability. The same kind of data was not available for all countries. In addition to primary sources, the analysis refers to secondary sources in order to use the expertise and competence of experts for the particular country in each of the seven cases. The translations of foreign-language citations are all by the author.

Structure of the book

In a first step, the explanatory factor of the theoretical approach will be given further empirical foundation and operational structure. In chapter 2, the causes and the development of global markets will be systematically analysed in the areas of finance, production / investment, and trade. Building upon this research, the fundamental impact of global markets on states will be further discussed and explained in order to test the plausibility of the three pathways 'crises, interests and instruments'. How do global markets affect inward-looking interventionist policies and economies? How do they change domestic interests? How do they influence governmental instruments? As chapter 2 represents a deepening of section 1.3, a certain overlap is not only unavoidable, but also necessary, as the explanatory factor and its pathways are thoroughly developed.

Chapters 3, 4 and 5 are dedicated to the seven case studies, structured according to the three regional agreements. These chapters are organized symmetrically in order to employ the explanatory approach equitably across all the cases and to achieve comparability of results. At the beginning of each chapter (section 1, respectively), the regulations and goals of the cooperative treaties will be examined with regard to the following questions. Does the treaty represent a new strategy compared to former cooperation? Is it pursuing a liberalizing, world market approach? Is it justifying cooperation as an answer to the challenges of global markets? Subsequent sections will investigate the impact of global markets on the preference formation in the decisive countries for the agreement on the European single market (France, Germany, the UK), on MERCOSUR (Argentina, Brazil) and on NAFTA (Mexico, USA). The case studies are each divided into two parts: the first analyses problems of inward-looking interventionist policies deriving from the influence of global markets; the second investigates the liberalizing reforms and the formation of preferences for new regional cooperation.

All seven case studies follow the reasoning of the GMA: the pathways 'crises, interests and instruments', the preference building according to changes in the costs and benefits of policy options, the advantages of cooperation regarding the 'economic efficiency' and 'political acceptability' of adjustments, and the methodological elements focusing on figures and perceptions. In addition to the country studies, section 3.3 will investigate the impact of global markets on the regional European level: on European institutions, interest groups and debates. This is necessary because the SMP was built upon three decades of European integration, decades in which regional organizations and a regional 'identity' emerged, which could have been relevant for the formation of government preferences. At the end of chapters 3, 4 and 5, the results of the case studies will be brought to a conclusion that attempts not a detailed summary, but rather a systematic aggregation of individual country results. The concluding chapter (6) will begin with a comparative summary of the empirical results with regard to the question 'to what extent was the GMA able to explain the preferences of governments for regional cooperation in the cases analysed?'. This section will be followed by theoretical remarks further developing the GMA. Section 6.3 investigates the implications of the results for theories of international relations and cooperation.

2

Global Markets: Development and Impact on States

This chapter will expand on the analysis of the explanatory factor 'impact of global markets on states' by further developing its empirical foundations and its operationalization. Two questions guide the following examination. What has caused the emergence of global markets since the 1970s? How do global markets affect states' – that is, governments' – economic policy and national economies? In examining the latter question, the pathways 'crises, interests and instruments' will be explained with more precision and detail.

2.1 Global Financial Markets

The increasing mobility and transnational integration of financial interactions is a gradual process. Therefore, no 'date' can be specified on which global financial markets emerged in their present form. The decisive question for the GMA is: to what extent did the growth of private financial actors' transnational activities over two decades (the 1970s and 1980s) influence the policy options of states in such a way as to stimulate states to prefer a liberalizing regional cooperation?

Causes, development and dimension

The central causes of the growth of global financial markets were (1) the end of the Bretton Woods System, (2) the competitive deregulation in the UK and the USA, followed by the emergence of euro-dollar and 'off-shore' markets, and (3) the sudden increase in transnational banking, primarily due to the recycling of 'petro-dollars' and the expansion of TNCs. These developments partly reinforced each other and became driving forces for the world economy in the 1970s.

(1) As Helleiner (1994: 4) and Ruggie (1982) have shown, the Bretton Woods System of 1944 regulated a world economic order that gave preference to free trade at the expense of a liberal financial system. In order to secure national economies' openness to trade, a relatively restrictive financial system was established based on the Gold Dollar Standard, international stand-by support for balance of payment problems and capital controls.[1] These regulations secured financial stability in order to prevent protectionism in trade. The neo-Keynesian consensus of the 1940s to 1960s saw the regulation of international capital transfers as necessary in order to avoid speculative and destabilizing international capital flows that would restrict the new interventionist welfare states' policy autonomy.

The system of fixed currency rates and liberal trade had become increasingly unstable since the end of the 1960s, primarily due to the USA's growing indebtedness (in part due to the cost of the Vietnam War) and to the relative decline of US economic power, resulting from the economic recovery of Europe and Japan. As a consequence, the USA was no longer able (or willing) to guarantee the exchange of dollars for gold at a fixed rate, and in 1971 President Nixon terminated the guarantee. A system of flexible ('floating') exchange rates developed and led to a rapid increase in exchange rate fluctuations and currency swaps. The fluctuations of exchange rates increased the possibility of making a profit on currency transactions. At the same time, it became necessary to denominate business and capital holdings in several currencies – that is, to diversify currency holdings, in order to reduce the exchange rate risk.

(2) Both to improve their attractiveness as locations for financial markets and in response to pressure from private business, the USA and the UK started to deregulate their financial sectors in the mid–1970s. The need for an influx of capital had risen in the USA (in part because of a recession after 1973, current account and budget deficits) and induced it to expand its dominant position in world finance by lowering restrictions on transnational financial activities. This deregulation was also a response to pressure from financial groups that had threatened to withdraw their capital because of new regulations established in the 1960s. The liberalization of the 1970s freed transnational banking from many of these constraints and strengthened the 'Euromarkets'. The latter are also called 'off-shore' financial centres because they operate nearly without restrictions and thus quasi 'outside' national jurisdiction (Dombrowski 1996: 70–9).

Geographically speaking, the most important 'off-shore' markets are located in London and New York. The deregulation of national financial markets was competitive in that it forced other countries to take similar steps if they wanted to avoid a massive outflow of capital. Competitive deregulation therefore imposed considerable costs on states that chose to defend their autonomy of policy by retaining a high level of regulation (Thierstein and Langenegger 1994: 504). Deregulated financial locations are attractive for both investors and creditors because they can expect higher profits, better interest rates, more liquidity and easier transfers as a result of the lower or non-existent taxes, minimum reserve requirements, restrictions and controls on the 'off-shore' markets. The USA tried, quite successfully, to counterbalance its external deficits by using more profitable conditions to entice capital out of other currencies into the dollar – as higher interest rates did in the 1980s (Helleiner 1994: 91, 100).

(3) At the same time as the financial restrictions of the Bretton Woods System were being dismantled, the volume of international investment and lending rose dramatically. This was due, on the one hand, to the expansion of TNCs, whose investment and trade activities increased transnational financial flows. On the other hand, the explosion of oil prices created a unique need for additional investment sites. The enormous revenues of the Organization of Petroleum Exporting Countries (OPEC) were deposited primarily with European and American banks, especially on euro-dollar markets. Because of the ongoing recession in the industrialized countries after 1973, these 'petro-dollars' could not be entirely absorbed. While private banks were having a hard time finding profitable investment sites for their 'petro-dollars', a number of developing countries were desperately seeking external financing for their respective industrialization strategies. As a consequence, transnational banks started lending to developing countries. Thus, while the volume of private global lending was expanding, so too was the range of countries to which private lenders were extending credit. Some of these countries had previously been only marginally integrated into global financial markets.

In principle, there is consensus on these causes of the growth of global financial markets and the interconnectedness of private financial transactions. The central controversy surrounds the role of states in this process (B. Cohen 1996: 271–9). Helleiner (1994: 81–168; 1996) and Ruggie (1982) argue that government decisions were decisive: global markets were made possible by liberalization and deregulation, by the creation of 'off-shore' locations and by renouncing the possibility of reinstating controls. According to this argument, it was also important that states secured the stability of the newly liberalized financial system by crisis management – for example, during the debt crisis of developing countries after 1982 and the stock market crash in the industrialized world in 1987. Other authors, like Sobel (see B. Cohen 1996: 271), emphasize the influence of domestic interest groups and see liberalization towards the outside world as a response to internal necessities and the interests of domestic pressure groups (the 'inside-out approach'). A different approach, proclaimed predominantly by private business circles, regards the role of innovation (information technology, new financial products) and autonomous market forces as central to the emergence of global financial markets (the 'outside-in approach').[2] According to this view, the states' deregulation was only a reaction to non-political driving forces.

In the light of the evidence presented, it seems plausible that states' choices made a decisive contribution to the expansion of global financial markets. But Helleiner also confirms the partly autonomous, non-governmental character of this process by stating that several attempts by governments to reregulate – for example, by instituting capital controls – failed as early as the 1970s because of the expected costs in the form of probable capital flight (Helleiner 1994: 121–45).[3] Ultimately it seems difficult and possibly of little cognitive value to prove a primary cause. Obviously government policies, such as deregulation, and pressure from technologically and market-induced 'globalization' (that is, the higher cost of maintaining regulations) reinforced each other.

As for the dimensions of global markets, the decisive factor for the influence of higher mobility and transnational integration is not whether they *dominate* the financial sector of a specific national economy, but to what extent the *growth* of transnational activities has changed the costs and benefits of governments' options. Transnational financial activities are still small in comparison to domestic economic transactions (Wade 1996). Therefore, the following will focus on evidence of the growth of global activities in comparison to national ones in the 1970s and 1980s. For the analysis in this book, only quantitative changes from the 1970s until the 1990s matter, as the preferences for national liberalization and for regional cooperation were formed during this period.

Cross-border sales of bonds and equities grew from less than 10 per cent of the GNP of G7 industrialized countries in 1980 to well over 100 per cent in 1995; in Germany those figures went from 7.5 per cent (1980) to 169.4 per cent (1995) (IMF 1997: 60). Worldwide trade in currencies increased from $188 billion in 1986 to $1190 billion *per day* in 1995; compared to national currency reserves, currency trade went from 36.7 per cent (1986) to 84.3 per cent (1995) (IMF 1997: 64). In the last thirty years of the twentieth century transnational bank loans grew three times as much as world trade (Cable 1995: 29). Deposits on euro-markets grew from $110 billion (1970) to $1515 billion (1980) (Dombrowski 1996: 71). By the beginning of the 1980s, transnational portfolio activities had increased dramatically. Germans, for example, bought and sold foreign securities for a total of 86.4 billion DM in 1981, but traded 399.9 billion DM worth in 1986 (Schröder 1988: 382). The existence of global financial markets made it easier to exploit the much higher interest rates in the USA in the first half of the 1980s. However, these indicators have to be placed in context. Whereas global financial activities grew rapidly by comparison to national ones, domestic investment remained dominant in absolute terms. Moreover, the separation of the domestic investment from the propensity to save that one could expect from a completely globalized market cannot yet be observed (Epstein 1996: 213).

Impact on states: crises, interests and instruments

> The key difference for governments today is that, unlike their predecessors in the period from 1945 to 1980, they confront unprecedented levels (and speeds) of capital mobility, which make the reaction of international financial markets a major consideration in policy formulation. (Milner and Keohane 1996a: 23)

(1) *Crises of inward-looking interventionist policies.* With the increase of transnational capital mobility, the incentive for governments grew, to offer attractive conditions in order to attract or retain financial flows. The cost of not taking such measures rose to the same extent in the form either of low capital influx or of actual capital flight. Governments had to give more consideration to private investors' criteria and thus found themselves restricted in their autonomy to act. Stronger competition among investors (especially institutional investors) is projected onto states because even small interest rate differentials or

expected currency rate changes can provoke considerable portfolio shifts. Private financial actors (banks, investment firms, stockbrokers, and so on) register every detail of new laws, growth prognoses, budget deficits or modifications of interest rates by central bankers and immediately incorporate them into their investment decisions (Krupp 1997: 4). There was a rise in the costs (outflow of capital) of an inward-looking neglect of global markets and a rise in the incentives (influx of capital) for an adjustment to global markets.

Following the USA, the UK (1976, 1979–), France (1983–), Germany (1983–) and other countries were also induced to lower controls and ameliorate the profitability of transnational financial activities on their territory. As in the production and service sectors, the transnationalization of activities had provided financial actors with new 'exit options'. States themselves had contributed to the creation of an alternative to national business by stimulating the emergence of the euro-dollar markets and by legally and technically facilitating access to these markets. Since the 1980s it seems difficult to reverse this situation using new restrictions unless all OECD states are prepared to introduce controls. The viability and efficiency of even this option seems doubtful given the proliferation of economic centres – especially in the form of NICs. A *unilateral* reregulation would cause a massive capital outflow and a de facto isolation from new inflows: 'Capital is now so mobile that markets will ensure that holders of financial assets receive roughly the same, risk adjusted, real return everywhere. Any country that offers significantly lower returns will experience capital outflow and a rapidly depreciating exchange rate' (Cable 1996: 27).

(2) *Efficiency of economic policy instruments.* Global markets do not lead to 'The End of the Nation-State' as Ohmae (1995) argues, neither do they induce the complete inefficiency of governmental instruments. Rather, global markets modify the efficiency of instruments. Because of the increased mobility, a considerable amount of capital can be transferred more quickly from one currency or location to another. These capital transfers can derive from speculative considerations or represent the results of profit calculations on the basis of real developments in the respective country – like inflation (which devalues nominal interest rates), growth, productivity and production costs (wages, taxes, norms). The assessment of such 'financial market fundamentals' can have considerable impact on prices, interest rates, exports and jobs.

An increased demand for dollars, for example, leads to a stronger exchange rate of these currencies vis-à-vis others. From this follows, on the one hand, a deterioration of the conditions for US exports, as their prices in other currencies rise. Correspondingly, the prices of imported goods sink. As a result, pressures on the balance of trade, job losses, lower tax revenues, lower wages and a higher share of foreign goods in national consumption can be expected. In this situation, neo-Keynesian demand stimulation (by raising government expenditures) would benefit foreign producers through 'import-leakages' of the newly created demand to the extent to which a country integrates into global markets (Lerda 1996: 74). If the government reacts to an appreciation of its currency by broadening its monetary base or by buying foreign currencies, then the impact of global markets is transferred from the economic situation (currency) to political action and indicates changing policy options.

On the other hand, a negative evaluation of 'financial market fundamentals' by global actors can trigger a decrease in the demand for a currency and thus weaken its exchange rate. If the government or the central bank reacts by raising the interest rate level (for example, through a restrictive monetary policy) in order to keep mobile capital in the country, it takes externally induced steps, which could possibly counteract preceding goals. Higher interest rates can have negative effects on domestic investment and thus on growth and jobs as capital becomes more expensive.[4]

The volume of capital handled by global financial markets dwarfs any national currency reserve and diminishes the capability of governments to influence exchange rates (for example, via support purchases): worldwide trade in currencies amounts to one trillion dollars per day – a higher sum than the combined currency reserves of all governments (Cable 1996: 27). The global financial system sets its own interest rate, the London Interbank Offered Rate (LIBOR): transnational banks borrow from each other at this rate. The LIBOR is considered the point of reference for transnational private loans as well as for loans between private banks and governments. Loans to high-risk debtors such as Brazil and Mexico are calculated as LIBOR plus x per cent 'spread'. The interest payments of debtor governments can vary considerably as transnational credit is increasingly tied to the LIBOR, which is fixed every six months by private banks. While real interest rates ('LIBOR on US dollar deposits minus the US wholesale price increase') averaged -0.8 per cent from 1971 to 1980, they jumped to 7.5 per cent in 1981 and 11 per cent in 1982 (Cline 1984:

8–11). Consequently, the states' ability to shape national economies is restricted by the impact of global markets, which affects governments' policy options in securing their economic performance. In principle, the causalities outlined here do not require global markets; they also hold in the interactions between two national economies. But the emergence of global markets increased the extent and the speed of the impact considerably.

Moreover, the efficiency of governmental control is also undermined by the increasingly 'virtual' (electronic) way business is conducted, reducing the ability of government agencies to obtain the information necessary for monitoring global financial transactions. The evasion of taxes and regulations was facilitated and new duties could hardly be enforced.[5] Even states that were only partially integrated into global markets – such as Latin American countries – had experienced growing capital flight since the 1970s without being able to control it. The ongoing discussion in the EU about the taxation of revenue from interest and the low efficiency of this kind of taxation attest to the restriction of governmental instruments incurred by the increasingly transnational scope of financial interactions.

In order to avoid a reductionist picture, it has to be mentioned that governmental instruments are efficient mechanisms for steering national economies, but since the 1970s this efficiency has been in the process of change. States are less able to determine real exchange rates by using currency reserves or prevent capital flows by implementing controls. But they can still influence the exchange rate – for example, through national interest rate levels – if they agree to subordinate their monetary policy to this goal. The 'transmission belt' between governmentally influenced interest rates and inflation is valid – although no longer to the same extent as it was until the 1970s: 'Whereas national banks, which reacted reliably and predictably to monetary policy, previously dominated the securities market, external factors were able to gain considerable influence and temporarily even a leading role over capital market interest rates through globalization' (Schröder 1988: 383).

(3) *Transnational interests strengthened*. Domestic interests and interest groups changed in correspondence with the impact outlined in points (1) and (2): to the extent that global financial markets (such as euromarkets) offered attractive investment options and investors favoured better access to these transnational markets and / or better

conditions in their home location. As a consequence of the global markets' greater attractiveness, a growth in disposable income – for example through tax cuts – became more important for entrepreneurs than the formerly dominant neo-Keynesian goal of 'growth of production through demand management'. In proportion to the increased profitability of financial markets, private actors placed a higher priority on being able to invest in financial assets rather than in production – except where the latter offered more attractive possibilities.[6] Thus, the emergence of global markets altered the interests of private actors in favour of a supply-side opening and deregulation to the detriment of inward-looking demand management. The significance of these actors grew with rising capital mobility and increasing engagement of investors in global markets, as they had more access to an 'exit option' than others. In principle, they gain political relevance to the extent to which they can threaten a government with the removal of their assets. These actors are not necessarily organized into a lobby, instead, they may 'vote with their accounts', resulting in capital flows that increasingly and rapidly reflect a negative evaluation of government policy, as outlined above. Consequently, the government faces high opportunity costs if it implements inward-looking interventionism.

2.2   Global Production and Foreign Direct Investment

Global division of labour and foreign direct investment (FDI) are not historically new phenomena. This global market reached a peak at the end of the nineteenth century, at which point the worldwide colonial economic structures were particularly well developed. For example, the first treatment of a raw material frequently took place in a colony and the half-finished product was then sent to the colonial power for finishing. Direct investment in the construction of manufacturing sites in the colony was also common (Hirst and Thompson 1996: 18ff). The two world wars and the economic crisis following 1929 interrupted this version of global capital, investment and production mobility. By the end of the twentieth century, global markets were considered new because they differed in form and magnitude from the worldwide economic developments of the period before the 1970s.

Causes, development and dimension

Important causes of the growth of the mobility and volume of investments as well as the worldwide division of labour were (1) the expansion of transnational corporations (TNCs), (2) industrialization in developing countries, (3) new liberalizing economic policies in industrialized countries and (4) the resulting increase in competition, which forced producers to use every possible comparative advantage. In part, these developments were contingent upon one another, and they are closely connected with the development of the global financial market. TNCs that shift productive capacity and technology out of the realm of their country of origin by transferring capital are the primary forces behind FDI. This is always associated with productive capacity and differs from portfolio investment, which flows into the stock market as speculative capital. FDI cannot thus be withdrawn as quickly and at as little cost as speculative capital can. For the most part, it becomes 'sunk investment' within a short period of time, since factories and machines cannot shift locations in a matter of seconds, even in the age of cyberspace. Consequently, governments hold direct investments to be considerably more important than portfolio capital in securing growth and welfare (production, jobs, technological development, etc.).[7] TNCs' production both domestically and in foreign countries is usually not financed exclusively from their own capital stock; instead they borrow from national and global capital markets. The demand for capital to finance the growing level of FDI was one of the most important causes of the development of the global financial markets. The latter in turn stimulated the expansion of TNCs.

(1) It is necessary to differentiate two types of production connected with the expansion of TNCs. First, they can build up companies outside their countries of origin in order to produce complete goods in the target market. The motivation often lies in the desire to avoid transportation costs and to circumvent tariffs and non-tariff barriers to market entry in the target country ('jump the tariff'). Protectionism can thus be a cause of FDI, and, as a result, liberalizing the market can lead to the substitution of FDI flows by exports from the country of origin. The goal of constructing complete production sites in the target market is to achieve better sales opportunities than were possible on the basis of deliveries from the corporations'

original production sites. This type of TNC production was predominant in the 1950s and 1960s and was still important in the 1990s (Gereffi 1995).

Since the 1970s, a second form of TNC activity has moved into the foreground: dividing the production of a good among several countries. In order to achieve the most efficient allocation of productive factors, individual stages of production are shifted to those sites where, for example, wage costs are lower, access to raw materials is easier, the proximity to the suppliers is closer or the conditions for research and development (educational levels and legal frameworks) are better than in the previous site.[8] Global division of labour refers not only to the production of a good at the various sites of *one* corporation (subsidiaries), but also to 'global sourcing' – that is, drawing components, primary products, licences and personnel from various sites and from external companies (Germann et al. 1996: 26).

(2) Successes in industrializing developing countries, visible in the emergence of newly industrializing countries (NICs), are also a *result* of the expansion of TNCs, which contributed considerably to the industrialization of Brazil, for example (Schirm 1990: 74–81). However, these successes are also a *cause*: on the one hand, these countries, especially the East Asian ones, brought forth their own TNCs, such as Hyundai and Gold Star in South Korea, which are now among the *global players*. On the other hand, 'sunk investments' tended to attract further funds in order to guarantee the optimal use of the previously invested resources. The costs of withdrawing would then include the loss of the already invested capital. Moreover, the successful development in NICs raised the purchasing power in many of them, making their markets more attractive. Although the inequality of income distribution frequently rose,[9] TNCs found these markets increasingly interesting as sites for production and investment.

(3) Market liberalization also encouraged the expansion of TNCs, particularly in the industrialized countries, because it lowered the costs for transnational activities and increased the pressure to use global comparative advantages. The lowering of tariff barriers achieved by various GATT rounds and by regional agreements promoted 'global sourcing' by making the import of components and primary products for further processing within the country cheaper (Lerda 1996: 69). At the same time, the opening-up of various OECD countries (especially the USA and the UK) enlarged the competition in their markets.

Companies that had focused exclusively on the 'national' markets were faced with new rivals and obliged to transnationalize their activities in order to reach world market competitiveness.

(4) Foreign investment in industrial nations also grew rapidly because the stronger competition for technological innovation led companies to capitalize on ever smaller comparative advantages as well as on research and development output. This refers to both of the types of TNC activity depicted in (1): complete production 'on site' and manufacturing a good using a number of production sites. The increasing transnational competition in the last two decades of the twentieth century stimulated the global expansion of business activities (Germann et al. 1996: 28). Thus, the stronger competition between companies is both cause and effect of global markets. Because of greater mobility and more foreign involvement, enterprises are faced with more foreign competition in their home markets, which forces them to expand their own transnational activities in order to be able to compete.

As to the magnitude of global production and investment: in the period at stake in this book, the 1970s and 1980s, the volume and scope of direct investment and TNC activity grew by leaps and bounds. Between 1980 and 1996, FDI rose three times as quickly as the total amount of investment (including investment in domestic economies), but in 1996 it was still only 6 per cent of the industrial nations' annual investment activity (UNCTAD statistics, from *The Economist*, 22 Nov. 1997: 108). The vital aspect is that this increase was substantially *larger than the growth of national economic activity and therefore the shares of aggregate economic output shifted in favour of transnational activity*. Transnational investment as a proportion of the growth of worldwide GNP best illustrates this shift. FDI inflows increased from 1986 to 1990 by 24.4 per cent, whereas world gross domestic product grew by only 10.7 per cent. Between 1982 and 1994, the sum of FDI stock doubled as a percentage of worldwide GDP to reach 9 per cent (UNCTAD 1997a: xv, 3–4). Total worldwide direct investment from 1980 to 1987 was higher than the accumulated amount of *all* previous foreign investment (Junne 1994: 86). At the end of the 1980s, about 80 per cent of direct investment flows were concentrated on the industrial nations of the 'Triad' – that is, North America, Western Europe and Japan (Petrella 1996: 69). During that decade two-thirds of all the worldwide influx of investment had gone to the

EU and the USA, not including the intra-EU investment (Wade 1996: 70). Thus, 'global' markets encompass primarily the OECD countries.

Foreign investment also raised the level of corporations' transnationality. For example, between 1970 and 1984 the share of FDI stock as a percentage of the total corporate assets in Germany rose from 2 per cent to 7.2 per cent, in Japan from 0.4 per cent to 1.7 per cent and in the UK from 22 per cent to 31 per cent (1983). In the USA, on the other hand, this share dropped – an indication that American companies were losing some of their dominance in the world economy during this period (UNCTC 1988: 26). In particular, the large industrial enterprises demonstrated a high level of involvement in global markets. In the mid-1980s, the subsidiaries' share of the total turnover of the sixty-eight largest industrial enterprises was almost one-third, and over one-third of the TNCs' jobs were located in their subsidiaries (Wade 1996: 63). As transnationally oriented companies contributed substantially to the total economic output of their countries of origin, the governments of these states became more receptive to the economic policy requests of the 'global' sectors. Between 1975 and 1990, the turnover of the fifty largest TNCs grew by 3.5 per cent, the GNP of the OECD countries only by 2.9 per cent. In the USA the turnover of the fifty largest industrial TNCs rose from 28 per cent of the American GDP in 1975 to 39 per cent in 1989 (Carnoy 1993: 49).

These statistics show that transnational activity as a share of worldwide output has made significant advances and that the share of purely domestic economic activity, which can be more easily steered by the state, has decreased proportionately. This tendency is self-reinforcing to the extent that producing at a number of sites strengthens TNCs' competitiveness against enterprises that produce only in one country for that domestic market. Globally active firms can achieve a higher level of productivity in comparison to their national rivals because they operate transnationally and are forced to face global competition (Lerda 1996: 68). As a result, increasing numbers of companies feel obliged to bring their production into line with the competitive requirements of global markets. In the 1980s, this pressure also contributed to the increase of 'strategic alliances' between TNCs in order to take advantage of synergies in research and marketing without necessarily having to swap equity.[10] Examples of transnational networks are airline cooperations ('Star Alliance'), and of equity mergers car manufacturer takeovers (DaimlerChrysler). Corporate alliances strengthen global markets by encouraging a worldwide network of private economic activity and thus establish a global system partly outside the jurisdiction of one individual state.

Impact on states: crises, interests and instruments

In judging the effect of global markets on states, it is necessary to remember that most of the economic output, even of an industrial nation, is produced and consumed domestically. At the completion of the European SMP, in 1993, only 5.7 per cent of Germany's domestically accumulated capital was invested abroad (France: 9.1 per cent; UK: 18.6 per cent; USA: 3.7 per cent) (World Competitiveness Report 1993 statistics, cited from Hoffmann 1994–5: 59). Investors still tend to invest primarily in their own countries. Although 'global' production and investment is an increasingly important factor, it is not (yet) a dominant one for these economies. However, the depicted developments are gaining relevance not only because of their rapid progress, but also because they affect the most productive sectors. Like the mobility of financial capital, global production and investment (1) raise the competitive pressure on governments and the costs of inward-looking policies, (2) alter the interests of societal groups and (3) lower the efficacy of individual state instruments.

(1) *Competitive pressure and the crisis of inward-looking interventionist policy.* The growing share of transnational corporate activity as a proportion of national and worldwide output expresses the increased mobility of production and investment. It places additional pressure on the state to improve the country's attractiveness as a production site by implementing supply-side deregulation – if the country is interested in participating in the dynamics of the global economy. States increasingly compete with one another on the worldwide market for production sites. A country's competitiveness is indicated not only by its share of world trade, but also increasingly by its ability to attract or retain mobile capital: the attractiveness of infrastructure, deregulated markets, low corporate taxes and monetary stability in global comparison influence competition among locations for investment and production (Cable 1995: 32). Comparative advantages can also lie in a good educational system, rule of law (fair and effective jurisdiction), low crime rate and so on. In the long run, these public goods, which are financed by taxes, might be more important than low taxes for companies. The task for governments is to secure the sustainability of locational advantages vis-à-vis global markets and to

combine world-market-oriented liberalizations with social competence (Schirm 1999b: 489).

Neglecting global locational competition through the pursuit of inward-looking interventionist policies produces suboptimal investment rates of transnationally oriented companies on the location, which in turn stimulates economic crises. One vital factor is that companies have found it easier to shift production and capital and that growing numbers of firms are enlarging the transnational part of their operations. In principle, TNCs could shift their activities abroad more easily than companies not engaged in or experienced in doing business abroad, and they therefore have a more realistic 'exit option' – that is, the option of abandoning their current site, at least partially. Using Hirschmann's concept of 'Exit, Voice, and Loyalty' (1970; 1978), it can be presumed that the TNCs' 'exit option' will also provide them with more influence on the government – that is, 'voice'. Immobile companies do not have the same potential to use the political threat of withdrawing their activities, with the corresponding loss of jobs and tax revenues.

(2) *Interest groups.* In accordance with their interests, the political influence of globally active companies in the Western industrial nations is directed at improving their competitiveness by means of market liberalization, lowering surcharges, achieving economies of scale by expanding regional markets, and so on. The lobbying efforts of domestic companies that depend substantially on exports (and therefore compete on the world market) are likely to tend in the same direction. With regard to economic policy conditions, the producers of *tradables* are oriented towards global prerequisites for competitiveness. Unlike the producers of *non-tradables*, they have an interest in the transnational mobility of economic factors. Since global trade has grown more quickly than the sum of national domestic products, the share of sectors oriented towards the world market as a proportion of the total economy has also grown more quickly than the share of domestically oriented sectors. The pressure the global market exerts on governments to offer better conditions for competition affects two intersecting levels: the microeconomic and the macroeconomic. TNCs and the national export sector will want to persuade governments to provide them with better working conditions by global comparison and to implement economic liberalization.[11] This is the microeconomic or sector-specific projection of the effect of global markets on the political arena. At the macroeconomic or societal level, governments

will feel bound to act when they see their ability to ensure 'welfare' endangered – for example, by the deterioration of aggregate statistics (exports, investment influx and outflow, tax revenues, etc.).

Since the growing competitive pressure and the liberalization it stimulates can affect societal sectors negatively (for example, companies that were previously protected by tariffs), governments will presumably also face pressure in the opposite direction. A number of factors, including specific national characteristics, such as political institutions and culture, will determine which group is more relevant and more likely to influence the government's behaviour. Corporative and consensus-driven political institutions in large countries like Germany make adjustments difficult, while small countries such as the Netherlands or competition-driven political institutions like the British can implement reforms more quickly. One of the most important determinants is the degree to which the country depends on the outside world, in the form of exports, loans, investments or technology. A further vital aspect might be the extent to which alternatives to a world-market-oriented liberalization are available and capable of gaining political relevance. In Western Europe and Latin America, the inward-looking models based on state regulation (neo-Keynesianism in Europe, import substitution in Latin America) of the 1970s and the beginning of the 1980s respectively, were no longer able to secure growth or 'welfare'. The alternative concept to market liberalization and to an orientation towards global competition was therefore both politically and economically discredited.

(3) *The effectiveness of state instruments.* The expansion of TNCs, direct investment and global division of labour changes the efficiency of some of the state's economic policy instruments and raises the opportunity costs of policies that ignore the pressure of global competition. This is particularly important in view of liberalizing regional economic cooperation because some of the instruments that have been undermined were fundamental to the inward-looking economic strategy. As in the case of capital controls, the effectiveness and the expediency of trade barriers have been reduced (but not entirely removed). For example, global division of labour makes it more difficult to protect 'national' sectors from 'foreigners' politically by means of tariff or non-tariff barriers because the distinction between the 'internal' and the 'external' became less clear. In 1990, Robert Reich, later Clinton's Secretary of Labor, asked, 'Who is Us?': if the components of a product are made in several countries, then the

effectiveness of political measures to protect or to prohibit a good is reduced. Political campaigns, such as 'Japan-Bashing' and 'Buy American', lack substance if the relevant car or hi-fi is not produced predominantly in Japan or the USA. Offering preferential treatment to American-owned companies will have little effect on American jobs if these companies produce mainly abroad. By contrast, discriminating against the products of foreign companies would be counterproductive if these were manufactured to a large extent in the USA.

Intra-firm trade is hard to control, as invoices need not indicate prices that reflect the actual production costs. In this way, price setting can be used to shield profits or losses from the state. Intra-firm trade makes it more difficult to tax corporate profits, and offers TNCs the possibility of declaring losses wherever they would reduce the burden of taxation most (Lerda 1996: 75). However, these caveats to the effectiveness of state instruments should not be exaggerated. Even the large TNCs, whose job creation and turnover are most relevant, pursued the majority of their activities on their 'home site' in the 1980s. For example, in 1989, 70 per cent of General Motors' jobs and 70 per cent of its assets were located in the USA. American TNCs undertook 90 per cent of their research and development in the USA, Japanese firms did 98 per cent in Japan (Wade 1996: 79). Thus, TNCs are still subject to the economic policies of their countries of origin. The relationship between the state and the TNC is one of interdependence. Global markets and those who are active in them affect the state gradually. TNCs are not independent of states; rather, their global orientation can facilitate their ability to shift locations and thereby exercise both their 'exit' and 'voice' options to persuade governments of the benefits of competition-friendly policies. In absolute numbers, economic activity is still predominantly national, even in the OECD states. However, in *relative* terms, the share of global business as a proportion of the total economic activity has risen since the 1970s.

2.3   World Trade

Since the three markets capital, production and trade are closely related to one another, the analysis of the first two has already examined the most important determinants and developments of transborder trade.

Causes, development and dimension

The heightened significance of global goods markets for national economies and their economic policies is manifested in the growing share of foreign trade (exports and imports) in proportion to GDP. Since the 1960s, this share has grown rapidly compared to the previous decades. The essential causes of this were (1) the liberalization achieved in multilateral intergovernmental negotiations, (2) the rapid decline of transport costs, (3) the expansion of TNCs and (4) the development of NICs. Since a number of these factors have already been examined, the following explication will be kept brief.

(1) The reduction of tariff barriers by means of multilateral agreements between nations under the aegis of various GATT rounds was particularly important (Kahler 1995: 23–48). GATT laid the foundation for the Kennedy, Tokyo and Uruguay Rounds, which finally achieved a substantial facilitation of trade. The Uruguay Round also managed to reduce non-tariff barriers and to include trade in services. By the time it was concluded in December 1993, it had further eased world trade and founded the World Trade Organization (WTO), into which GATT was absorbed. As a result of the lower barriers, some exports and imports that tariffs had made uncompetitive became profitable. This made foreign trade increasingly attractive and contributed to the fact that world trade grew more rapidly than the worldwide domestic product, thus increasing the foreign trade share in world GNP.

(2) Lower transport costs and faster transportation also contributed to the rise of transborder exchange of goods. Like the lowered customs duties, the savings in costs increased the attractiveness of international trade. The transport of goods benefited from technical innovations, such as the large-scale introduction of container shipping since the 1960s, which made the slow and expensive loading and unloading of individual goods by dock workers as unnecessary as expensive individual packaging (*The Economist*, 15 Nov. 1997: 89–90). The growing percentage of industrial goods in world trade also reduced transport costs in relation to the value of the goods, because, in comparison to many raw materials, a greater value-added per tonnage or volume could be transported. This tendency culminates in technical innovations such as the Internet, in which valuable information can be transported in real time and (almost) at the cost of local

telephone rates. The costs of obtaining information about other markets or products as well as the break-even point of transfers also dropped.

(3) The expansion of TNCs also caused a sudden leap in the amount of world trade, as it stimulated the exchange of parts and finished products between the various subsidiaries of a corporation. As a consequence of the expansion of corporations' production sites, intra-firm trade increased considerably. However, the role of TNCs must be relativized, as the construction of production capacity in target markets was undertaken to a certain extent at the cost of the prior exports to that market.

(4) Successes in the industrialization of some NICs led them to produce a wider range of goods. Thus, they were increasingly able to export not only primary goods but also finished products. Moreover, industrialization in developing countries was tied to the import of capital goods and increased efforts to export more goods in order to earn foreign currency. Both of these aspects increased some NICs' involvement in foreign trade. Given their high growth rates, these NICs became very attractive markets for durable consumer goods. This in turn led to some substantial involvement by companies from industrial nations, in the form of both direct investment by TNCs and higher exports to NICs.

The growth in world trade compared to worldwide GDP is clear: World Bank data show that worldwide trade grew by 5.6 per cent from 1965 to 1980 (exports + imports/2), while the world product grew by 4 per cent. Between 1980 and 1990 worldwide trade grew by 4.4 per cent, the world GNP by only 3.2 per cent (World Bank 1992: 221, 245). Thus, the growth of worldwide trade came to about 140 per cent of the growth in the world economy in both time periods and increased the transnationally produced share of the world economy considerably. According to calculations by Hirst and Thompson (1996: 22), throughout the twentieth century only in the period from 1913 to 1950 was the growth of worldwide GNP, which averaged 1.9 per cent, higher than that of world trade (0.5 per cent). In the period from 1950 to 1973, world trade was already growing by 9.4 per cent, much faster than the worldwide GNP (5.3 per cent). Between 1973 and 1984, the increase in world trade (3.6 per cent) was 75 per cent larger than the growth of the worldwide GNP (2.1 per cent). Whereas the share of world trade as a percentage of the worldwide GNP was about 11.9 per cent in 1965, by 1987 it had reached 19 per cent.[12]

Bairoch (1996: 178) calculated that the proportion of merchandise exports in the domestic product of the Western industrial nations rose from 7.8 per cent (1950) to 14.3 per cent (1991–3) – most of the growth took place between 1959–61 (8.6 per cent) and 1974–6 (14.1 per cent). Clearly, the expansion of TNCs contributed to this development. UNCTAD (1997a: 18) estimated the share of intra-firm trade in total world trade at about one-third. These numbers clearly show an increase in the relevancy of global markets in the years leading to the new preferences for liberalizing cooperation in Europe and the Americas.

Impact on states: crises, interests and instruments

Like the effects of global financial markets and global production, the expansion of world trade contributed to (1) the crises of the inward-looking interventionist model, (2) a shift in interests, and (3) a limitation of states' instruments.

(1) A growing share of foreign trade as a proportion of the GNP is always accompanied by a growing orientation of production towards world market standards. The costs of not taking the supply and demand conditions on the world market into account rise, as do the incentives to adjust to the conditions of the world market. Thus, an economy is stimulated to adapt to the quality and price requirements on global markets to the extent that it is dependent upon exports. In other words, the pressure (costs / incentives) to adapt to global competition rises in proportion to the share of the domestic product that is subject to the supply and demand conditions of the world market. This is primarily a condition that private producers must fulfil. For the government, this concatenation implies that it will be less free to set policy according to inward-looking criteria to the extent that economic performance (and thus also 'welfare') is no longer dependent solely on the domestic market. Most importantly, rising export quotas reduce the efficiency of inward-looking interventionism because the allocation of resources and the production conditions are increasingly tied to a market the government cannot control. If a government wants to retain or expand production in its country in the face of a growing dependence on exports, it must offer conditions that can compete on the world market in terms of quality, price, innovation and so on. Thus, inward-looking interventionism eventually reaches a crisis of efficiency and can, in principle, no longer assure 'welfare' to

the extent it could before the growing integration into world trade. This is also true for imports in so far as producing for the world market requires easy and cheap (barrier-free) access to the import of primary products, capital goods and technology in order to be competitive.

(2) The growing foreign trade share of GNP changes the interests of private actors and the importance of interest groups to the detriment of inward-looking interventionist economic policy. The interest group that is negatively affected by inward-looking interventionism grows and gains priority. In proportion to the increase of global tradables as a share of GNP, the interest in and lobbying for an economic policy that improves competitiveness on the global market for goods also rises (Frieden and Rogowski 1996). On the other hand, a declining share of non-tradables induces a reduction in the interest in and lobbying for trade protection mechanisms. The liberalizations especially of the OECD countries encouraged competition on their markets. As a consequence, companies that had previously been active only 'nationally' were obliged to orient their activities more towards the world market or even to structure their production transnationally. In this way governments contributed significantly to the strengthening of anti-protectionist and economically liberal interest groups.

(3) The limitation of those instruments necessary for the implementation of neo-Keynesian or import substituting policy follows a pattern for trade similar to that for the financial and production markets. Global markets react to measures undertaken to steer the domestic economy by countering or undermining the effects. In the case of trade, this relates primarily to 'import leakages' — that is, to the outflow of demand stimulation (increased state expenditures) through higher imports. Depending on the country's integration into world trade, the increase in purchasing power is absorbed by imports and has only a moderate ability to encourage the intended expansion of domestic production and job creation. The dependence on the openness of the target markets (which has grown proportionally to the dependence on exports) limits the feasibility of countervailing measures, such as blocking imports. In the light of the growing support for 'fair trade' and 'reciprocal trade' in the OECD, this openness of target markets would be endangered if the government of an exporting country imposed trade barriers for imports in order to retain stimulated demand domestically. Consequently, the government finds itself restricted in its choice of foreign trade instruments. The state's basic

source of funds, its tax income, also becomes harder to steer according to inward-looking priorities in the course of integration into the world economy because a large part of the GNP is then made on the global market. Politically motivated protection from the latter would directly cut the government's income.

2.4   Conclusion: Crises, Interests and Instruments

Global markets are only one determinant of national economies and economic policies among others, even if their importance has increased since the 1970s. National economic policy, political institutions, culture and mentality, natural resources, education and geography also have a bearing on the political and economic development. The empirical significance of global markets will be examined in the case studies. The previous sections have demonstrated at what levels global markets influence states on the pathways 'crises, interests and instruments'. These three pathways are closely connected; they augment one another and they are not necessarily equivalent. For example, the restriction of instruments for an inward-looking interventionist steering of the economy can contribute to a crisis of this economic model, as can the growing influence of liberally oriented groups. However, the aforementioned crisis symptoms can emerge because of the effects of the global markets even in the absence of reform-minded national interest groups.

Crises. The degree to which an economy is receptive to exogenous influences rises with the increase in the transnational share of the economic output and the reduction of state controls. If the transnationally active (or interested) capital brokers, investors or producers see the overall conditions for their involvement deteriorating or conditions at some other site improving, one can expect capital outflow or a decline in production, which would in turn have a negative effect on the country's economic situation. Any government wishing to participate in the growth and efficiency dynamics of the global economy must subject itself to the global markets' judgement of its policies. Global markets could damage the overall economic situation in a country in that the higher mobility makes it possible for ever more actors to shift their ventures if in their opinion 'bad policies' are being pursued. For this reason, global markets have made it expensive to pursue inward-looking interventionist policies, since the opportunity costs have risen proportionally to the growth of the transnational sector.[13]

Interests. We can presume that increased transnational business (including exports) as a share of total economic output leads to the growth of those interest groups that prefer economic policy frameworks that provide them with good prerequisites for competing on the world market. This includes such aspects as economies of scale by increasing market size, liberalization through deregulation, cheaper access to foreign primary products and components by lowering tariffs, a stable monetary environment and low taxes. The rising importance of these interest groups as a result of the growth of global markets is a consequence not only of their quantitative increase (as a proportion of GNP), but also of their ability to demand. In contrast to local or national sectors, they can threaten to 'exit' more realistically and gain more political influence ('voice') than firms that do not produce for the world market or cannot lay claim to foreign involvement and experience. Apart from these differences, the development of global markets and the associated liberalization *fundamentally* facilitate transnational activities. Attractive conditions have to be offered not only to those already involved in transnational activities, but also to *potential* transnational actors to entice them to the country and to retain them. This is especially important for the first group.

Instruments. The effectiveness of state instruments is limited primarily by the greater mobility of capital, production and investment, but also by the globalization of the division of labour. Controls on capital transactions and business taxes no longer have the same effect, government expenditures cannot influence business cycles as they once could, demand stimulation flows out of the country through imports and so on. In conjunction with the incentives for market liberalization, the reduced efficiency of some measures can lead governments purposely to dismantle them further. The combination of the declining efficacy of some instruments of government regulation and the growing competitive pressure has altered the cost effectiveness of neo-Keynesian or interventionist import substituting economic policy and has made a liberalizing competition policy attractive.

Thus, global markets modify the governments' policy options in a number of ways and increase both the incentives to pursue a policy oriented towards global competitiveness and the costs of a more inward-looking interventionist strategy.

The delineated reduction in the efficacy of state instruments and the increase in the costs of measures that do not take into account the competitive pressure of global markets are not, however, processes proceeding independently of states. On the contrary, the causes of the emergence of global markets made it clear that governments were decisive promoters of this development. 'The state' is, therefore, not exposed to an exogenous force that it is unable to influence. Rather, it is itself a co-generator of global mobility and competition. Boyer and Drache's title, *States against Markets* (1996), is misleading in so far as it suggests an antagonism that although it holds true for the different tasks, ways of functioning and territorial range, neglects the fact that global markets emerged only as a result of state measures aiming at the promotion of growth.

3

GLOBAL MARKETS AND
THE EUROPEAN SINGLE MARKET

3.1 Liberalization Strategies in the Single Market Project '1992'

The realization of a single market in the European Community was a constitutive element of the Treaty of Rome of 1957. However, in the following three decades, only some steps towards the free movement of goods, services, labour and capital were undertaken. The reasons for this were first the maintenance of national regulations that could be only partially harmonized in time-consuming negotiations, second, the widespread effort of governments to protect national sectors by keeping domestic markets relatively closed and, third, the desire to retain the largest possible autonomy in steering their economies (Tsoukalis 1992: 14–147; W. Wallace 1994: 58–86). These motives of national governments for opposing the Europe-wide liberalization necessary for a single market corresponded with the neo-Keynesian economic policy dominant in most EC member states in the 1960s and 1970s. Protecting national sectors from outside competitors, steering the economy by means of neo-Keynesian demand management and maintaining the efficiency of their instruments required a degree of interventionism and control over their own economies that contradicted Europe-wide factor mobility.

Although a considerable reduction in customs duties had been reached by the mid-1980s and a number of norms had been harmonized, the European 'Single Market' remained incomplete. Thus, the project to complete the single market by 1992 represented a distinct step, not only in the European integration, but also in the strategies of national economic policy. The EC member states gave up neo-Keynesian economic policies and with them the hesitant attitude towards full integration at the European level. They anchored this change of strategy towards a deregulated opening of their economies in a regional – and therefore also in a national – framework. Substituting the former paradigm of harmonization by the mutual recognition of standards implied a fundamental change in the integration process. It would no longer be necessary to negotiate detailed compromises at the technical level; instead different national regulations would be allowed to compete. Consequently, the liberalization strategy of the single market was less a continuation of earlier integration methods and more a new approach to economic policy and integration.[1]

Regulations

The Treaty of Rome (Arts 2, 3a, 3c) and the supplements to the treaty by the SEA of 1986 (ratified in 1987) on the completion of the single market by 31 December 1992 (Art. 8a–c) are the foundations of the single market. The SEA's most important goal was the realization of the *four freedoms* – that is, the free movement of goods, services, labour and capital. The principle of the *mutual recognition* of norms and standards was the central instrument in achieving this goal and thus reducing the alternative strategy of harmonization to a minimum. Until that time, harmonization had been the rule and was one of the main reasons for the inadequate implementation of the 'four freedoms' in the decades following the signing of the Treaty of Rome (Moravcsik 1991: 41). Whereas direct tariffs had been reduced to a great extent, much less progress was achieved in lowering the non-tariff barriers such as norms. However, harmonization was also the instrument – very popular with the member states' governments – that allowed them to retain the regulation of market forces and to minimize the negative political effects of competition. By accepting the principle of mutual recognition, the states had to relinquish this instrument. The foundation for '1992' was henceforth the automatic acceptance on the domestic market of all goods that had been legally produced according to the regulations of their (EC) country of origin.

Except for minimum standards (such as environmental, health and consumer protection),[2] mutual recognition eradicates all non-tariff trade barriers and stimulates intra-European competition. The further dismantling of protective tariffs enhances this effect. Additional measures for completing the single market were:

- providing free transfer of investment and portfolio capital by removal of capital controls;
- improving the decision-making and implementation process by introducing qualified majority voting in the European Council for most of the directives pertaining to the single market (the previous need for unanimity had often blocked liberalization);
- restricting the role of the Council of Ministers to the formulation of basic requirements for standards not subject to mutual recognition and leaving the technical specifics to the Centre Européen de Normalisation (CEN; European Norm Organization);
- opening the public procurement markets to bidders from other member states;
- dismantling the entry barriers for other EC suppliers of financial (banks and insurance) and transport (airlines) services;
- encouraging transborder movement of labour by mutual recognition of education, training and qualifications;
- aligning taxes (e.g. value-added tax) to remove competition distortions.

All in all, the Commission presented to the Council 282 measures for the reduction of material, technical and tax barriers, which were considered necessary for the realization of the single market. The single market regulations followed the strategy of 'negative integration' – that is, integrating by dismantling national restraints and regulative competencies (Schreiber and Woolcock 1991: 26). In contrast to the previous harmonization strategy, integration was supposed to progress not by means of new joint regulation ('positive integration'), but rather by competition between the (mutually recognized) national requirements. Although the exceptions to the deregulation strategy (such as the agricultural, coal and steel sectors) and the discrimination against third parties provided some protectionist sectors with privileges, the SMP's liberalizing orientation was the dominant characteristic.

Goals

The single market's primary goal was to stimulate economic growth. This was to be achieved by freeing market forces through liberalization as well as by reaching economies of scale through an enlargement of the market and by enhancing the efficiency and specialization advantages following from greater competition (Jacquemin and Sapir 1991). Thus, the single market pursued a supply-side-oriented economic policy and broke with the tradition of the national neo-Keynesian demand management followed in the 1960s and 1970s. By improving conditions for European enterprises on the European market, lowering production costs by means of a larger market, strengthening competition and reducing transport costs and non-tariff barriers, the price level was to be lowered and production was to be expanded. The expectation was that this would improve the competitiveness of European suppliers on their own markets and on the world market. The desired consequences included a growth in the European GDP and a reduction in the level of unemployment in the EC.[3] The Checchini Report, written by a group of experts at the request of the EC Commission, details examples of the economic strategy and expectations that the SMP would pursue:

> The release of these constraints will trigger a supply-side shock to the Community economy as a whole. The name of the shock is European market integration. Costs will come down. Prices will follow as business, under pressure of new rivals on previously protected markets, is forced to develop fresh responses to a novel and permanently changing situation. Ever-present competition will ensure the completion of a self-sustaining virtuous circle. The downward pressure on prices will in turn stimulate demand, giving companies the opportunity to increase output, to exploit resources better and to scale them up for European, and global, competition.   (Checchini 1988: p. xix)

One central concern was improving the competitiveness of European companies: 'At present in many key sectors, companies are operating without the specialization and size necessary to compete globally' (Checchini 1988: 21). Shifting from the previous harmonization strategy to mutual recognition was supposed to strengthen market forces, as henceforth the national regulatory frameworks would compete with one another for production and investment (Winters 1995: 220). In this way, the governments of the member states were obliged to formulate their national regulations such that their enterprises would not suffer from competitive disadvantages in the area of Europe. The single market was to provide even the already strong and globally active 'national champions' with an improvement of their position so that they could function as 'European champions' on the regional and world market. The orientation towards external competition became a maxim – to the detriment of domestic steering measures. Apart from the economic policy shift from demand to supply-side orientation, the single market therefore also changed the governments' influence on European and national economic policy. Substituting mutual recognition for the former harmonization procedures was also intended to reduce the influence of interest groups that might be negatively affected by competition and consequently interested in seeking state protection: 'Another advantage is that harmonization is not undertaken ex ante at the political bargaining table under the influence of interest groups, but follows from an anonymous market process in which the power of interest groups evaporates' (Siebert 1989: 6).

The goal of strengthening market forces in order to stimulate growth and competitiveness went hand in hand with the reduction of the state's and interest groups' regulative influence on the economic process. This lowers the likelihood of political protection for national sectors and therefore of *rent-seeking* – that is, of drawing profit from state protection, instead of from marketable goods. Thus, the single market also envisioned the use of the European level for pushing through necessary structural changes in the members' economies. Stronger competition in conjunction with an acceptable reduction in governments' ability to secure regulative protection from market forces was aimed at encouraging an adjustment that would be less subject to political influence than had previously been the case in the national arenas (Clement 1988). As the costs of adjustment to stronger competition (job losses, closing of production sites, etc.) were expected to be greatest in the least developed regions of Western Europe, the SEA also included a scaling-up of the transfer payments to these regions (possibly via the structural fund). The industrialized countries of the EC used these *side-payments* to secure the support of the SEA by countries such as Greece, Portugal and Spain.

According to the Checchini Report's optimistic prognoses, the completion of the single market was meant to achieve the following macroeconomic goals in the 'medium term' (Checchini 1988: 97; for critics, see Herrmann et al. 1990: 65–73):

- additional growth of the EC's gross domestic product by an average of 4.5 per cent;
- reduction of inflation by an average of 6.1 per cent;
- an easing of public budgets by 2.2 per cent of GDP and an improvement of the EC's balance of trade by 1 per cent of GDP.
- creation of 1.8 million new jobs and thus a reduction in the unemployment rate of 1.5 per cent.

According to a 1996 report by the Commission, the SMP had the following results (*The Economist*, 15 Mar. 1997: 23ff; Monti 1996):

- the GDP of the EU in 1994 was about 1.1–1.5 per cent higher than it would have been without the single market;
- 900,000 additional jobs were created;
- because of the single market, the inflation rate in 1994 was 1.1–1.5 per cent lower than it would have been otherwise; the low inflation is attributed primarily to the competition enhancing measures of the single market;
- the intra-European (EC/EU) trade grew from 61.2 per cent (1985) to 67.9 per cent (1995) of the member states' total trade;
- the investment among the EC/EU countries quintupled between 1985 and 1993;
- the EC/EU's share of worldwide direct investment rose from 28.2 per cent (1982–7) to 44.4 per cent (1990–5);
- the EC/EU's productivity climbed during 1986–91 by 2 per cent per year, as opposed to 0.97 per cent in the USA and 1.8 per cent in Japan.

Although these figures clearly deviate from those of the Checchini Report, the single market's substantial contribution to the economic development of Western Europe can be documented. Europe's considerably larger share of worldwide direct investment derives not only from more attractive conditions and a larger economic growth, but also from the efforts of companies from third countries to obtain the same competitive conditions the single market offers their European rivals by producing 'on site'. Apart from the quantitatively measurable macroeconomic dimension, the outcome of '1992' also includes the multilateral contractual and political anchoring of competition-oriented liberal economic policy and thus the continuation of the reversal of the regulatory, inward-looking national policies of the 1960s and 1970s: 'In truth, this 1992 project is an adventure in deregulation: that is why Britain likes the sound of it. That, curiously, is why the French and the West Germans go along with it. Deregulation is the economic treatment of the decade – a fashionable medicine which European countries know they should swallow like good patients, even if they dislike its taste' ('Survey: Europe's Internal Market', *The Economist*, 9 July 1988: 12).

The examination of the role of global markets in forming national preferences for decisions on liberalizing cooperation can concentrate on France, Germany and the UK. These countries were decisive for constituting the single market and providing its qualitative direction (Moravcsik 1991: 42). They were not only the largest economies in the EC, but also the politically most influential member states, with the highest number of votes in the European Council. Germany and France were at that time also the decisive driving forces of European integration. Moreover, the smaller member states demonstrate a higher level of foreign economic integration, are thereby more strongly affected by global markets and have even less scope for individual policy initiatives. In other words, if global markets have contributed to changes in economic preferences and economic policy in France, Germany and the UK, then we can presume that the smaller countries were subject to this effect at least to the same extent, if not more.[4]

3.2   France

In the 1970s, the liberal-conservative President Giscard d'Estaing pursued a careful policy of opening up by exposing the French economy to world market influences in addition to the integration into the EC. The resulting structural adjustment was accompanied by a growing internationalization demonstrated by the GDP's rising export and import dependency and more intensive capital flows. The export share of the French GDP rose from 16 per cent (1970) to 22 per cent (1980), while that of imports swelled from 15 per cent (1970) to 23 per cent (1980). This level of foreign economic relations was maintained throughout the 1980s (in 1990 both exports and imports amounted to a share of about 23 per cent of the GDP) (UNCTAD 1997b: 295). France's economic and political development in the years prior to the SMP of 1986 experienced two distinct phases. In 1981, the newly elected government of the Parti Socialiste (PS; Socialist Party) and President François Mitterrand began a 'socialist experiment' of neo-Keynesian, inward-looking economic steering that had to be relinquished in 1982–83 in favour of an increasingly liberal austerity policy, the *rigueur*.[5] Thus, in the case of France it is important to examine to what extent global markets contributed to this change of course or were seen as a cause of the reversal of policy.

Mitterrand's 'experiment socialiste'

The election of François Mitterrand to the presidency in 1981 and the winning of a majority in the National Assembly for the coalition led by the PS marked the first accession to power by the left in France since the late 1940s. The *projet socialiste* in economic policy was based on a classic mix of neo-Keynesian demand stimulation by a state-ordained increase in purchasing power and dirigistic allocation of resources (raising the minimum wage and state expenditures, nationalization, more regulation). It was an experiment in 'redistributive Keynesianism' (Hall 1987: 55) with which unemployment was to be lowered, economic growth was to be encouraged and, most of all, the distribution of wealth (wages and property) was to be shifted in favour of the lower income groups. For example, the purchasing power of the minimum wage – to which many other wages were pegged – was briefly raised by 10.6 per cent in 1981–2 (compared to 3.3 per cent in 1979–80).

Together with a sizeable expansion in the number of public sector jobs and a noticeable rise in social benefits, the socialist government's programme came to 2 per cent of GDP (OECD 1988: 59). As a result, domestic demand grew by 4 per cent in 1982, while in other OECD countries it fell slightly, in keeping with the tendency of the worldwide recession. It sank by 2 per cent in Germany, France's most important trading partner (OECD 1988: 59). As a result of an extensive programme of nationalization (especially of banks and large enterprises), the nationalized sectors' share of the total economy grew considerably in 1982 (employees: from 13 per cent to 16 per cent; exports: from 11 per cent to 23 per cent; investment: from 29 per cent to 36 per cent) (Uterwedde 1987: 105). At the macroeconomic level, this policy in conjunction with France's integration into the world economy had the following effects.

(1) The initial growth in domestic purchasing power led to a distinct reduction in exports (more of the production was consumed domestically) and to a considerable rise in imports. Because of the foreign trade penetration of the French economy (around 20 per cent of GDP), a disproportionately large share of the growth in demand could flow out of the country. The increase in the growth rate between 1981 and 1982 by 1.6 per cent led to an expansion of the volume of imports by about 5 per cent in 1982 (Albert and Ball 1983:

40). The balance of trade (goods and services) for 1982 showed a record deficit of FF 69 billion (1980: FF 34 billion) (OECD 1990: 227). Thus, although the new economic policy did stimulate domestic demand, it was much less successful in stimulating domestic production and the creation of jobs in the private sector. One reason why domestic suppliers were unable to expand production to meet rising demand was the deterioration of their profits.

(2) The profit margins of many enterprises were reduced by wage hikes and higher taxes as well as by the growing social security contributions from companies (*The Economist*, 31 July 1982: 56). This led to a noticeable decline in investment, which further damaged the competitiveness of the French industry. Productive investment fell by almost 8 per cent from 1980 to 1984 (OECD 1988: 61). This took place against the background of a French economy whose competitiveness had already declined in the 1970s by comparison to that of Germany, the USA or Japan. France functioned as an 'intermediary' economy, whose competitiveness lay neither in capital goods (Germany) nor in high technology (Japan, USA), but, rather, in technologically less demanding products, which it exported with political support primarily to developing countries. In 1983, France ran its largest bilateral trade deficits (excluding oil) with Germany, the USA, the Netherlands and Japan, whereas it achieved surpluses in trade with countries such as Egypt, Tunisia and Greece (*The Economist*, 24 Mar. 1984: 61). This already precarious competitive situation was further undermined by the increase in companies' costs in 1981–2.

(3) The rapid increase of interest rates as a result of the *crowding-out* of private lending by the state also contributed to the decline of investment. In order to finance extensive social programmes and nationalization, the French government was obliged to issue public bonds on the open market. In this way, the state drove the interest rates up, making private loans for investment and consumption purposes more expensive. In view of the worldwide increase in interest rates (caused primarily by the USA's high interest rate policy) during these years, a deflationary policy – not Mitterrand's reflationary rate-increasing strategy – would have been a means of countering the negative effects of the global wave of high interest rates on the investment level in France.

(4) The franc came under international pressure, especially because of the rapidly deteriorating balance of trade, the equally negative trend of the balance of payments and inflation driven by *deficit*

spending. The rising difference in inflation levels between France and important trading partners like Germany and the UK, which were following deflationary stability-oriented policies, was decisive for the weakness of the franc. In October 1981, the socialist government was obliged to devalue the franc for the first time; a second depreciation followed in June of 1982 and a third in March of 1983.

(5) The inflation rate increased substantially, in part because of higher domestic production costs, exploding state expenditures (partially financed by printing money), rising interest rates and growing imports at a time when the franc was falling against other currencies.

(6) The budget deficit grew quickly as a result of the rapidly increasing government expenditures for the 'experiment's' programmes: in 1981, the budget deficit came to FF 64 billion (as opposed to FF 24 billion in 1980); in 1982, the government planned to spend FF 93 billion more than its income (OECD statistics, from Uterwedde 1987: 111).

Failure of the experiment, rigueur *and the single market*

In view of the costs of the 'socialist experiment' in the form of budget deficits, depreciation pressure, rising interest rates and inflation as well as the outflow of demand, by 1982 a change of policy was already necessary. If the French state had taken on further debt to finance its programme or its budget deficits, the foreign trade balance would have deteriorated further, and an additional increase in the inflation level would have placed even more downward pressure on the currency. In principle, the government had two options. On the one hand, it could have withdrawn from international arrangements or partially severed France's links with the world economy. The discussion of possible measures included quitting the European Monetary System (EMS) to enable the government to devalue the currency[6] at its will, as well as a selective disassociation from the world economy via capital controls and restrictions on imports (Hall 1987: 56). On the other hand, France could have adapted its policies to the foreign economic pressure by improving the competitiveness of its economy and the stability of its currency. This would have required better conditions for investment (lower interest rates and inflation), for production (wages, taxes and social security contributions) and a generally more stable economic situation. In view of the high costs and low efficacy of 'redistributive Keynesianism', the government chose the second option, which it implemented from 1983 on in the framework of the *rigueur*, an austerity policy led by Finance Minister Jacques Delors. The following causes were decisive for this reversal of policy.

(1) Even a careful withdrawal from the world economy and from international agreements would have heightened the pressure on the franc and capped access to external sources of financing *deficit spending* and supporting the exchange rate. France's creditworthiness would have declined, access to capital markets would have become more difficult and international sources of assistance (EMS, Bank for International Settlements (BIS), International Monetary Fund (IMF)) would have dried up. Instead of ameliorating the situation, this would have heightened the compulsion to austerity. According to the Finance Ministry's estimates of 1983, leaving the EMS would have resulted in a 20 per cent devaluation of the franc, which would have forced the government to institute drastic savings measures (deflation) to avoid a sudden leap in inflation and a substantial deterioration of the balance of payments (Goodman 1989: 177) Moreover, membership in the EMS provided an external anchor for an anti-inflationary policy (OECD 1988: 62). Import restrictions for strategic (preventing the outflow of demand) or financial reasons (insufficient foreign exchange) would have led to substantial cost increases or scarcity for one-fifth of the goods bought in France at that time and thus a decline in the standard of living, more inflation and an increase in the cost of production (due to more expensive imported components and primary products).

(2) Introducing trade barriers would have been a break with the careful strategy of opening the French economy – pursued since 1958 in the context of the EEC – which had formed the basis for the relatively successful economic development of the 1960s and 1970s. Besides the political costs (international isolation, rupture with the EC/Germany), the French exporters would have had to expect massive countermeasures from those countries excluded from the French market – that is, lower exports for French producers. This would have threatened the *c*.20 per cent of GDP and jobs dependent upon exports.

(3) The 'socialist experiment' was unable to achieve its two main goals to the expected degree: as production failed to expand, unemployment could not be substantially reduced and the initial

increase in purchasing power was in part balanced by the rising inflation. The low effectiveness of the inward-looking neo-Keynesian strategy led to a weakening of the traditional faction in the governing PS and to a strengthening of the 'internationalist' faction – that is, those politicians (foremost among them, Jacques Delors) who advocated a strategy of stability, opening up, and global competitiveness (Gourevitch 1987: 186ff). A similar shift took place among the economically relevant *interest* groups. The problems associated with the inward-looking experiment weakened the position of the 'anti-capitalist' trade union, the Confédération Générale du Travail (CGT) and strengthened the 'internationalist' faction in the more moderate Confédération Française Démocratique du Travail (CFDT) (see Uterwedde 1987: 96, 181–203). On the business side, the exporters (*tradables*) turned out to be the losers of the 1981–2 developments (in part owing to sinking competitiveness because of higher costs for labour, investment and taxes), while the *non-tradable* sector's expectations of higher profits remained unfulfilled because of the demand outflow to imports, the high inflation and interest rates, and growing taxes.[7]

(4) All in all, the pressure of the *contrainte extérieure*, the external economic restrictions, was decisive for relinquishing redistributive Keynesianism and for introducing a stability-oriented neoliberal policy after 1983. For one thing, the French economy's external connectedness did not offer the socialist experiment the expected success, since, because of the degree of internationalization, important *instruments* were not sufficiently effective. To a large extent, the expansion of demand to stimulate growth (job creation) flowed out of the country, and the control over interest rates and inflation necessary for realizing the total nominal growth in purchasing power did not function. As a result, the desired effects of demand-oriented domestic steering were largely offset by the integration with global markets. For another, the *contrainte extérieure* led to considerable *costs* – that is, to a crisis that necessitated a change in strategy in order to secure the population's support.

(5) The radical rise in government spending in 1981–2 had led to a sharp increase in public debt, including foreign debt (in dollars to private banks). According to the Finance Ministry, a trade surplus of FF 20–30 billion would have been needed annually to service the external liabilities, but this surplus could not be achieved with the 'socialist experiment' ('Survey on France', *The Economist*, 9 Feb. 1985: 9). If the government did not want to speculate on the dollar

or the international interest rates dropping, it had to change its economic policy with respect to settling its debts to transnational creditor banks as well. Regarding the role of global markets for the change of course in 1982–3, an OECD study concludes that: 'At the political level it was above all the pressures in the exchange market, reflected in a fall in reserves, as well as mounting foreign debt, that seem to have persuaded the government to act' (OECD 1988: 64).

The decision in favour of openness to foreign trade and a deflationary reduction of demand through *rigueur* was thus a direct result of the costs of the inward-looking interventionist policy that was due to France's integration into global markets. A close adviser of Mitterrand and Secretary-General of the Élysée at that time, Hubert Védrine, wrote about the contemporary perception of global markets as a cause of the change in the economic paradigm: 'And March 1983 clearly reminded us that France is not an island, but rather part of an ensemble, the global market, in whose midst an open economy cannot afford to be a debtor for too long a time without risking monetary sanctions and [external] tutelage' (Védrine 1996: 294).

Védrine later became Minister of Foreign Affairs. The austerity policy beginning in 1982–3 still showed strong state intervention in the economy but shifted increasingly to a more liberal policy before Chirac's conservative government (1986–8) replaced the PS. Finance Minister Jacques Delors played a decisive role in the *rigueur* until he was appointed president of the EC Commission in 1985. The *rigueur* aimed foremost at reducing inflation and improving the competitiveness of industry, which was supposed to counter the foreign financial (devaluation) and trade (deficit) pressures. The central measures of the new policy were a diminution of the purchasing power (freezing wages and salaries), a limitation of the public budget deficits to 3 per cent of GDP (in 1982 alone the expenditures were cut by FF 20 billion) and an improvement of the French economy's competitiveness. Social security contributions and taxes for entrepreneurs were lowered or frozen. The inflation and the budget deficit were to be tackled by throttling purchasing power through tax hikes (see Fröhlich 1986: 80–4; Hall 1987: 57; Uterwedde 1987: 111–40).

While the costs of redistributive Keynesianism in 1981–3 were shouldered mostly by companies, the burden of the deflationary austerity policy was borne to a great extent by wage and salary earners. The only reason this did not result in the government's loss of public support was that high inflation, the foreign trade deficit, the lack of global competitiveness and the franc's weak exchange rate secured a relatively high level of acceptance for the austerity programme with the majority of the population. Prior to the change of course due to the 'socialist experiment', the PS had experienced substantial losses at the local elections of 1982–3. Electorally, Mitterrand was more dependent on votes from the political centre than on those of the Communists, whose quitting of the coalition could therefore be consciously taken into account. In contrast to the neo-Keynesian deficit spending and purchasing power stimulation of 1981–2, the effects of the austerity programme manifested themselves only in the mid- and long term. Despite a relatively efficient implementation of the new policy, unemployment remained high and economic growth got off to a slow start. Only in 1985 did an improved economic situation become visible: inflation was reduced from 12.6 per cent (1982) to 5 per cent (1985), the balance of payments was in equilibrium in 1985 (after deficits in 1981– 4), and investment (1982: −7 per cent; 1983: −4 per cent; 1984: +10 per cent) and growth rose again after years of stagnation (Hall 1987: 61, 64). However, domestically the new economic policy was successful only in so far as the conservative opposition could hardly find points of criticism prior to the 1986 elections (*The Economist*, 25 Jan. 1986: 48). As a result, the positive economic developments materialized too late for the government to benefit from them domestically, since the conservatives were able to win the 1986 elections for the National Assembly.

In view of the unrelentingly high unemployment rate, the decline in real wages and the moderate growth figures, the government's political survival depended on its ability to give the new course political legitimacy, which would make it possible for the PS to stay in power. The appointment of the reformer Delors to the presidency of the EC Commission in 1985 can also be seen from this perspective: using new EC initiatives to secure the national reform programme politically and to flank it economically appeared to be an effective means. On the subject of the French strategy in 1985–8 with regard to the EC SMP, Deubner (1989: 85) concludes: 'Thus, to a certain extent, Europe is blamed for the present impossibility of a national policy against unemployment – which all the parties seem to find equally difficult and thankless – while the hopes for once again attaining competitiveness, growth and more employment in the future are also projected onto Europe.'

The experiment of 1981–2 also demonstrated to the populace that France's economy was too strongly intertwined abroad to follow a successful strategy that did not take the *contrainte extérieure* into account. The losers of this policy had voiced their concerns and the state had reached the limits of its financing and steering abilities. The change of course to *rigueur* not only made the advantages of a liberal EC single market more compatible with national preferences; the government also considered the single market a desirable option for an economically more effective implementation of its own growth strategy. Mitterrand's adviser Védrine wrote (1996: 286) about the causal importance of *rigueur* for Mitterrand's liberalizing strategy in his efforts for a 'relance européenne': 'De fait, son [Mitterrand's] forcing européen des années 1984–92 est impensable sans le préalable de la rigueur de mars 1983'.

An efficient implementation of the new austerity and competition policy implied further liberalizations. This stimulated the preference for a liberalizing strategy on the European level and made the single market attractive as an external legitimation of the competition-oriented strategy's costs, which would have arisen anyway. The latter, for example, became clear when Prime Minister Rocard's government (socialist again after 1988) had to deal with the public sector's strikes. The President, the Prime Minister and the Minister of the Economy all explained their refusal to make any concessions to the unions by referring to European competition (Deubner 1989: 85). They had successfully acquired a new and contractually legitimated justification for the implementation of policies, which had become necessary since 1983 because of external economic pressures. The SMP turned national liberalization into a regional obligation. President Mitterrand stated in 1989 that 'we [the EC members] have mutually committed ourselves to eliminate protectionism in all its forms, also the hidden ones' (Mitterrand 1989: 2).

The French government did not give the SMP approbation for its own sake, but rather as an instrument 'in order to adapt the country fundamentally to the realities of a new world' (Zibura 1989: 11). In addition to this legitimating function, it was possible to attach various contradictory hopes to the SMP (improved global competitiveness as well as better protection against the USA and Japan) and at the same time to accommodate the awareness, growing since 1982, that it is ever less possible to limit economic development to national impetus (Lequesne 1988: 361). With regard to the legitimizing effects of the single market, Deubner concludes (1989: 84):

> Furthermore, in the last three years 'Europe' and '1992' have been placed so prominently in the foreground by all the parties (except Le Pen-supporters and Communists) in part simply because these concepts fill important gaps in the domestic policies parties are offering to the voters. They fill them – and that is especially important – with a challenge from the outside, through which in France itself the necessity of austerity and hardships is given new legitimacy, while the demand for a stronger social component in the battle against unemployment has its legitimacy withdrawn from the outset.

The entrepreneurs – except for the traditional sectors of protectionistically secured rent-seekers – saw the SMP as an instrument to deepen the liberalization strategy. The president of the Conseil National du Patronat Français (CNPF; French Employers' Association), François Perigot (1987), stated: 'In order to be successful, the French employers... need a liberal and competitive Europe. The Europe of 1992 should not become an overregulated superstate, it must be a liberal space.'

Moreover, the SMP represented the most effective mechanism in order to assure that the (business friendly) economic reforms since 1983 would be made irreversible by international treaties. Regarding the connection between the liberal reforms and the SMP, a representative of the economically liberal faction in the political spectrum, the leading politician of the Parti Républicain, Alain Madelin (1988: 42), declared: 'But in order to make this change irreversible, nothing is better than external pressure exerted by competition on the European market... The French and British must join forces to construct this Europe, to preserve the magnificent European dream from the ever returning temptation of *dirigisme*' (emphasis in the original).

As opinion polls showed, the legitimating aspect of the SMP in France was successful, since the criticism of the negative aspects of *rigueur* did not aim at its legitimation by the European treaty. Whereas public opinion was very positively attuned to European policy matters after the decision on the SEA and anti-European attitudes had declined, some groups of voters remained dissatisfied with the inability of the liberal economic policy to lower unemployment (Deubner 1989a: 84ff). The European explanation was even accepted for measures that were contested by segments of the population. In view of these indications, we can presume that implementing the new policies without tying them into the obligations of the European treaty would have resulted in higher domestic political costs. A further indication of the single market's domestic policy functionality is the PS's victory in the elections for the National Assembly and the presidency in 1988, after a campaign in which the SMP was one of the central elements (Lequesne 1988: 369). Mitterrand and the protagonists of the liberalizing change of course of 1983 were able to stay in power – until Chirac was elected president in 1995. The liberalizing strategy since 1983 and the SMP's liberalizations, which commenced in 1987, also contributed to the success of the French economy in the second half of the 1980s: exports (as an indicator of global competitiveness) rose in 1985–90 by 15.3 per cent (compared to 1980–5: –2.6); machinery and transport goods' share of total exports was higher in 1990 than in 1980; the gross domestic product grew in 1985–90 by 3.1 per cent (1980–5: 1.5) (UNCTAD 1997b: 14, 118, 286).

3.3   Germany

Problems of neo-Keynesianism

The use of demand-stimulating instruments with a concomitant focus on exports was characteristic of the economic policy of the coalition of the social democratic with the liberal party in the 1970s (Deubner 1984: 526–31). The involvement of the FRG in foreign trade had grown substantially since 1970: exports' share in GDP had risen from 21 per cent (1970) to 26 per cent (1980), that of imports from 19 per cent (1970) to 27 per cent (1980). In the subsequent decade, exports increased further to 32 per cent (1990), while the share of imports in 1990 (26 per cent) was slightly lower than in 1980 (UNCTAD 1997b: 295). The shift in economic policy from variations of neo-Keynesianism to a more supply-side-oriented stability policy had already begun in the last year of Helmut Schmidt's government and was continued after 1982 by Chancellor Helmut Kohl. For this reason, it is useful to examine the last years of the Schmidt government in order to study the causes of the political shift. Of course, other factors that had nothing to do with global markets (such as the rise in oil prices in 1979 through the OPEC cartel) also played an important role in this transition. However, the effects of the West German economy's integration into global markets (then called 'Internationalization') contributed decisively to the crisis of neo-Keynesian policy, to a shift in the structure of interests and to the limitation of state instruments – that is to say, to the impression that the previous path had become inadequate. Global markets produced costs, weakened instruments and thus raised the incentives for a change of course (Giersch et al. 1992: 240–50; OECD 1988: 45–55; Scharpf 1987: 185–98):

(1) The consequences of relinquishing fixed exchange rates at the end of the Bretton Woods System hit the DM especially hard, since it became the second most important reserve currency and object of speculation as transnational capital investors and currency traders lost confidence in the dollar. Between 1975 and 1978 the DM's cumulative appreciation against the US dollar amounted to 25 per cent (OECD 1988: 47). Depending on estimates of the respective German or American economic situations, the consequences were first short-term changes in the DM's exchange rate and second an equally short-term influx or outflow of capital to or from Germany.

(2) As a result, Germany's balance of payments depended more strongly than before on the global markets' estimate of economic data (growth, productivity, costs) in comparison to other countries. Thus, the government – and the Bundesbank's money supply management – were less able to influence the balance of payments than they had been in the 1950s and 1960s.

(3) Exchange rate fluctuations tended towards an appreciation of the DM against other currencies – especially against the dollar – and therefore made German exports more expensive. In conjunction with the already high production costs (wages, taxes) by international comparison and tougher global competition, the result was a repeated deterioration of German industry's ability to sell its goods abroad. The increased fluctuation of exchange rates hit Germany especially hard, since its export share of GDP, about one-third, was the highest of the G7 industrialized nations.[8] The DM's appreciation affected a greater proportion of production and employment than was the case in other countries.

(4) One outcome of the deregulation and integration of the capital markets was that the rise in interest rates in the USA after 1979 forced other countries to follow similar policies. Thus, neo-Keynesian *deficit spending* and private investment became more expensive leading to contractionary, restrictive pressures. The higher price of borrowing for states, investors and consumers slowed domestic demand and thereby limited a key neo-Keynesian instrument, despite underutiliza-

tion of production capacity and unemployment, which would in principle have made demand stimulation beneficial. But retaining interest rate differentials at the beginning of the 1980s would have led to massive capital outflows and to a weakening of exchange rates against the dollar after 1979, as well as to a reduction in the currency reserves in the case of support purchases by the Bundesbank and subsequently to a depreciation of the currency.[9]

The foreign trade influence resulting from the development of global financial markets led to a dilemma for the government in its attempts to steer the economy. Simultaneous achievement of growth (by demand-stimulating state expenditures), low inflation and an equilibrium of foreign transactions (balance of trade and payments) became increasingly difficult. The Schmidt government's solution[10] of giving neo-Keynesian growth policy priority over price stability was made more and more impracticable by the reactions of transnational market participants towards the end of the 1970s and particularly in 1980 and 1981, since exchange rate crises raised the costs of the neo-Keynesian measures as well as the incentives for deflationary stability. The OECD (1988: 54) stated with reference to the exchange rate crisis: 'The exchange-rate crisis of early 1981 was essentially the sudden and short-lived reaction of the market to growing evidence of problems in the German society . . . and the view that the authorities were not paying sufficient attention to them.'

The crisis resulted essentially from the convergence of four factors. First, in 1979 the USA began a high interest rate policy that forced other countries to raise their real (inflation-rate adjusted) interest rates, in order to avoid massive capital outflows that were due to increasingly integrated and open capital markets. Second, the oil shock of 1979 substantially increased the costs of imports and the inflationary trend in Germany as well. That year the West German balance of goods and services slid into a deficit for the first time. Third, the DM exchange rate was still overvalued and this obstructed an improvement of exports. Fourth, imports rose due to the domestic pursuit of demand stimulation, for which the government had taken on an international obligation at the G7 summit in Bonn in 1978 ('economic locomotive'). The trade deficit climbed from 6 billion DM in 1979 to 16 billion DM in 1980.[11]

Scharpf (1987: 189) distinguishes three means, in principle, of reacting to exchange rate crises, all of which have 'uncomfortable side-effects'. First, the government and the Bundesbank could have accepted a deficit in the balance of goods and services: the DM rate would have dropped as a result of global investors' withdrawal, and consequently exports would have been stimulated, inflation would have risen and the real purchasing power would have declined. Second, the Bundesbank could have financed the deficit by selling its currency reserves and stabilizing the exchange rate – risking heavy speculation against the DM, rising inflation and sinking real incomes. Third, the Bundesbank could have attracted capital imports by raising interest rates, which would have redressed the deficit and stabilized the DM exchange rate. As a result of the very high interest rates in the USA since the beginning of the 1980s, this option of a restrictive monetary policy would have been possible only by raising the interest rates equally high in Germany, and that would have diametrically opposed the government's goal of achieving full employment by stimulating demand through fiscal expansion. The Bundesbank chose the third option, the deflationary course, in order to retain the trust of global financial markets. In tandem with the tightening of the USA's restrictive policy and the accompanying further increase in interest rates, the Bundesbank also stiffened its policy by raising the discount and Lombard rates as well as by intervening in the currency market. However, these measures obviously did not suffice: in 1980 the DM proceeded to depreciate against the dollar and other currencies, and the Bundesbank responded by further tightening its restrictive monetary policy.

As a result of the exploding interest rates, the costs of the government's expansive fiscal policy rose dramatically and led to a considerable increase in the public debt (interest payments climbed from 25 billion DM in 1979 to 45 billion DM in 1982 (Scharpf 1987: 191)). In 1981, the federal government also began to make the transition to stability by reducing spending and by limiting demand stimulation. Because of the high interest rates, further indebtedness was no longer considered as acceptable as it had been. Economic problems such as the deficit in the balance of goods and services, high interest rates (low investment) and diminished economic growth[12] contributed to the enlargement of state expenditures and to the reduction of its revenues. In the last analysis, the effect of the American high interest rate policy and the speculation against the DM made possible by the expansion of global financial markets intensified the costs to the German economy of continuing an expansive neo-Keynesian policy and led both the Bundesbank and the government to pull the 'emergency brake'. The OECD (1988: 54) concludes: '1981 marked a watershed for fiscal policy and the role of government in the economy. The foreign exchange crisis certainly contributed to speeding-up the decision making process.... external considerations played a major role in the adjustment of monetary policy in early 1981 and may have imposed a degree of stringency beyond what was called for by domestic conditions.'

The 'Wende' and the single market

In October 1982, Helmut Schmidt (Sozialdemokratische Partei Deutschlands (SPD – Social Democratic Party)) was dismissed from office by a constructive vote of no confidence by the Bundestag and Helmut Kohl (Christlich Demokratische Union (CDU – Christian Democratic Union)) was elected chancellor. The change of government was made possible because the Freie Demokratische Partei (FDP – Liberal Party) left the social-democratic–liberal coalition and provided the CDU/CSU (Christlich Soziale Union) with a majority in parliament. This change of coalition partners was essentially but not exclusively due to a growing incompatibility of the interests of the SPD's and FDP's most important clientele groups. The effects of global markets had caused the preferences of these interest groups to diverge. As Scharpf (1987: 194–8) explains, the social-democratic–liberal coalition was based on the two groups' mutual interest in the growth of the goods sector. Simplified, this means that the profits of the entrepreneurial group (represented by the FDP) were stimulated by the demand management policy (sale of goods), whereas labour (represented by the SPD) was able to realize a real increase in purchasing power through wage agreements above the inflation level and through expanding state expenditures. This convergence of interests collapsed in 1979–82. The growing unit labour costs lowered the profit margins of entrepreneurial activity, while at the same time alternative opportunities for profit (transnational capital investment) became more attractive because of the globalized wave of high interest rates. Whereas in the case of low (1975: 2.3 per cent) or negative real interest rates in the mid-1970s almost every profitable business had been worth investing in, real interest rates of up to 5.9 per cent (1981) meant that production now had to compete for funds with portfolio investment on capital markets. The opportunities for making a profit on global financial markets were completely independent of national growth and employment rates. However, in order to seek these profit opportunities, it was more important to have a greater share of freely disposable capital (a redistribution, for example, by means of tax reductions) than higher aggregate demand – that is, economic growth.[13]

In view of the rising opportunity costs for productive investment, the Schmidt government began to ease the burden on entrepreneurs and cut back the labour-friendly measures as early as 1981. However, this led to problems with Schmidt's party (the SPD) and the trade unions. All in all, the SPD neither could nor wanted to follow the FDP's proposals to the extent the CDU was prepared to offer (*The Economist*, 30 Jan. 1982: 70). At the same time, the FDP clientele exercised a growing pressure on the party to effect a change in the government's policy. This pressure became obvious in an opinion poll conducted by the Allensbach Institute: if the FDP had not left the Schmidt government, its electoral support would have fallen below 5 per cent, and after the next election, the party would no longer have had a seat in the Bundestag (*The Economist*, 25 Sept. 1982: 37). The most influential FDP politician of that time, Minister of the Economy Otto Graf Lambsdorff, conducted the negotiations with the CDU and in his '10 Theses' of September 1982 he formulated the programme for the change of government on 1 October. In addition to the depicted reasons for the FDP's change of coalition, the Schmidt government also had to accept a loss of the populace's confidence, in part due to NATO's missile deployment (which a majority of the population opposed), the rising public debt (the opposition spoke of a 'looming state bankruptcy') and the persistently high level of unemployment (which discredited neo-Keynesian recipes).

In the last analysis, the new Kohl government did not carry out a comprehensive deregulation and liberalization of the economy, as Prime Minister Thatcher had done in the UK after 1979. Instead, Kohl continued the policy that Helmut Schmidt had begun in 1981 of consolidating the budget (reducing the deficit and the public debt) by 'cutting into the social security net' and supplemented this policy with tax reductions for business, careful deregulation and measures to fight inflation. In the mid-1980s, the budget deficit found a new level, down from 4 per cent (1981–2) to 1–2 per cent of GDP; in 1986 the balance of payments reached a surplus of 4.4 per cent of GDP after negative accounts in 1979–1; in 1983 a slow recovery set in, but only in 1988 did it achieve more than 2 per cent growth. The reduction of the inflation rate from 6.2 per cent (1981) to 0.6 per cent (1987) was considered one of the biggest macroeconomic successes of the new government. However, between 1983 and 1989 unemployment did not fall below the two million mark (statistics taken from Giersch et al. 1992: 193ff; 236ff).

All in all, the Kohl government was unable to liberalize the economy, return to the growth rates of the 1960s or massively reduce unemployment. However, the 'architect' (*The Economist*, 4 Feb. 1984: 4) of Kohl's economic policy, Minister of the Economy Otto Graf Lambsdorff, was able to push through substantial measures to reduce business costs – for example, tax breaks and investment bonuses. This was also supposed to encourage investment – a goal that was only inadequately achieved given the high global interest rate level and the strongly regulated domestic economy. The announced deregulation was only gradually implemented.[14] This was due primarily to the corporativist organization of the West German society and economy, coupled with the narrow majority the government had in the Bundestag, which made it unwise to annoy even the smallest group of voters, if these were well organized. Lobbying groups in areas that seriously needed reform, such as agriculture, the 'sunset' sectors (coal, shipbuilding, textiles, steel), trade unions and in part the entrepreneurial side often hindered the orientation towards competition that would have taken account of growing global competition in the goods and capital markets (Giersch et al. 1992: 235). The government's credibility was particularly undermined by delays or cancellation of already announced measures such as the dismantling of subsidies, the privatization of state enterprises and the reduction of competition-hindering regulations.

Although the profitability of business in Germany had risen in comparison to the years prior to 1982, no significant increase of investment over the 1982 level was registered in the years up to 1988. The attractiveness of other locations within global markets is a major reason for this. The USA drew an especially large proportion of transnational investment in production despite its growing budget deficits. After 1982 President Reagan had increased the USA's microeconomic efficiency by deregulating and its competitiveness as an investment site by offering special incentives (see section 5.3). The subsequent rapid recovery of the American economy was primarily 'investment-driven' – to a large extent by investment from Europe and Japan. The investment activity in the USA rose from 14.4 per cent of GDP in 1982 to 19.1 per cent in 1984, whereas in the FRG it remained unchanged in 1982–4 at 20.6 per cent and 20.5 per cent, respectively (Giersch et al. 1992: 246). The fact that a rise in investment took place despite the – investment-hampering – increase in both interest rates and the dollar's value emphasizes that these capital flows were also attracted by the positive economic situation in the USA.

Germany's asymmetry between the slight aggregate recovery, the improved profit situation of entrepreneurs, investment incentives and a higher propensity to save, on the one hand, and a stagnating rate of investment, on the other, indicates that potential investors' trust in the recovery was not sufficient and / or that the investment alternatives on 'global markets' – especially the USA – were more attractive. Thus, the Kohl government was missing a vital element for the success of its moderate supply-side policy: the improvement of the locational attractivity of Germany relative to its global rivals. The costs of the insufficient locational attractivity in global comparison had grown and so had the incentives for an economically more efficient reform by opening markets and encouraging competition through liberalization in the European setting.

The costs also included the more frequent shift of German firms' production out of the country because of *push* and *pull* factors. While production costs in Germany were high, economies of scale were limited by the size of the market and innovations were hampered by state regulation, other locations became more attractive as a result of deregulation (such as in the UK) and because of industrialization successes coupled with the still relatively low wages in NICs.[15] But the indicator 'production site relocation' is somewhat problematic, because it can be based on a number of causes that would hold even without the effect of global markets, such as high tariffs in target markets ('jump the tariff' production) or the goal of avoiding exchange rate fluctuations. Given the relative weakness in foreign trade competitiveness, the slight recovery after 1983 was achieved mainly through domestic demand, which was not sufficient to put a real dent in the unemployment rate.

In the mid-1980s (that is, before the Bundestag election in January 1987), a slowdown of the moderate recovery during the CDU–CSU–FDP government's first term became apparent.[16] Given this constellation, the foreign and domestic demands for the completion of the EC single market fell on fruitful ground: the project promised to stimulate growth and investment and to push deregulation along, without the government having to take responsibility for the political costs of the various measures. Thus, the government could first counter the world economy's pressure by improving competitiveness, second accommodate the growing criticism from some of its entrepreneurial clients for failing to liberalize and third remove at least in part the topic of 'deregulation' from domestic responsibility. The business community's criticism of the government's policy had become more pointed in 1986–7. The President of the Bundesvereinigung der Deutschen Arbeitgeberverbände (BDA; Federal Association of German Employers), Murmann (1987), wrote, for example: 'to date real structural reforms, worthy of the name, have not been implemented . . . The international top level of German labour costs and social security contributions has prevented a larger increase in employment because it limits the possibilities for entrepreneurial involvement . . .'

In a memorandum on European policy, the Bundesverband der Deutschen Industrie (BDI; Federal Association of German Industry) called on the government to 'apply all its power of conviction to combine the creation of the single market with a European deregulation offensive' (BDI 1987: 5).[17] Businessmen were not the only ones aware of the strategy to use the SMP in order to realize domestic liberalizations that the government had previously been unable to implement. The chairman of the Deutscher Gewerkschaftsbund (DGB; German Association of Trade Unions), Ernst Breit, made exactly this use of '1992' as a means for a politically more acceptable and economically more efficient deregulation the focus of labour's criticism:

> We are concerned that behind the excuse of realizing the European single market, a deregulation of social protection measures is to be introduced. One cannot avoid having the impression that some people are taking advantage of the detour Europe to achieve ideological goals that they could not implement on a national basis due to opposition from the trade unions.   (Breit 1987)

After 1987, the political discussion and the economic debate focused on how well the German economy was prepared for the competitive challenge of the single market (Hinze 1989: 74). Like the government, proponents of further liberalization could counter critics with the reasoning that adjustment measures were now necessary and unavoidable because of the external (European) commitments. In addition to stimulating economic efficiency, the Kohl government had gained a new means of justifying its policies. This use of the SMP for externally legitimizing measures that were domestically either contested or previously not implementable was also criticized by the chairman of the opposition party, SPD, Vogel (1987). Even the co-initiator of the *Wende* and former Minister of the Economy in the Schmidt and Kohl governments, Otto Graf Lambsdorff (1987), accused German

politicians of 'all too gladly pointing to Brussels' in the case of un-
popular decisions. One example of the way the governing coalition
utilized 'Europe' to distract from its own responsibility was the attack
of CDU Secretary-General Geißler on the 'Commission in Brussels',
which supposedly bore the responsibility for the disadvantages of the
competition and agricultural price policies.[18] Presumably, Geißler was
also fully aware of the role that the Commission plays as an executive
body for the decisions taken by the governments of the member states
(in the Council).

The exposure of the German Vice-President of the EC Commission,
Karl-Heinz Narjes, is typical of the causal connections that the proponents of the SMP considered decisive.[19] It will be quoted extensively
at this point, as it is excellent evidence of how free market-oriented
politicians represented the logic of '1992' to governments and interest
groups and explained the connection between global competitive pressures, internationalization of national economies, domestic policy
problems and the European solution (Narjes 1987).

- *Regarding global markets.* 'Global interdependence has grown to
  such an extent that today no economy ... is master of its destiny
  any more. This is particularly true of an economic area as strongly
  integrated into world trade as the European Community.'
- *Regarding the necessity of a regional response to global competition.*
  'The creation of a continent-wide economic area with over 320
  million inhabitants is a necessary condition for the assurance of
  European industry's competitiveness. Without the possibility
  of community-wide cooperation and the realization of "economies
  of scale", which can only be secured by a large home market, it
  will be very difficult to gain and defend a leading position as an
  innovator against the competition from the US and Japan.'
- *Regarding the economic superiority of a regional strategy over national options.* 'The goal of a single market in 1992 thus stands for
  an economic policy strategy which combines the long-term growth
  and employment effects of a continent-wide deregulation with investment incentives effective in the short-term while conforming to
  stability criteria. This chance at a highly effective investment promotion programme free of cost to the minister of finance should
  not be declined without serious consideration.'
- *The argument of 'Europe' in responding to interest groups.*
  'Here ... in the future the forces of market and competition will
  play a greater role. The compulsion to adjust will increase – for

the German economy as well. This will activate resistance...It should be made clear that narrow-minded interest-group policies and complaints will not aid in surmounting the ostensible adjustment difficulties. "Resistance to change" or bureaucratic obstruction are not appropriate responses to the pressing problems of the future and to what is probably the only chance Europe has to assert itself.'

It is interesting to see how closely these arguments of the late 1980s resemble those of the debate in the late 1990s on Europe's global competitiveness and the EU monetary union. Apparently the problems and arguments had not changed much since the decision on the single market and its realization in 1992. This highlights the fact that, although the completion of the single market in 1992 did lead to the economic achievements outlined in section 3.1, it was not sufficient to offer a sustainable solution to Western Europe's problems. However, in the second half of the 1980s, Germany did experience a distinct improvement in its economic situation. The new economic strategy and the liberalization through the SMP will also have contributed to the overall success: exports as an indicator of global competitiveness rose in 1985–90 by 15.7 per cent (in comparison 1980–5: −1 per cent) and machinery and transport goods' share of the total exports was higher in 1990 than in 1980, GDP grew in 1985–90 by 2.9 per cent as opposed to 1.5 per cent in 1980–5 (UNCTAD 1997b: 14, 118, 286). In addition, the completion of the single market included a comprehensive deregulation programme, which previously the German Social Democrats had not wanted and the Christian Democrats had not implemented. The UK's development was different in so far as a radical policy of deregulation had already been pursued after Margaret Thatcher had come to power in 1979.

3.4   The United Kingdom

Problems with Labour's neo-Keynesian policies

The shift in the UK's economic policies from an interventionist demand management to a supply-side strategy differs from the developments in France and Germany primarily in three ways. First, global markets' pressure to deregulate was not as strong, as the British economy was traditionally less regulated and was more open to financial markets (Schmidt 1995: 93ff). Second, the shift in the economic policy took place as early as the second half of the 1970s – hesitantly under the Labour government of Callaghan and more distinctly under Margaret Thatcher after 1979. Third, the influence of global capital played a greater role than on the continent, since London's 'City', given its position on the cutting edge of capital markets' internationalization, was globally connected both earlier and more thoroughly than other financial sites. With the Euromarkets it joined New York in forming the centre for global capital transactions in the 1970s. Because of London's traditional function – reaching back to the nineteenth century – as a focal point for financial transactions, the British balance of payments in the 1950s–1970s was more strongly influenced by speculative transfers than that of Germany and France, and this was still the case at the beginning of the twenty-first century.

In terms of economic policy, both Conservative and Labour policies after the Second World War showed neo-Keynesian characteristics, similar to the French and German cases. In the UK, the trade unions were particularly influential – especially the Trades Union Congress (TUC) – in raising the purchasing power of private households by closing wage deals above inflation. The growth rate of the UK's foreign trade involvement stayed below that of France and Germany but started from a higher level. Exports' share of the UK GDP rose from 23 per cent (1970) to 27 per cent (1980), that of imports from 22 per cent (1970) to 25 per cent (1980). In 1990, the share of exports was lower (24 per cent), while that of imports (27 per cent) had risen slightly (UNCTAD 1997b: 296). What influence did global markets have on the crises of the UK economy, on the configuration of interests and on the state's instruments?

In addition to a domestic escalation of the confrontation between trade unions and the government, two global factors were decisive for the change of course in the second half of the 1970s. These were first the decline of UK industry's competitiveness relative to its rivals in the world economy (because of high wages, low productivity and the low level of investment) and second the exchange rate problems, which had come to a head in the Sterling Crisis of 1976.[20] The latter marked the turning point in economic policy and ushered in the period of neoliberal and stability-oriented policy that has lasted into the twenty-first century. Domestic and foreign investors had lost confidence in the pound principally because of the rising inflation, which reached 24.2 per cent in 1975, and a high trade deficit (1974: −$7.9 billion; 1975: −$3.5 billion). They were concerned that their capital stock would lose value through the seemingly inevitable depreciation of the British pound. The consequence was a massive outflow of funds and an equally large speculative run on the pound. The exchange rate sank from $2.32 per pound (1973) to $1.70 (1976). The price of imports rose rapidly and the inflation rate continued to climb. The Bank of England's efforts to support the exchange rate by selling other currencies to buy pounds led to a drastic reduction of the country's currency reserves and undermined its ability to meet interest payments in foreign currencies.

By the end of 1976 it was obvious that loans from private banks and the IMF could not be repaid as had been agreed. In this situation, the government – like many Latin American debtors after 1982 – only had a choice between (open or hidden) international insolvency and a special loan from the IMF, which would be followed by further loans from private banks. In order to qualify for an IMF loan, governments must sign a 'Letter of Intent' committing them to measures that enhance their credit standing – that is, to a supply-side and monetary stability policy, to reducing state expenditures and to improving the trade balance and the investment climate (Overbeek 1990: 172, see also the appendix to chapter 4). The thus improved financial standing strengthens the country's creditworthiness for private transnational banks as well. In that way, an agreement with the IMF leads to further credit opportunities.

The UK government chose the IMF option in part because a new consensus on the need for a consolidation of state finances and a reduction of neo-Keynesian demand management had emerged within the Labour leadership. Neo-Keynesian policy had also been discredited by the fact that traditional measures had not reduced the growing unemployment and had contributed considerably to the foreign trade imbalance and the competitive difficulties. By taking on the commitments entailed in the IMF agreement, the government was attempting not only to restore the confidence of transnational investors but also to use the external pressure to legitimize the new course domestically (Overbeek 1990: 172; Scharpf 1987: 111).[21]

Despite the more restrictive policy after 1976 and because of pressure from the trade unions, the government was able to restrain the real growth of wages only in 1977 (−9.7 per cent). By 1978 wages were already growing faster than inflation again (8.4 per cent). As a result, the price level rose above the average in OECD states (1977: 15.8 per cent, 1978: 8.3 per cent, 1979: 13.4 per cent) and the trade balance did not improve fundamentally (1976: −$1.6 billion, 1977:

−$0.2 billion, 1978: +$1.9 billion, 1979: −$1.6 billion (OECD statistics, from Scharpf 1987: 106ff). The propensity to invest remained low. In the winter of 1978–9, internal trade union problems contributed to a radicalization of individual trade unions and to a dramatic strike by the public sector employees in the 'Winter of Discontent'. The government's new priorities conflicted with the neo-Keynesian demands for rising real wages made by some of the trade unions. Since the trade unions had brought large segments of the state's functions to a halt through strikes in the public sector, many voters lost confidence in the Labour Party's ability to govern.

At the same time, within the opposition Conservative Party, the faction that wanted to push through a policy of laissez-faire, a reduction of state intervention, a deregulation and monetary stability was strengthened: 'the Tory right critique grew in strength. It articulated the growing difficulty that British manufacturers faced from foreign competition' (Gourevitch 1987: 196). The neo-Keynesian consensus of the post-war period was thus ruptured. While the trade unions increasingly voiced their opposition to free trade in order to protect the immobile factor of 'labour' from global contenders, the capital investor side (both production and assets) increasingly oriented itself towards the profit opportunities and the competitive pressure of global goods and capital markets. In May 1979 Margaret Thatcher won the general election with a neoliberal programme.

Thatcherism and the single market

The new prime minister's economic policy was characterized mainly by the consistent fight against inflation using a strategy of monetary stability. This approach was coupled with the privatization of state companies and state functions as well as with a reduction of social services and business taxes. Besides price stability, the goal was also to enhance the global competitiveness and attractiveness of the UK for capital investors. On the whole, however, the actual policy pursued was in part far removed from the rhetorical intentions: the state expenditure's share of GDP even rose from 39.5 per cent (1979) to 42 per cent (1980 and 1984) and the tax revenue grew from 34.4 per cent of GDP (1979) to 35.7 per cent (1980) and 38.3 per cent (1984) (statistics from Ball 1985: 9ff). Thatcherism achieved its greatest success – as did Kohl in Germany and the policy of *rigueur* in France – in reducing inflation, which dropped from 13.4 per cent (1979) to 4.6 per cent (1984). The interest rates fell parallel to inflation from 13.7

per cent (1979) to 9.7 per cent (1984). As a result of the lower inflation and interest rates, the investment rose and with it the competitiveness of the UK economy. The latter was also stimulated by a limitation of the protection against dismissal and by lower wage agreements. The slower nominal growth of wages was also a consequence of a relative loss of the trade union *association*'s power, which was reached in part by replacing sectoral wage contracts with agreements negotiated at the level of the individual company. The balance of trade improved via rising exports, and after 1981 the economy began to grow again. This growth was driven primarily by domestic demand, in part because consumers and investors were able to take out loans at lower interest rates and consumption was stimulated by the sinking inflation rate.

However, Thatcher left the problem of mass unemployment unsolved: in her opinion the number of unemployed, which rose drastically between 1979 and 1984 from 1.2 million to 3.1 million, was less the concern of the government than that of business and particularly the trade unions that had prevented an expansion of employment by demanding too high wages (Scharpf 1987: 117). As a result, the factor 'labour' was increasingly devalued, while stability, growth and competitiveness – that is, the returns accruing to the factor 'capital' – improved considerably for private transnational actors. This manifested itself in a new asset boom for the City of London as a first-class global financial site and in direct investment now preferring the UK to its European rivals such as Germany and France. Between 1980 and 1988, $64.7 billion FDI flowed into the UK, $9.1 billion went to Germany and $27.9 billion went to France.[22] The new stability of the UK economy led to a 'historic' rise in the stock markets and to an influx of foreign funds, particularly in London's euro-market (Ball 1985: 11; *The Economist*, 23 Aug. 1986: 68).

In 1983 Thatcher was elected to a second term in office – with the help of nationalism accompanying the Falkland/Malvinas War (1982). In 1985–6, before the SEA had been signed, the situation for a third term in office appeared somewhat different: despite the resuscitated growth and low inflation, the government came under increasing pressure from public opinion, particularly because of rising unemployment. The dissatisfaction of many voters threatened Thatcher's re-election in 1987–8. *The Economist* (11 May 1985: 13) wrote: 'At bottom, though, voters are unimpressed by the government's economic record, and for one big reason. Unemployment is still rising, from 1.2m adults when the Tories took office in June, 1979, to 3.2m last month. The government's electoral fate in 1987 or 1988 depends on the jobless figures: if they are still rising, it will probably fall.'

Although Thatcher had implemented the neoliberal opening for years by that time and the British electorate was therefore already well acquainted with the social costs of Thatcherism, it does not seem to have become 'accustomed' to this aspect. Evidently voters were worried enough about the costs of Thatcherism for a third re-election to be jeopardized. In the mid-1980s a greater consideration for public opinion on the part of the government could therefore be discerned than had previously been the case. Thus, the search for new growth impetus and a new or improved justification of the social and political costs of deregulation played a leading role for the government.[23] Therefore, Thatcher's argument that her government had imposed the 'successful British model' on Europe in the form of the SMP can be interpreted as an attempt to present a domestically disputed policy as multilaterally supported and sanctioned. Thatcher portrayed her government not only as a pioneer of the SMP '1992', but also as a champion of the spirit of the Treaty of Rome, which had in any case envisioned deregulation and free trade. In her memoirs Thatcher (1993: 547) writes: 'The Single Market – which Britain pioneered – was intended to give real substance to the Treaty of Rome and to revive its liberal, free trade, deregulatory purpose.'

The second reasoning behind the British preference for '1992' was the announcement – aimed at the voters' expectations – of growth due to rising British exports through the SMP. These expectations were shared by the enterprises (Woolcock 1991: 63). Because deregulation, higher profitability and investment in the Thatcher years did actually lead to a rising competitiveness vis-à-vis the European rivals, the government justified the SMP on the basis that UK firms had better chances of selling on the continental markets than continental companies had on the UK market (H. Wallace 1990: 163). According to Thatcher, in order to obtain these economic advantages, it was necessary to accept a limitation of sovereignty by majority decision making in the EC: 'British businesses would be among those most likely to benefit from an opening-up of other countries' markets.... The price which we would have to pay to achieve a Single Market with all its economic benefits, though, was more majority voting in the Community' (Thatcher 1993: 553).

As in Germany and France, the SMP was also an instrument to enhance companies' *global* competitiveness and to raise the attractiveness of the country for investors. '1992' was seen by the government as a key instrument for further liberalization. The Minister for Industry and Trade Lord Young (1988: 40) emphasized that the SMP was an important element in the government's competition-oriented strategy of opening-up. Foreign Secretary Howe (1985) stated that the completion of the SMP was 'of decisive significance, if we wish to create an atmosphere in which the European industry is more competitive both within the Community as well as on the world market and thus secure work and prosperity for our citizens.'

UK companies' propensity to invest abroad and to shift production out of the country had continued to increase in the 1980s – even though, as a result of Thatcher's policies, the UK offered a better location than Germany or France (Thompson 1992: 203). The relatively strong attraction the UK had for global investment was to be further enhanced by the single market. The year after the single market was decided upon, the influx of FDI to the UK leapt from $11.4 billion (1985) and $16.5 billion (1986) to $30.5 billion (1987) (1988: $27.1 billion); (statistics from Julius 1990: 116). Since, in comparison to the other large EC members, the country provided the most deregulated, cost-effective investment site[24] with monetary stability, it was also able to use '1992' to gain ground in global markets because, for transnational actors, it combined the advantages of an EC internalization of their activities (access to markets, acknowledged standards) with the above-mentioned advantages (Bressand 1990: 57). Thus, the single market followed the logic of the previous national deregulation: in order to realize the advantages of national reforms, it was necessary to have a larger playing field. The UK financial sector also saw the single market primarily as a 'stage in the internationalization of markets' (Woolcock 1991: 65), for which it was better qualified than its continental European competitors.

Interest groups were less relevant in forming public opinion on the SMP than in Germany and France, since they generally had less influence on the economic policy process (Woolcock 1991: 59). This was due to the less corporativist structure of British society and to the conviction of the Thatcher government that organized interest groups were a central cause of inflexible and uncompetitive economic structures. The extent to which the SMP was a government matter, removed from economic actors, is demonstrated by opinion polls. According to these, in 1988 only 15 per cent of British entrepreneurs were cognizant of what '1992' meant, while 62 per cent of French and 36 per cent of German entrepreneurs had already started making plans for new business opportunities (statistics from Volle 1989: 342).

One indicator of the government's relative independence from interest groups was its clear refusal to join the EMS despite requests from the Thatcher-friendly financial markets (the City of London), the business association the CBI and the Bank of England.[25]

After the experiences of the 1970s, the government saw the trade unions as a basically negative institution for the UK economy and treated them as political opponents (Gamble 1988: 103ff; 115ff). However, apart from their minimal influence on the government, trade unions had a very positive attitude towards '1992'. Given their experience of deregulation in their own country, they were hoping for a 'social dimension' through a single market that was co-designed by corporativist states such as Germany and France (Volle 1989: 344; Wallace 1990: 166). EC Commission President Delors nourished this hope by introducing his idea of a 'social charter' at trade union conferences in the UK. In the end, the social charter was made non-binding, the Thatcher government did not sign it and the single market stimulated primarily economic competition.[26] The UK's economic growth accelerated at the end of the 1980s, because of the single market, and Thatcher was elected in 1987 for the third time. Despite social hardships, a broad support for economic liberalism emerged in the UK, which Tony Blair transferred to 'New Labour' and which helped him to win the election in 1997. The acceptance of the neoliberal course and the European SMP can also be explained on the basis of the UK's economic success in the second half of the 1980s: exports as an indicator of global competitiveness rose in 1985–90 by 12.7 per cent (in comparison to 1980–5: −2.1 per cent) and the machinery and transport goods' share of the total exports was considerably higher in 1990 than it had been in 1980; the GDP grew in 1985–90 by 3.5 per cent, as opposed to 2.1 per cent in 1980–5 (UNCTAD 1997b: 14, 130, 286).

3.5   The European Level

The analytical focus of the previous sections lay on how global markets changed the decision-making environment of national governments, which were responsible for the decision to complete the single market by 1992. Evidence was analysed on global markets' influence in turning away from neo-Keynesian strategies and in the shift of interests and instruments. These changes paved the way for an economically more efficient and politically more tolerable logic of the SMP as opposed to national solutions. In the following section, I will examine to what extent global markets stimulated the preference for the SMP at the *European* level. This seems relevant, in so far as the SEA had been preceded by three decades of European integration, which had contributed to the creation of a European debate in academia, politics and the media and thus led to the perception of 'Europe' as a definitional and analytical category (on a par with 'the USA' or 'the world economy'). Moreover, particularly on the part of enterprises, interest groups began to organize on the European level, pursuing their agendas also with supranational strategies. Finally, the integration process had created European institutions, such as the EC Commission, which, although they could not decide on the SEA, may have made relevant contributions to the formation of public and government preferences. Did global markets cause perceptions, interest groups and institutions to form or articulate at the European level in a way that promoted the SMP?

Perceptions: Europe's 'lagging behind' in global competition

At the end of the 1970s and the beginning of the 1980s, the economic problems of European states and the possibilities of coming to terms with them were increasingly seen and discussed as a common European concern. This was primarily due to two factors. First, the crises of the neo-Keynesian welfare model, the limitations of the instruments necessary for its demand management and the shift of interests demonstrated similar patterns and thus stimulated an awareness of European commonalties regarding the economic dilemmas and possible political solutions. Second, and at the same time, Europe's development increasingly diverged from that of the USA and Japan, which differed ever more from the Continent in terms of economic policy approaches and regarding European problems such as competitiveness, unemployment and growth. Thus, the similarities within Europe and the growing differences to OECD rivals strengthened the awareness of a common ground. This paved the way for common solutions through stimulating public debates and European identity.[27] What role did global markets play in the European debate? To what extent was the necessity of a deregulating single market argued on the basis of global markets?

In 1980–85 the analysis of the problem and the debate on possible solutions at the European level – that is, in those media[28] and research[29] that reached a Europe-wide audience – concentrated on the following arguments:[30]

1 Europe's falling behind the USA and Japan economically was attributed foremost to the fact that the Continent had not succeeded in preventing a leap in the level of unemployment: whereas the USA created fourteen millon jobs between 1973 and 1983 and Japan three million, Europe lost two million jobs in the same period (*The Economist*, 24 Nov. 1984: 99).[31]

2 Technological deficits in comparison to the USA and Japan, 'Europe's Technology Gap' (*The Economist*, 24 Nov. 1984: 99–110), were also cited as important reasons for the sinking global competitiveness in innovation-intensive goods (Mucchielli 1991: 36ff). In figures on trade in high-technology goods ('specialization indices'), the EC countries had fallen from 1.01 (1963) of the OECD average (1.00) to 0.87 (1981) (USA: 1.27 (1963) and 1.19 (1981); Japan 0.72 (1963) and 1.37 (1981)) (statistics from Albert and Ball 1983: 32a).

3 Europe's situation in terms of GDP growth rates had also clearly deteriorated in comparison to the two rival regions: whereas the EC countries could still attain rates of 2.3 per cent in 1973 (USA: 2.2 per cent, Japan 3.7 per cent), by 1981–3 growth was down to 0.1 per cent (USA: 0.8 per cent; Japan: 3.1 per cent, estimates) (OECD statistics from Albert and Ball 1983: 11a).

4 These problems of growth, employment and innovation were identified as being caused primarily by the weak competitiveness in global contention as a result of markets in Europe being too regulated and too fragmented: 'European firms will never have an even chance of competing with their American and Japanese rivals so long as western Europe remains sliced up into a dozen or more semi-separate markets' (*The Economist*, 24 Nov. 1984: 110). The competitive disadvantages of a fragmented and regulated market had intensified following Europe's integration into global markets to the extent that the USA under Jimmy Carter in 1979 and under Ronald Reagan since 1981 had pursued a policy of deregulation.

5 Together with an awareness of European companies' global competitive disadvantages due to small national markets and regulation (especially after the French experience of 1981–2), the realization had spread that a nation's ability to steer its domestic economy had been eroded by foreign economic integration. Albert and Ball's report to the European Parliament (EP) states: 'Only in

1982 did one begin to realize clearly that there was practically no margin left for a mid-term autonomous up-swing. As we have seen, the foreign economic pressure becomes more peremptory, the greater the foreign trade involvement' (Albert and Ball 1983: 40).

Thus, Europe's problems were considered directly in connection with its position in global markets and the solution propagated was deregulation and a merging of national economies to a unified market. This causal logic is reflected in the official reasons for the SMP. For example, after signing the SEA in 1986, the highest decision-making body of the EC, the Council, came to the conclusion 'that technological co-operation and innovation at the level of the Community will provide an indispensable contribution to the European industry's ability to survive in a world of pitiless competition. Corresponding efforts should concentrate strictly on completing the single market ...' (Europäischer Rat / European Council 1986: D 486).

As a consequence, the completion of the single market was given a significance that it did not have at the time of its inception in 1957. It was now declared, in conjunction with deregulation, a necessary response to global competitive pressure and to the weakened ability of states to steer their economies individually. Global markets had changed the distributive leeway of national economic policy and caused states to implement the adjustment to global competition through regional commitments that were declared 'practical necessities', in order to carry out reforms more effectively and to give them more legitimacy than they would have had if justified solely as a single-handed national effort.

European interest groups and institutions

Since the beginning of the 1980s, interest groups at the European level have increasingly articulated their demands for a deregulating completion of the single market. This lobbying emanates from both existing organizations and newly formed initiatives. To a large extent, entrepreneurial groups and the party organizations close to them influenced public opinion in a number of European countries and exerted pressure on various national governments. The trade unions were less stringently organized on the EC level and less interested in a liberalizing SMP. Like the social-democratic parties, the workers' representatives saw their position in the political discourse weakened by the perceived failure of the neo-Keynesian strategies. The leadership in forging public opinion had shifted to the supply-side and stability-oriented groups, as represented by entrepreneurs, conservative parties (UK) and 'new' socialists (France) (Moravcsik 1991: 73). The entrepreneurial side was also not homogeneous. Many sectors still clung to a protectionist attitude, as they feared a threat to their existence in the strengthened competition (Philip 1987). However, these positions were not new. On the contrary, they had moulded the development of the European integration from its inception and contributed substantially to the incompleteness of the single market, to complicated efforts at harmonization and to a lasting fragmentation of the markets. The new aspect in the 1980s was the increasing pressure of those enterprises that experienced a deterioration of their global competitiveness because of the fragmentation and regulation of their markets. To what extent can these changes be attributed to the development of global markets? How is the influence of entrepreneurial initiatives on the preference for '1992' to be assessed?

The most important group was the Round Table of European Industrialists (REI), founded in 1983, in which some of the largest transnational enterprises of Europe had come together, such as Siemens, Philips, Olivetti, Fiat and Daimler Benz. Prominent representatives, like the Chairman of the Board of Directors of Philips, Wisse Dekker, used the presentation of strategy papers, public appearances and direct discussions with government representatives and the EC Commission to further their goal of the rapid completion of a liberalized single market.[32] In essence, his argument is based on the perception of European companies in global competition: 'And only a truly European single market can serve as a launching pad for the world market' (Dekker 1985: 13).

Besides Dekker and the REI, other associations were also involved in promoting the completion of the single market, such as the Union of Industrial and Employers' Confederations in Europe (UNICE) and party organizations like the Liberal Democratic Group and the economically liberal, multipartisan 'Kangaroo' Group in the EP. These lobbying groups' main arguments also revolved around the competitive requirements on the world market, the increasing rivalry amongst global suppliers to the European markets and the concern over the perceived advantage of the USA and Japan.[33] Among the numerous initiatives, the European Market Economy Organizations, a group of economic institutes and associations from six EC countries, stood out. In January 1985, this group presented a single market concept, in which the essence of the argumentation was first an interpretation of

European problems as a result of interventionist–neo-Keynesian policies and second the pronouncement that liberal economies of scale are a precondition for a solution: 'a free market is the only way for Europe to compete in the changing markets of the world.'[34]

It is difficult to estimate what influence these activities and arguments actually had on the forming of governments' preferences and the decision for the SEA, just as it is to judge the effect of the debate in the media and academia. Moravcsik (1991: 65), for example, disputes a substantial influence from transnational lobbying groups and sees governments and domestic policy considerations as the only relevant factors. He does not take into account, however, that the actors who joined together in REI, UNICE, 'Kangaroo' or the forum of the economic institutes were also influential on the national level, in 'domestic politics'. Companies like Philips and Daimler Benz have access to considerable means of exerting pressure (taxes, jobs) on their national governments. It seems plausible that this influence is intensified when it is coordinated at a European level and simultaneously and uniformly directed at the most important governments in the EC/EU, at public opinion and at EC/EU institutions.

In contrast to Moravcsik, Sandholtz and Zysman (1989: 117) conclude from their interviews and discussions that the REI was a 'powerful lobby vis-à-vis the national governments'. According to their research, the interest groups were particularly effective because they influenced not only national governments and domestic policy debates, but also the EC Commission directly. However, they argue that influence was mutual between the entrepreneurial lobbies and the EC institutions. Both of them together had exerted 'substantial influence' on national governments (Sandholtz and Zysman 1989: 116ff).

There is a large number of research papers on the relevance of the EC Commission in the decision making process for the single market (Fligstein 1993; Garrett and Weingast 1993; Pierson 1996). Evidently, Commission President Delors (1985–95) – sent by Mitterrand and previously concerned with the French Socialists' reforms – was able to push the single market along. According to Delors's own statements, he used the formal visits to member states' heads of governments on the occasion of his inauguration 1984–5 to resuscitate various projects in the European integration process (Delors 1996). Of the suggestions presented, only the completion of the single market found the governments' approval. Closer cooperation in defence matters and the establishment of a monetary union, also suggested at that time, were not as well received. Delors's comments make it clear that the Commission's role in the '1992' project was dependent upon the extent to which its ideas found member states' approval and upon preferences among the governments that were already present. As the country studies have shown, the development of global markets made a decisive contribution to creating a preference for a deregulating single market with the governments.

The Commission had long been striving for the completion of the single market, but, because of the lack of corresponding preferences by member states until the mid-1980s, its suggestions were not accepted.[35] As section 3.1 explains, the Commission (White Book, Checchini Report) and other community institutions (EP, Albert and Ball 1983) also based the necessity of a deregulating single market on the requirements of foreign economic competition. The Commission's role in the forming of government's preferences seems in general to have been more of catalytic-supportive relevance than of causal importance. The Commission was able to push the rapidity of the final decision-taking, the organization and the quick implementation of the SMP along substantially by means of directives and concrete catalogues of measures – but it was not able to create government preferences.

3.6   Conclusion

The empirical results of the case studies confirm the hypotheses of this book in so far as the GMA explains the forming of governments' preference for the SMP. It could be plausibly demonstrated that governments' preference for new liberalizing regional cooperation in the three countries examined was essentially stimulated by the effect of global markets on their national economies. The influence of global markets made a decisive contribution to the replacement of inward-looking neo-Keynesian economic policy by a competition-oriented liberal course that could be implemented in an economically more efficient and politically more acceptable way by means of regional cooperation.

Global markets' influence on the change of economic policy

The case studies clearly showed that the three pathways 'crises, interests and instruments' are closely connected and in part strengthen one another. Global markets' contribution to the crisis of neo-Keynesian policy and to the change of paradigm to a competition and stability-oriented policy in the countries examined essentially took on the following forms.

Through the integration of national economies in growing and more mobile global financial markets, the countries were confronted with a rising external influence on their balance of payments and their exchange rates. These reacted negatively to political measures of a neo-Keynesian type – that is, to measures that did not aim primarily at securing monetary stability and global competitiveness. In France (1981–3) and the UK (1976–9), a massive outflow of capital led to repeated devaluations of the currencies and consequently to waves of inflation (due to the higher cost of imports). In order to slow this trend, the interest rates were raised. The overall result was a loss of purchasing power and a reduction of investment. Thus, the effectiveness of neo-Keynesian measures for expanding production by raising demand was restricted and employing these measures was associated with substantial macroeconomic costs in the form of capital flight, high interest rates and rising public debt. Furthermore, global financial markets produced costs for the productive sectors of national economies by raising interest rate levels. Inward-looking mechanisms not only lost some of their effectiveness, but also became more costly. Reforms that met the expectations of globalized financial markets were stimulated.[36]

As a result of the increased foreign trade involvement of the economies examined, the neo-Keynesian measures intended to revive growth and production no longer had the effect the governments had planned. The example of France clearly demonstrated that a state-stimulated increase in demand flowed to a disproportionate extent into imports and thus no longer had the desired effect of boosting domestic production. Because of the strong dependency on exports, political measures that raised the domestic production costs were accompanied by macroeconomic (and therefore also political) costs because they lowered firms' competitiveness on the global markets. In the *tradables* sector, which had been growing since the 1970s, such measures enlarged the incentives to shift production abroad (FRG, UK) or to replace productive activity with stock market investment. This last point was particularly important in 1982 during Germany's change of government, as it represented a substantial part of the differences in interests between the SPD's and the FDP's clientele.

In all three countries it was possible to observe that neo-Keynesian interest groups lost importance while sectors oriented towards global competition and stability gained influence. This shift could be found within the trade unions (France, 1993) and parties (the Conservatives in the UK, 1978) as well as in government coalitions (Germany, 1982) and in the political debate. In the latter, the proponents of neo-Keynesian steering were increasingly backed into a defensive position, whereas the offensive reform positions were usually concomitant with demands for liberalization. In the private sector, these demands for liberalization grew in importance. First, in the course of growing foreign trade and rising involvement in global financial markets, those sectors that depended on open, stable and globally competitive conditions for their business activities grew. Second, the alternative of 'global markets' raised the opportunity costs of domestic economic activity under circumstances of neo-Keynesian regulation.

As a result, global markets have substantially contributed to:

- limiting the effectiveness of inward-looking neo-Keynesian policy instruments;
- increasing the costs of inward-looking neo-Keynesian policy;
- enhancing the incentives for stability and competition-oriented policies;
- raising the level of interest and the domestic relevance of interest groups oriented towards global competitiveness.

Economic efficiency and political acceptability through regional cooperation

In the last analysis, global markets have stimulated the formation of a preference for the SMP in two ways. First, '1992' became attractive as an economically more efficient and politically more acceptable means of implementing national reforms, which – as demonstrated – were essentially a consequence of the impact of global markets (*indirect causality*). Second, global markets exerted a direct pressure on the examined states to adjust to the harsher global competition by improving the appeal of their countries to transnational investors – a measure that could be achieved in an economically more efficient and politically more acceptable way by means of regional cooperation (*direct causality*).

Indirect causality   The change in the economic policy paradigm was the prerequisite, not for cooperation per se, but for *liberalizing* co-operation: global markets' limitation of inward-looking steering reduced the price of sovereignty loss through the EC single market. Since governments were less able to steer their national economies effectively anyway, the contractual limitations of national autonomy implied by the SEA were no longer the serious reductions of actual abilities that they would have been in the 1960s. Thus, the states' *de jure* renunciation of national autonomy of action was made easier by the previous *de facto* loss.

Moreover, the change in economic policy course was the substantial condition for '1992': only by replacing neo-Keynesian maxims with the new reform course's goal of supply-side 'global competitiveness' – that is, only by substituting a more market conforming openness for the interventionist domestic orientation – did the advantages of a liberalizing cooperation become compatible with the priorities of national policy. A single market project such as '1992' could have contributed to a more efficient allocation of resources through economies of scale and increased competition in the 1960s as well. But it would not have been compatible with the dominant neo-Keynesian model because at that time it would have taken still relatively effective instruments for steering the economy out of the hands of the governments, and because governments, in forming their economic policy preferences, still placed direct distribution policy over the criteria of global competitiveness.

Indirect causality also includes the necessities connected to the new economic policies: as the case studies have shown, the governments justified their preference for the SMP with the goal of making the nationally launched course irreversible and more efficient. The justifications for '1992' and the goals of the SMP were largely congruent with the declared reasons for the change of economic policy at the national level. The purpose was to continue more effectively at the EC level what had been begun by the individual states previously. Moreover, the governments of all three countries used their corresponding contractual obligations to justify and legitimate national stability and liberalization policies. In all three countries the government tried to shift the responsibility for the costs (social hardship) of the national liberalization policy onto the regional level. There are some indications that this regional justification argument and the actual or expected increase in growth as a consequence of the single market led to a rise in the acceptance of the new economic policy.

The indirect causality between the impact of global markets and regional cooperation can also be seen in the activities of interest groups. In all three countries representatives of globally oriented firms, for example, declared that more competition and economies of scale in regional markets were a precondition for the successful implementation of a liberal policy. They also emphasized the possibility of tightening national reforms and making them irreversible by means of regional cooperation. Representatives of the trade unions (FRG) also saw this logic as valid but criticized it as an attempt to use regional instruments to force through liberalization not achieved nationally.

Direct causality   Part of the global markets' direct influence on the formation of the preference for a single market is the change in the cost–benefit relation of fragmented and regulated markets. That includes both the change in materially measurable costs as well as the changing perception of such costs. Because of the higher mobility of capital and production as well as the stronger integration of national economies into global markets, the global competition for these factors had risen and had intensified the disadvantages of the relative fragmentation, the high density of regulation and the relatively strong inward focus of Western Europe. This was demonstrated in the 1980s by Europe's so-called 'dropping behind' its rivals (USA, Japan, NICs) in terms of growth, job creation, investment and innovation criteria. The fact that this connection was not only based on (interpretable) statistics, but also perceived in this way by political decision-makers could be seen in the Europe-wide debate on this subject and the reasoning behind the SMP.

The declarations of government representatives as well as the Europe-wide discussion and the requests of interest groups emphasized that Europe could best meet the new demands of global competition and global mobility of capital and production by means of a liberalizing single market. It was repeatedly pointed out that the improvement of Europe's attractiveness for investment and production could be more efficiently achieved through the single market than by individual national efforts. The necessary precondition of governments' *simultaneous* preference for regional cooperation was therefore stimulated not only indirectly via the partial causation of similar economic reforms due to global markets, but also directly through the perception of Europe as a unit with similar problems vis-à-vis global markets and competing regions. In view of the relative success of other regions by means of better competitiveness on the world markets, there was a growing perception of the relatively strong fragmentation and regulation of European markets as a growing cost factor and of the advantages of a liberalizing regional cooperation as a rising incentive.

4

GLOBAL MARKETS AND MERCOSUR

4.1 Liberalization Strategies in the Common Market of the South

Until the beginning of the 1980s, the two initiating countries of MER-COSUR,[1] Argentina and Brazil, were rivals for dominance in South America (Schirm 1994b: 121–35). Only as a result of Brazil's success in industrializing in the 1960s and 1970s and Argentina's economic stagnation did Brazil become the more relevant regional power. As late as the 1970s, military conflict scenarios were still part of their bilateral relationship and contributed to the legitimation of a dominant role for the military in the domestic politics of both countries. After the 1950s, this rivalry also included a race for the development of nuclear warheads. In 1979, the agreement of Corpus–Itaipú initiated a first détente, which developed into cooperation after the military withdrew from government in Argentina (1983) and Brazil (1985). Until the late 1980s, however, trade remained marginal. Both countries had traditionally oriented their foreign trade towards the industrial nations – Argentina primarily towards Europe (especially the UK) and Brazil towards the USA.

With regard to regional economic cooperation, both states had belonged to numerous pan-Latin American integration mechanisms of the 'first generation'. Organizations like the Asociación Latino-Americana de Libre Comercio (ALALC; Latin American Free Trade Association) founded in 1960 (renamed Asociación Latino-Americana de Integración (ALADI) in 1980) and the Sistema Economico Latino-Americano (SELA; Latin American Economic System, 1975) were established in the framework of the Comisión Economica para America Latina y el Caribe (CEPAL), the UN Economic Commission for Latin America's propagated development strategy of ISI. According to this model, integration in the 1960s–70s served primarily to expand the protected and state-directed domestic markets. The state's effort to steer economic development and to protect national production from external competitors often led to low efficiency and expensive, technologically outdated production and contributed substantially to the failure of the 'first generation's' attempts at integration, as the development model was diametrically opposed to free trade (Schirm 1997a: 28–48). *Rent-seekers* dependent on monopolies and protection did not want to lose their privileges to competition and were supported in this endeavour by their governments.[2] At that time, the integration strategy was a state-designated and 'complementary' trade, which sought to avoid any adaptation to competition. Thus, member states lost the essential advantages of free trade, as there was no competitive rise in productivity and specialization, little economy of scale effects and equally little improvement in the efficiency of the allocation of resources due to regional cooperation. The result was a regionalization of underdevelopment.

Compared to these earlier developments, the founding of MERCOSUR in 1991 embodies a change of course in various ways. First, it ended the historic rivalry between Argentina and Brazil and institutionalized friendly cooperation between the erstwhile enemies.[3] Second, it symbolizes both states' rejection of the traditional inward-looking development strategy of protectionist import substitution. Third, along with NAFTA, MERCOSUR belongs to the 'second generation' of cooperation agreements. Their concern is less the state-regulated enlargement of protected domestic markets, but rather the support of national – free market – reforms, the achievement of improved efficiency and the enhancement of the members' competitiveness on the world market for goods and capital.

However, this economic policy has characterized the cooperation process only since 1990. In the first bilateral agreements, such as the Programma de Integración y Cooperación Argentina–Brasil (PICAB) of 1986, the two countries were still relying on concepts of the 'first generation' (Hirst 1989). Protected domestic markets were to be expanded and in selected areas a state-decreed industrial cooperation would be arranged. After early increases in trade, the exchange of goods collapsed again. Most of the projects for industrial cooperation did not get beyond the planning stage. Only in the course of structural reforms on the national level was the regional dimension also oriented towards a free market economy. Fundamental reforms began in

Argentina in 1988 (Brazil in 1989) and gathered momentum in 1989 (1990). In line with this time sequence, PICAB contained only little and sectoral easing of trade barriers in 1986, whereas in 1988 a common market was agreed upon, and in 1991, at the founding of MERCOSUR, 'universal and automatic' reductions of tariffs and a common market were agreed upon as a 'springboard for the world market'.

Regulations

The foundations of MERCOSUR are the Treaty of Asunción (1991), the complementary protocol of Ouro Preto (1994) and a number of additional agreements as well as implementation directives.[4] In these documents, the signatory states – Argentina, Brazil, Paraguay and Uruguay – agreed to create a common market by 1 January 1995. The project is composed of three dimensions of economic cooperation. First, a free trade zone was to be established – that is, the free exchange of goods, services and capital was to be secured by dismantling the tariff and non-tariff trade barriers. The mobility of labour was exempt. Second, a customs union was to be instituted by raising a common external tariff and by implementing a common foreign trade policy towards third parties as well as by coordinating positions in international economic fora. Third, a Common Market was planned, with harmonization of the members' economic policy in the areas of foreign trade, agriculture, industry, capital, fiscal policy, monetary policy, exchange rate policy, customs duties, transport and communication. Furthermore, the member states' laws were to be adjusted to one another.

In contrast to earlier efforts at cooperation, the main instrument for implementing these decisions was a general reduction of tariffs, applicable to all products, which was to come into force automatically and progressively. Moreover, the establishment of a common customs regime towards third parties was to assure that goods from non-member states would not be imported by way of the state with the lowest customs level. Specifically, the MERCOSUR regulations comprised the following elements.[5]

1 *The dismantling of customs within MERCOSUR.* A gradual and automatic reduction of tariff barriers between the members began in 1991 and was supposed to make entirely free trade possible by 1 January 1995. A customs level of 0 per cent was reached by the

end of 1994 for 90 per cent of all products. For the remaining 10 per cent, an extended adjustment period was arranged. The dismantling of non-tariff barriers was still unresolved in 2001.

2   *Exceptions to the rule.* Every member state has the right to protect especially 'sensitive' branches of production – that is, those whose existence is threatened by competition. Such goods are placed on a list of exceptions, which may not exceed 300 product positions and will not be subject to the general rule on tariff reductions. These exceptions cover a total of 10 per cent of all customs categories, such as the car and computer industries.[6]

3   *External tariff.* A Common External Tariff (CET) against non-members between 0 and 20 per cent was established.[7]

4   *Foreign direct investment.* In principle, foreign capital from MERCOSUR states and investment from non-members are to be comparable to national investment, protected from expropriation and not subject to any limitations in transferring profits.[8]

5   *Rules of origin.* Because the CET could not be completely achieved, rules of origin had to be determined for goods not covered by the CET. In order to prevent goods produced mostly abroad – for example, products assembled only in MERCOSUR – from taking advantage of the intra-regional freedom from tariffs, a minimum local content rule was agreed upon, amounting to at least 60 per cent and determined according to the product.

6   *Services.* Equal competition conditions are to hold for the service sector in the future. However, in 2001 this rule still did not hold for important sectors such as banks and insurance because the decisive non-tariff barriers were much more difficult to dismantle or adjust than the tariffs.

7   *Public procurement.* In the case of public contracts, suppliers from MERCOSUR states were to be treated as equals to national firms before the law.

8   *Economic policies.* A harmonization of macroeconomic policies and technical norms was agreed upon in order to reduce trade diversion and to give the regional trade stable conditions. The creation of a body of common law follows from the most rapid possible implementation of common decisions into national law, to which all the members have obligated themselves.

The regulations of MERCOSUR demonstrate a clear tendency towards market liberalism, but the exceptions indicate the lingering influence of protectionist sectors. In its institutional structure,

MERCOSUR slightly resembles the construction of the EU, but with entirely intergovernmental processes. There was no transfer of national competencies to a common body. The Additional Protocol of Ouro Preto to the Treaty of Asunción designated the Council, the Group and the Secretariat as the most important institutions of MERCO-SUR. The Consejo del Mercado Común (CMC; Council of the Common Market) is the highest common body and determines MER-COSUR's policy via decisions which are binding for the members and must be transferred into their national law. The CMC takes all of its decisions by consensus. The Grupo Mercado Común (GMC; Group of the Common Market), composed of representatives of the national ministries, is the executive body of MERCOSUR. The GMC converts the CMC's fundamental decisions into operational resolutions and represents MERCOSUR in negotiations with third parties (it does not have an independent mandate). The Secretariat in Montevideo, the Secretaría Administrativa del Mercosur (SAM), serves as a documentation and organizational body. Thus, MERCOSUR lacks a technical-administrative authority, analogous to the Commission in Brussels.

Goals

As in the case of the EC single market, MERCOSUR's foremost goal was to promote economic growth. This was to be reached by means of more competition (division of labour and efficiency effects) and the production of larger quantities (economy of scale), as a result of which the competitiveness of MERCOSUR products on the world market would improve, consequently attracting more direct investment from abroad (Manzetti 1993–94: 112–16). These effects were expected to lead to self-sustaining growth, lower prices, better product quality, technology transfers from abroad and innovation for the adjustment to the competitive requirements of the world market. Thus, MERCO-SUR was pursuing the goal – limited by the various exceptions to the rule – of extensive liberalization and the freeing of market forces. By improving the conditions for companies on the regional market, each country hoped that its own economy would be better equipped to compete on the world market. The result was a renunciation at the regional level of the decade-long dominance of state regimentation. One of the Argentinian chief negotiators of the Treaty of Asunción and then Adjunct Under-Secretary in the Foreign Ministry, Felix Peña (1992: 1), summarized MERCOSUR's goals in an exemplary way:

MERCOSUR was conceived as an instrument for facilitating the consolidation of democracy, productive transformation and competitive integration of its member states into the international economy.... Moreover, MERCOSUR is an integral part of the national strategies which aim at making each of these countries more competitive on all markets, that is, on their own domestic markets, on those of MERCOSUR and those of the world.

The Brazilian negotiator of the Treaty of Asunción and Head of the Department for Latin American Integration in the Foreign Ministry (Itamaraty), Renato L. R. Marques (1994: 12, 15), emphasized that MERCOSUR was created in the framework of an 'open economy and competitive integration into the international market'. MERCOSUR serves primarily to attract direct investment, which would increase only with an enlarged market and macroeconomic stability. The regulations and goals make it equally plain that the regional cooperation agreement secured a liberalizing strategy at the national level through a multilateral treaty. An individual nation's sole return to the earlier strategy is made more difficult, if not practically impossible, by the contractual obligations. The MERCOSUR expert of the most renowned Brazilian institute for economic research, Fundaçao Getúlio Vargas (FGV), Lia Valls Pereira (1993: 40), emphasized MERCOSUR's possible disciplinary effect ('marco disciplinatório') with respect to the economic policy of the member states, 'that responds to the challenge of the new global scenarios'. These challenges can be found principally in the strong competition for productivity, technology and investment capital – areas in which the members could reduce their relative backwardness through competition-oriented regionalism (Pereira 1993: 29, 39ff).

Although MERCOSUR, like the EC single market, is market oriented with regard to its economic policy, the parallels between the two treaties are clearly finite. MERCOSUR is considerably less consistently planned, its goals are less obvious, its binding properties are less precisely laid out. Moreover, its members' governments have much less economic policy competence and implementation power than the Western European governments. In comparison to the industrialized countries, the Latin American states serve much more to satisfy the particular interests of elites and corporatively organized clienteles and place less emphasis on societal or macroeconomic considerations. This does not mean that European governments do not pursue particularistic interests – the difference is one of degree. The liberalizing strategy and goals of MERCOSUR, which – like the EC

SMP – incorporate a world-market-oriented rejection of earlier tendencies towards etatistic inward-looking approaches, are confirmed in the preamble of the MERCOSUR Treaty of Asunción of 1991: '...in view of international events, especially the consolidation of large economic spaces and the relevance of achieving an adequate international integration of its countries, [the signatory states] emphasize that this integration process constitutes an adequate answer to these events' (Republica Argentina, Republica Federativa do Brasil, Republica do Paraguai and Republica Oriental do Uruguai 1994a: 87).

In contrast to the EC single market, the prognoses on the effects of MERCOSUR were not specified as precisely as they were in the Checchini Report of the EC Commission. If one takes stock of events since the beginning of the cooperation process in 1991, however, distinctly positive results of the economic cooperation can be noted: regional trade (imports + exports) between the member states rose continuously from $10.2 billion (1990) past $21.7 billion (1993) to $34.7 billion (1996) (*Latin American Weekly Report*, 28 Oct. 1997: 510ff). At the same time, the percentage of MERCOSUR goods as a share of total imports in the member states grew only slightly from 15.1 per cent (1990) to 18.8 per cent (1995), while Europe's share of MERCOSUR's total imports increased from 23.3 per cent (1990) to 28.5 per cent (1995) (Devlin 1996: 3). This is an indication that the trade diversion through discrimination against third parties may have remained small, and that, on the contrary, MERCOSUR acted primarily towards trade creation as well as actually implementing a strategy of opening up to the world market.

In the case of MERCOSUR, the examination of the role of global markets in forming the national preferences for competition-oriented cooperation can concentrate on Argentina and Brazil. These two countries were solely responsible for the Treaty of Asunción's constitution and its content. Paraguay and Uruguay were not relevant for the creation of MERCOSUR; Hirst (1993a: 34) assesses their role as that of 'observers'. They were obliged to join because, had they remained outside the organization, they would have suffered substantial disadvantages through the economic merger of their most important trading partners. Regarding the strategy of industrialization through substitution of imports, it should be noted that, although it clearly differed from the Western European neo-Keynesianism of the 1950s–1970s, it was also based on inward-looking steering of the economy and state intervention. A common feature of both models was that they were not primarily oriented towards liberal strategies and the competitive requirements of the world market and that they were founded on the state's ability to influence the national economy.

4.2   Argentina

Economic crises, indebtedness and pressure to reform

The case of Argentina differs from the European case studies primarily in two respects. First, its economic policy in the 1980s was marked more strongly by short-term decisions, which is also true of Brazil. Second, non-economic incidents played a greater role in the political events of the 1980s than in the other countries examined here. The war with the UK over the Falkland / Malvinas Islands in 1982 and the incisive manner of the transition from an extremely repressive military dictatorship to a democratic government determined the development of the country.

After decades of state-managed import substitution, the interests of the landed oligarchy and the financial sector (*patria financiera*) gained the upper hand following the military *coup* of 1976. Finance Minister Martinez de Hoz initiated the opening of the Argentinian economy towards the world market. This policy was particularly hard on national infant industries previously protected by high tariffs. For the most part, they were not able to compete with their foreign rivals and had to accept a substantial decline in production. Moreover, the interest rates had reached astronomical levels (in order to attract foreign capital despite the high inflation rate), which reduced the profitability of investment in production. The subsequent deindustrialization was actually intended by the government, in so far as it considered a 'healthy shrinkage' of the economy to be necessary for an improvement of global competitiveness (Kaufman 1990: 70). Encouraged by Milton Friedman's monetarist strategy ('Chicago Boys'), the military regime saw a radical liberalization as a means of modernizing the Argentinian economy, which had been stagnating for decades and which was still dependent on the export of agricultural products as a result of ISI.

This is the economic interpretation of the military's economic policy. According to power and elite coalition considerations, this policy can be explained as a result of the ability of the coalition between the agricultural oligarchy and the financial and trade sectors to prevail over the industrialists and workers dependent upon the protectionist ISI model (Simon 1988: 156ff; Waldmann 1985). Big agro-business, trade and financial sectors had suffered financial disadvantages under the import restrictions, export taxes, the inward orientation and the state dirigism of ISI. They had a structural interest in a liberal foreign trade policy, since they made their profit primarily in hard currency and not on the domestic market, as the ISI industry did. The agricultural oligarchy found the import restrictions particularly counterproductive, as it had access to foreign currency because of its exports and was able and willing to import high-quality goods from the industrialized nations. The military's general dismantling of trade barriers after 1976 led to a leap in the demand for imports by the middle and upper classes, which went far beyond the country's ability to earn foreign currency through exports.

This strategy was made possible by the expansion of the transnational financial markets' volume and their global reach since the beginning of the 1970s, which offered Argentina the ability to amass a huge foreign debt. Because of the national goods' low competitiveness and the liberalization of foreign trade, the country experienced a boom in imports that led to a large trade deficit. This, in turn, was essentially financed by taking out loans from foreign private banks. The military government's policy resulted in a structural crisis, since there was no foreseeable way that Argentina would ever be capable of repaying this massive debt. It is possible that the military hoped for extensive FDI – an illusion in view of the totally chaotic economic situation (high inflation and interest rates, overvaluation of the peso), the political instability (guerrillas, repression) and the country's international isolation as a result of the military's human rights abuses in the 'Dirty War' against the opposition. It should be taken into consideration that the then US president, Jimmy Carter, had chosen human rights as a central issue of his foreign policy. During the military dictatorship, the relationship with the USA was confrontational. In terms of economic policy, the reactionary generals made an effort to improve relations with the Eastern Bloc, and, by 1980, Eastern Europe (especially the USSR) was taking 22.4 per cent of Argentina's exports (UNCTAD 1997b: 90). The military was partly dependent upon the politically agreed exports to planned economy states, which, however, offered the country little hard currency. This demonstrates clearly that, although the Argentinian economic policy was based on financial integration into global markets, it did not demonstrate a world market orientation in foreign trade and production.

This structurally critical development was aggravated by a further important departure from the proposed liberalization. The state continued to set the exchange rate of the peso and to control foreign exchange (Kaufman 1990: 72ff). As a result of the strongly overvalued peso (devaluations lagged behind the inflation rate) concomitant with a state guaranteed exchange rate to the dollar, a bizarre constellation emerged at the end of the 1970s and beginning of the 1980s. At times, exchange rate speculators were able to make substantial profits exchanging the overvalued pesos for dollars at the guaranteed official rate and trading dollars for pesos at the black market's cheaper rate and then using these to buy dollars again at the official rate. The resulting 'sweet money' (*plata dulce*) was the outcome not of economic liberalization, but rather of the state-decreed regimentation of financial markets and exchange rates. Consequently, the inflation rate and interest rates rose considerably, leading to a further decline in foreign and domestic investment in Argentina.

At the same time, the amount of capital flight and the foreign debt of the country rose drastically – the latter in part because the government covered the greater demand for dollars as a result of speculation by taking out foreign loans. During the dictatorship, the foreign debt grew from $9.7 billion (1976) to $36.0 billion (1982) and $45 billion on 31 December 1983. The debt service (interest and repayment) increased from $1.5 billion (1976) to $6.3 billion (1982); in 1982, servicing the debt cost between 82 per cent and 107 per cent of exports (various estimates).[9] In the years preceding 1982, the country had financed its debt service to a growing extent by taking out new loans and had thus additionally raised its level of debt. When in 1982 the Mexican government declared its insolvency, this source of financing dried up rapidly, because transnational banks stopped lending to Argentina as well, for fear they would have to classify further outstanding debts as non-performing. The policy of exchange rate and currency control meant that the state was involved in servicing debts, even if the debtor was a private entity. Because of the state's exchange rate guarantee, the public sector was held responsible for about $13 billion of private debt between 1981 and 1985 (de la Balze 1995: 52).

The high rate of foreign debt meant that Argentina had extensively integrated into global financial markets and had taken on obligations that it could not fulfil or could meet only with great effort. In order to service its debts, it would have needed to orient its economy towards earning hard currency – that is, towards achieving export surpluses. In part because of the dramatic experiences during the dictatorship and the Falkland / Malvinas War, the democratically elected Alfonsín Administration (1983–9) was exposed to public pressure to make concessions to sectors whose interests had been neglected by the military – especially the industrialists of the import substitution model and urban labour. Alfonsín instituted a dirigistic, demand-stimulating programme and one of his government's first measures was to raise the minimum wage by 70 per cent. Instead of taking account of the precarious foreign economic (especially financial) situation, Alfonsín implemented neo-Keynesian redistributive measures for domestic policy reasons (Bouzas 1991: 5).

Alfonsín's presidency was characterized by a very chaotic economic policy, which essentially represented an attempt to reconcile state-directed import substitution following *cepalinic* objectives with the requirements of a high foreign debt. This failed completely. In its first years, the Alfonsín Administration engaged in direct negotiations with the creditor banks in an effort to reschedule the debt and thus reduce the burden of debt service. However, as an unstable and inward-looking economic policy offered creditors little hope that the country's ability to pay its debts from its earnings would be enhanced, the banks refused to comply with the government's request. Instead, they made concessions dependent upon Argentina's agreement with the IMF (Simon 1988: 161; see also appendix to this chapter).

The eruption of the debt crisis led to a crisis of the public budget as a result of the rising burden of servicing the debt, the growing capital flight and the fear of state bankruptcy (de la Balze 1995: 53). Since the return to an inward-looking demand stimulation in 1983 made the situation even more critical, the pressure to take the requirements of global financial markets into account increased. In December 1984, the Argentinian government signed the first letter of intent with the IMF, after the balance of payments situation had deteriorated further and transnational banks had threatened to cancel even those merchant loans necessary for trade.[10] However, Argentina was unable to reduce its inflation, and the IMF therefore blocked payment of further tranches of the loan. Private investors' lack of confidence in the country resulted in a further decline of the currency, which in turn drove the inflation rate up. After inflation had reached almost 1,000 per cent in June 1985, the Alfonsín government decided on a *partial* change of course. The Austral Plan introduced a so-called *heterodox* shock therapy, which was supposed to fulfil the IMF's requirements in an unorthodox way (de la Balze 1995: 68ff; Simon 1988: 163).

Dirigistic measures such as a state-decreed (and thus, in the last analysis, ineffective against inflation) wage and price freeze were combined with economically liberal ('orthodox') steps like the reduction of the budget.

As a result, the Argentinian economy plunged into chaos, since domestic demand was reduced (real wage losses, inflation, lowering of state expenditures) without achieving the economic liberalization and stabilization that would have increased domestic and foreign investment, productivity, competitiveness and the creditworthiness of the country. The outcome of the Austral Plan and other 'stabilization programmes' was instability. At the same time, Alfonsín used dirigistic, inward-looking measures further to reduce state expenditures and, after 1986, also domestic demand. This was intended to correspond superficially to the requirements of the IMF and the transnational banks and to produce an export surplus – not by raising competitiveness and production but by reducing the domestic demand for domestic goods and for imports. In order to stimulate exports, the peso was systematically devalued, with the effect that inflation continued to climb and real incomes sank.

In view of the general economic chaos, an inflation rate of 4,923 per cent in 1989 and the shrinking of the GDP by −1.5 per cent for 1980–9 (compared to +2.6 per cent 1970–9), Alfonsín lost the presidential election of 1989 (Hufy 1996: 161; de la Balze 1995: 59). In the last analysis, the debt to the transnational banks had made the pursuit of an ISI model impossible, as they forced the economy to earn export surpluses and withdrew from it the means necessary for expanding an import substituting industry. Moreover, according to Bouzas (1991: 8), the foreign economic weakness due to the high indebtedness repeatedly led to speculative pressure on the peso, which contributed decisively to the failure of the stabilization attempts. All in all, the state's integration with global financial markets not only abetted the crisis of the inward-looking, dirigistic economic policy, but also took away instruments (the use of loans and agricultural trade surpluses) for financing the model of development and reduced the leeway for attempts at redistributive stabilization.

Menem's reforms and MERCOSUR

The new president Carlos Menem belonged to the traditional representatives of the ISI clientele, the Peronist party (Partido Justicialista), but, from the start of his period in office, he pursued structural neoliberal reforms. This change of course was made clear by the choice of a manager of the country's most important transnational company, Bunge y Born, as finance minister. Although Menem appointed representatives of various political factions to ministries to raise the acceptance of his policies, economic policy remained firmly in the hands of a market-oriented minister. The final break with inward-looking policies was carried through by means of several reform plans between 1989 and 1991. However, only in 1991, under Menem's fourth finance minister Domingo Cavallo, could a lasting stabilization be obtained. The reforms essentially contained the following measures.[11]

1   The convertibility law of 1991 successfully reduced the inflation rate, which sank from 2,311 per cent (1990) to 171 per cent (1991), 24 per cent (1992), 10 per cent (1993), 4 per cent (1994) and 1.6 per cent (1995) (IMF statistics, cited from Starr 1997: 84). The *Plan de Convertibilidad* anchored the peso to the dollar at a rate of 1:1. This exchange rate was guaranteed by the currency reserves of the central bank. That means that the money supply could not rise above the level of currency reserves and that the state's monetary policy was limited to setting the interest rates. Thus, the previous policy of printing money to cover the state deficit, thereby expanding the money supply unrestrainedly, was prohibited. Restrictions on capital transfers were dismantled.

2   An extensive privatization of state companies contributed to the increase in competitiveness, reduced state expenditures for subsidies to these companies and earned the state sales returns of $24 billion between 1991 and 1994. The privatization programme was not, however, as successful as it could have been, because often the former state monopolies became private monopolies or oligopolies, which did not stimulate the competitiveness of the Argentinian economy.

3   Import duties were lowered unilaterally from an average of 50 per cent to 10 per cent and non-tariff barriers were reduced.

4   An increase in taxes (including value-added tax) and more efficient tax collection raised the state's revenues, and, together with drastic budget reductions, these led to a temporary budget *surplus*. A chronic cause of the high interest and inflation rates (the budget deficit) was thus removed.

5   As a result of the new economic policy, agreements with the IMF, the creditor banks and the USA (Brady Plan) became possible, on the basis of which a rescheduling of the debt (lengthening the

repayment period, years exempted from amortization, reduction of the interest rate) could be arranged.

6 Labour laws were made more flexible and sector-wide wage agreements were replaced by individual company contracts – similar to the Thatcher reforms in the UK. Thus, Menem diminished the trade unions' influence on the economic situation and moderated the nominal wage increase.

The causes for this change of course are to be found in the above-mentioned catastrophic economic situation, which had resulted to a large extent from Argentina's insufficient economic policy adjustment to obligations to the global financial markets. The economic crisis and the disappointment due to the lack of effectiveness of inward-looking, dirigistic concepts for overcoming the crisis led to a broad acceptance of liberalizing and stability-enhancing structural reforms among the population. In particular, the reduction of the inflation rate proved to be very popular, since the lower income groups especially had suffered from the high inflation rate. In contrast to the upper classes, they had been unable to avoid it by securing material goods, such as real estate, or foreign investment, but instead had seen their income, which was needed for day-to-day consumption, considerably lowered.[12] Opinion polls show that stability and a low inflation rate were among the highest priorities of the Argentinian population (Messner 1995, 152). An essential reason for the success of Menem's reforms was also the enhanced political and economic importance of neoliberally oriented bankers and entrepreneurs as a result of the integration into global financial markets.[13]

Because of the necessity of earning hard currency for servicing the debt with export surpluses, the government had also supported the export sector. These measures, and the pressure on the private sector to compensate for the decline in domestic demand caused by the recession, contributed to a growth in the exports' share of GDP – it rose from 10 per cent (1982) to 16 per cent (1990) (own calculations, based on statistics from BID 1992: 306, 309). With the Austral Plan, Alfonsín had already begun to reverse his original inward-looking concept and in part to accede to interest groups' demands for an anti-inflationary and world-market-oriented course. Under Menem, entrepreneurs, especially from the transnationally oriented industries and agricultural sectors, gained access to government decision making, while other sectors demonstrated 'fragmented articulation'. The trade unions were also – in part because of Menem's reforms – in a state of *desarticulación* and had lost importance as political actors (Hirst 1993a: 38; Starr 1997: 100–4).

The politically most influential groups in the 1990s were therefore those whose interest in economic liberalization had grown with Argentina's increased involvement in global financial markets. As, however, these groups were numerically not decisive for elections, Menem also needed politically to legitimize the social costs of his reforms, especially the drastic increase in unemployment and the periodic decline in real wages (*New York Times*, 5 Feb. 1995: 16; Haldenwang 1995: 691). In addition to its economic objective, the MERCOSUR was also given this function. As Hirst observed, the regional agreement offered a way out of the domestic policy dilemma of neoliberal reforms: the state's withdrawal from economic intervention and dirigism was secured in international contracts and 'locked in' for the future (Hirst 1993: 6). Government politicians repeatedly argued that MERCOSUR was a necessary instrument for the adjustment to the challenges of the world economy. In his speech at the signing of the Treaty of Asunción (26 Mar. 1991), President Menem made this task of MERCOSUR very clear: if Argentina did not adapt quickly and efficiently to the competitive challenges of the world economy's globalization, it would fall by the wayside of history – but the dimension of the challenge was matched by the response: regional integration (Menem 1991b: 190ff). The Deputy Foreign Minister Herrera Vegas (1994: 45–6) emphasized that even the closure ('desaparición de actividades') of some companies because of regional free trade had to be accepted in order to secure the 'multilateral stability of the rules of the game' necessary for attracting investment. In 1991 President Menem wrote: 'In any case, we must not forget that integration is not just a strategic alternative, but also and fundamentally a solution for the economic and social transformation' (Menem 1991: 138). Elsewhere, Menem writes with reference to earlier attempts at Latin American cooperation: 'today we are not integrating in order to close ourselves off, but rather to open ourselves up to the international economy – in the least traumatic way, in a balanced manner and with the possibility of competing efficiently on the world markets' (Menem 1991a: 85).

In addition to MERCOSUR's function as a source of legitimation and political reassurance as well as stabilization of liberal reforms, the cooperation project was primarily aimed at raising the Argentinian economy's competitiveness on the world market and its attractiveness for foreign investment. The latter was a central concern in so far as Menem's liberal policy was dependent upon an influx of foreign capital. The country needed hard currency both for payment of the rising imports following the lowering of tariffs and for the survival of the 'convertibility plan' – that is, to replenish the currency reserves. Moreover, currency was desperately needed for the planned modernization of the economy (importing technology, licences, etc.), since the focus was on gaining global competitiveness in industrial niches. Foreign investment was to be attracted by the multilateral guarantee for stable, investment-friendly conditions supplied by MERCOSUR combined with the attractiveness of an enlarged market. The Argentinian ambassador in Brazil, Guadagni (1993: 27), stated: 'MERCOSUR's goal is to achieve an improvement of global efficiency and an increase in the quantity, quality and variety of the goods and services as well as an open and growing market, which is capable of attracting international investment.'[14]

For Argentina, privileged access to the large Brazilian market was already a means towards industrial expansion and competitiveness on the world market through economy of scale and division of labour effects.[15] Argentina was actually able to realize its expectations to a considerable extent. A first accounting of MERCOSUR shows that the country was able to raise its intra-regional exports substantially: from $1,833 million in 1990 (imports: $833 million) to $4,209 million in 1994 (imports: $4,572 million) (statistics for 1990 from WTO 1995: 50; statistics for 1994 from IMF 1995a: 102ff). It should be remarked, however, that trade in MERCOSUR is in part dependent upon politically guided exchange of goods ('managed trade') and that as a result of exchange rate fluctuations Argentina and Brazil repeatedly reinstated protective tariffs (Schirm 1997a: 92ff). Seventy-five per cent of the Argentinian rise in exports in 1992–4 went to countries in MERCOSUR (Starr 1997: 96). Half of the Argentinian exports within MERCOSUR are processed goods. Since the industrial goods share of the country's worldwide exports is smaller, this serves as an indication that Argentina also successfully uses MERCOSUR as a crutch for its industrialization.

Economic growth rose rapidly – by an average of 7.65 per cent in 1991–4 – and halted abruptly in 1995 because of the 'Tequila Effect' of the Mexican currency crisis. The investment goal was also reached: whereas in 1989 only $1 billion of foreign capital flowed into the productive sector, in 1993 this figure reached $6.3 billion (direct investment without portfolio: IMF 1995b: 86). According to other calculations, FDI rose from $2.44 billion (1991) to $4.28 billion (1996) (*Latin American Weekly Report*, 14 Oct. 1997: 486). The investing

companies based their decisions to a large extent on the creation of
MERCOSUR – that is, on their intention to produce in Argentina for
the whole of the MERCOSUR area.[16] Menem's re-election in 1995
showed that the economic stabilization and renewed growth had contributed to a broad acceptance of the reform course, and that the
socio-economic costs and the unequally distributed benefits of growth
were obviously sufficiently politically legitimized to preserve his power
(*El Pais*, 22 May 1995: 6ff). Despite the social costs, the economic
course seemed to be acceptable enough for even the opposition alliance, which succeeded in winning the parliamentary elections of 1997,
not to demand a fundamental change in the economic model (*Süddeutsche Zeitung*, 28 Oct. 1997).

4.3   Brazil

Debt crisis and the pressure of problems

In the case of Brazil, foreign debt was also a major catalyst for a
change in the economic policy paradigm. In contrast to Argentina,
these loans had served the military, which ruled from 1964 to 1985, as
an *effective* instrument to finance an ISI model since the expansion of
the global financial system in the 1970s (Malan and Bonelli 1992:
84ff). Until the beginning of the 1980s, the foreign debt was used
primarily for building up new companies for durable consumer goods,
for infrastructural projects (for example, the Itaipú Dam) and for
heavy industries run by the state (such as steel and petro-chemistry)
and helped transform Brazil into a NIC (Schirm 1990: 74ff, 86). Thus,
the foreign indebtedness was also one of the most important instruments for Brazil's emancipation from the need to import manufactured goods from the industrialized nations and to have to export
primary goods to them. Whereas in 1965 the country almost exclusively exported primary goods, by 1990 the majority of its exports
were manufactured products (World Bank 1992: 249). Borrowing foreign capital was an attractive means of financing the development
model for two reasons. During the period of high indebtedness in
the 1970s, the real international interest rates – adjusted for inflation –
were negative or very low. Moreover, this way of financing development had the advantage of not being attached to any political conditions, as the loans were mostly made by private banks and not by
governments or international governmental organizations. In 1986,

the private creditors' share of total lending was 79.4 per cent, while in the early 1970s, it was still 52 per cent (World Bank 1988: 230).

Brazil made more productive use of the foreign loans than did Argentina and other developing countries, by building up new industries, improving the infrastructure and using the funds less consumptively. The high growth rates of the Brazilian 'economic miracle' (10.7 per cent p.a. 1968–74) could not be regained after the first oil crisis of 1973–4, *inter alia* because the dependence on imported oil led to a substantial burden on the balance of trade. However, the continuous influx of foreign loans secured the maintenance of a growth rate of about 7 per cent until the end of the 1970s (Bacha 1988: 19). Instead of reacting to the negative external influences (explosion of oil prices, recession in the industrialized countries) and endogenous structural problems (weak competitiveness, tight domestic markets) with internal adjustment measures, Brazil relied on a constantly rising influx of credit from transnational banks in order to avoid development hindrances. The level of foreign indebtedness rose from $13.1 billion (1973) to $53.9 billion (1979) (statistics of the Brazilian Central Bank, cited from *Veja*, 25 May 1988: 100). As of 1979, the ability to service the debt (interest and repayment) declined as a result of the second explosion of oil prices, the global recession and most of all because of the wave of high interest rates on the global financial markets (partly due to the interest rate policy of the US Federal Reserve Bank). Brazil began to take out new loans almost exclusively in order to service its old debts. Thus, its level of total debt continued to climb, even though the funds could no longer be invested productively, since they never even entered the country but rather were transferred to the debt service accounts of the creditor banks.

Jaguaribe (1991) estimated that in 1991 at least one-third of the then total foreign debt of $114 billion could be attributed to the cost of the high interest rates between 1979 and 1983. The tripling of LIBOR, the world leading interest rate calculated by transnational banks, from the end of the 1970s to 1982 had a considerable effect on the Brazilian debt service because the outstanding debt was subject to variable interest rates, which were anchored to LIBOR. Up to 76 per cent of the Brazilian foreign debt was subject to variable interest rates (Montoro 1987: 6; on LIBOR, see section 2.1). The debt crisis led to a reorientation of economic policy, the main goal of which was now servicing the debt, as opposed to continuing the strategy of industrialization.[17] Ever larger export surpluses had to be earned in order to receive the hard currency necessary for meeting interest payments.

This course was directed by the state and achieved both by pushing exports and by restricting imports (as well as by reducing domestic demand). By 1982, Brazil had succeeded in maintaining its solvency through a combination of a stabilization programme and further indebtedness. Moreover, it had avoided submitting to the IMF's conditions, which were perceived as irreconcilable with national autonomy and thus rejected by the (military) government as well as the opposition (Schirm 1990: 89). When Mexico declared its insolvency in September of 1982 and subsequently the international debt crisis broke out, the creditor banks abruptly reduced their lending to Brazil as well and persuaded the nation to turn to the IMF in the interest of its economic stability (Bacha 1988: 20).

Oil price hikes, worldwide recession and the interest rate explosion alone would not have forced Brazil to turn to the IMF. It needed the sudden retrenchment of loans by private banks following the Mexico shock to achieve that. They reduced their loans of $1.5 billion a month by half, which abruptly made the already precarious liquidity situation critical (Calcagnotto 1987: 64ff). The importance of the IMF as a precursor for the private banks is examined in the appendix to this chapter. Brazil signed a *letter of intent* with the IMF in order to continue obtaining loans from private banks, which it urgently needed to service its old debts. The IMF's demands (liberalization of the economy, opening up foreign trade and reducing the economic role of the state (e.g. by privatization)) ran counter to the previously held principles of the Brazilian development model. Within the framework of the ISI strategy, Brazil had built up national industries protected by high tariffs as well as state-run enterprises and introduced extensive subsidies. Consequently, the path to the IMF was a stony one for the government for two reasons: for one thing, it partially lost control over its economic policy and, for another, this move was not easily reconciled with the military's or the opposition's nationalism and therefore implied a loss of popularity and credibility for the government (*Veja*, 25 May 1988: 96).

As a result of the contradiction between the earlier objectives and the IMF policy, and the government's difficulty in implementing this move domestically (which continued after the democratization of 1985), Brazil demonstrated an ambivalent attitude to the demands of the IMF and the creditor banks. Until 1985 and after 1988 Brazil signed ten *letters of intent*, which were, however, often not fulfilled. Brazil also refused a number of times to accept the loss of sovereignty associated with signing a *letter of intent*: from 1985 to 1988 it thought itself strong enough to master the crisis of its own accord by intervening in the economy to direct the output into the export (Dinsmoor 1990: 73–114; *The Economist*, 22 Feb. 1992: 54). The Brazilian *assertiveness* was encouraged by the fact that the economic crisis did not reach the extent of the Argentinian one, but rather was temporarily interrupted by years of growth.[18] These fluctuations demonstrate the different costs of a continuation of inward-oriented policy and thus also the intensity of the pressure to adjust to the expectations of global markets. Because of the periodical resumption of growth, the first civilian government after the military dictatorship, led by President José Sarney (1985–1990), thought it could avoid the adjustment measures that global banks and the IMF demanded. Nonetheless, Brazil subordinated its development to servicing its debt (even without an IMF agreement), in order to receive new private loans and to avoid insolvency.

In February 1987, the country stopped paying interest on its loans from private banks ($65 billion) because of an acute scarcity of capital. As a result of this moratorium, Brazil was cut off from further credit by the transnational community of banks in 1987. This was a *de facto* isolation, which did not – as Citibank President John Reed had threatened – last 15–20 years but which nonetheless made Brazilian negotiations with the IMF appear necessary.[19] After three and a half years, these negotiations led to the signing of another *letter of intent* in 1988. Brazil's loan isolation, which was really overcome only in the mid-1990s, was due to the private banks' shock at the moratorium, which caused the stocks of the American banks involved to fall by 10 per cent in 1987 (Frankl 1991: 241, 265). With the signing of the *letter of intent* in 1988, Brazil returned to the circle of debtors who have submitted to the IMF's and the creditor banks' conditions for the restructuring of their outstanding loans and the obtaining of new funds (Schirm 1990: 90ff). The later change of course had become necessary because the economic crisis had returned with a negative growth of −0.1 per cent and a rapidly rising inflation – 1988: 684 per cent; 1987: 224 per cent (Dinsmoor 1990: 100). Furthermore, the previous interventionist economic programmes had proved to be inadequate. With the unsuccessful 'heterodox' plans (Plano Cruzado I and II 1986; Plano Verao 1988), efforts had been made to lower inflation and achieve stability through dirigistic shock therapy by freezing prices and wages and introducing new currencies (the cruzado and the cruzado novo).[20]

Not until 1988 did Sarney initiate a careful liberalization, which was to lead to an extensive reform programme during the administration of President Collor (1990–2). A group of technocrats under the leadership of Minister for the Economy Mailson da Nóbrega took over economic policy in 1988. This group did not support the political goal of the greatest possible inward orientation and autonomy from abroad, but rather preferred to pursue a 'pragmatic and professional' (Nóbrega) course of a liberal stamp (from Hirst 1989: 53). In view of the failure of previous economic plans and the lack of external support, the conviction grew that an adjustment to global markets by means of a liberal economic strategy would be the right way out of the crisis. At the government level, a process of rethinking former tenets could be seen, which was then also expressed by President Sarney: the country's fitting into the principles of the international financial world as a disciplined actor was a positive and deliberate measure, and the moratorium of 1987 was the biggest mistake that Brazil could have made (Hirst 1989: 53). Only a few years before, Sarney had denounced the 'dictates of the IMF'. The liberalization and the good behaviour in the matter of the foreign debt, however, remained an inconsistent patchwork: Brazil interrupted the payment of interest again in 1989. This inconsistency in the course of reforms can be attributed to an incomplete shift in government's preferences and to domestic opposition. The opinions of Brazil's political class were divided, in part as a result of the democratization process: concurrently with the government's careful liberalization, in 1988 the constitutive assembly passed a law for the regimentation of foreign enterprises (Baracho 1989–90: 105ff).

Collor, Cardoso and MERCOSUR

President Collor de Mello (1990–2) initiated extensive reforms of a liberal type, whose implementation, however, was sometimes chaotic and contradictory – owing to personal quarrels and a lack of support in parliament. The most important internal goal was the reduction of the hyperinflation, which was achieved temporarily only by the short-term nationalization of savings worth $80 billion. Finance Minister Marques Moreira's (1991–2) primary external goals were first 'to pacify foreign creditors' and second to clear up the points of conflict with the USA in order to benefit from the Brady Plan.[21] Collor lowered import restrictions drastically, assured foreign companies of patent protection, introduced a privatization programme for the *estatais* – in other words, initiated an extensive liberalization.[22] The inflation rate of over 2,000 per cent was to be reduced by increased competition – that is, lower prices and a short-term freeze of savings (demand reduction). With these reforms, the government completed a change of course by explicitly distancing itself from the political maxim that Brazil should master its economic crisis without the support of the creditor banks, the USA and the IMF. President Collor (1991: 809) explained his course of action during a visit to Washington: 'We know that despite our present hardships, our policies of liberalizing reform will not succeed without real cooperation and positive responses on the part of the international community regarding solutions to such problems as: foreign debt, removal of trade barriers, and access to advanced, clean technologies.'

Since the economic and debt policy, which ran counter to the creditor banks' interests, led to a dearth of external financial sources (e.g. loans, investment)[23] and to economic chaos in the second half of the 1980s, Brazil was confronted with the alternatives of an adjustment to global markets or a more extensive isolation. It opted for the first possibility. A longer *de facto* moratorium would have isolated the country from the world economy and cut it off from global flows of capital; import restrictions would have increased and the Brazilian economic crisis would have deepened. In particular, the export sector, which grew because of the debt crisis, had an existential interest in a greater opening-up. Exports' share of GDP grew from 7 per cent (1982) to 11 per cent (1990); in absolute terms, exports increased between the outbreak of the debt crisis to the introduction of market opening in 1990 from $20 billion to $36 billion (own calculations, figures from BID 1992: 306, 309).

Although Brazil has adapted to the expectations of the creditor banks and the USA since 1990, Washington used its influence at the World Bank and the IDB a number of times to enforce a disciplined repayment of debts to private banks. In 1990 and 1991, the US government stopped loans and project funds in the billions to ensure interest payments to private creditor banks.[24] Because of delayed debt servicing by the Brazilian central bank, in the first half of 1990 Washington refused to grant a $1 billion loan by the EXIMBANK, which prefinances American exports.[25] Private banks had not only instrumentalized the IMF to protect their interests, but also gained the US government as their advocate.

In sum, Collor's and Cardoso's (see below) stability-oriented and liberalizing reforms can essentially be attributed to the country's involvement in global financial markets:

1   The debt crisis contributed decisively to the – only periodically interrupted – recession of the 1980s, which, despite numerous

attempts, could not be managed with dirigistic inward-looking measures by the end of the decade. Instability, hyperinflation and the failure of etatistic solutions led to the perception that traditional development strategies had become inadequate instruments. An adjustment to the altered foreign economic situation seemed overdue.

2   The pressure of servicing the debt had forced a new orientation towards export surpluses and thus an improvement of the competitiveness on the world market.[26] Competitive sectors interested in global markets increased in importance while inward-looking sectors declined. The former approved of liberalization, as they were competitive and therefore not dependent on protective tariffs. They needed cheap access to the import of components and technology in order to remain competitive in world markets.

3   As a result of the precarious solvency situation, creditor banks and – brought forward by the former – the IMF, like the US government, received new means of influencing Brazil to change its economic policy.

4   The global financial market's withholding of new flows of capital denied Brazil the most important instrument for the continuation of the ISI strategy. It was no longer possible to replenish the insufficient internal savings through external sources in order to secure investment; and it was equally difficult to use hard currency to import capital goods and new technology. Currency surpluses now had to be earned on the world market and expended on servicing the debt.

In 1992 the Brazilian ambassador to Washington, Rubens Ricupero, emphasized that the main cause for the change of course was the economic crisis of the 1980s, which had persuaded Brazil to rethink its policy (Ricupero 1992c: 8). Thus, the recession can be considered the foundation of the later change of course. The depth of the economic crisis, in turn, came about essentially as a consequence of the debt crisis. This would not have occurred, or at least not to the same extent, without the massive growth of global financial markets' capital and their transmission of the interest rate explosion. The American high interest rate policy affected Brazil via the global financial markets and in terms of *indirect power* gave the USA an influence on the South American country that it would not have had without Brazil's and the USA's involvement in the global banking system.[27]

According to Ricupero (1992a), a 'consensus' regarding neoliberal reforms had grown since 1990. However, it did not reach the depth of the Mexican one and could not be implemented with the same amount of societal control that the Mexican leadership used within that countries' semi-authoritarian system. After 1991, Collor's reform programme won Washington's support at new negotiations of foreign debt.[28] In 1992, Brazil came to an agreement with the IMF and the creditor banks and thus fulfilled the condition laid down by the US government during Collor's visit in 1991 for access to the advantages of the Brady Plan (*Veja*, 26 June 1991: 23). Within the framework of the Brady Plan's options for creditor banks, Brazil was able to transform the conditions of its debts to the private banks: first, lower interest rates; second, a 35 per cent discount; and, third, extended amortization periods and collateral loans from the US government, the IMF, the World Bank and the IDB.[29] Brazil paid a high price for its chaotic economic policy and its refractory attitude towards fulfilling the expectations of the global banks, the US government and the IMF in the 1980s. This price was composed of delayed access to the benefits of the Brady Plan in comparison to other, more reform-friendly nations and of less advantageous conditions.

At the end of 1992, President Collor avoided being impeached by resigning. The immediate cause of this premature end to his administration was Collor's entanglement in a corruption scandal involving a former campaign manager. However, Collor had also made domestically powerful enemies – for example, through liberalization, in which he prevented important elite groups (e.g. import substitution industrialists, parliamentary groups) from sharing in the privileges to the same extent as before.[30] Collor's successor was Vice-President Itamar Franco, a political lightweight, who stepped into the limelight uttering diffuse dirigistic, inward-looking pronouncements (*Veja*, 30 Dec. 1992: 100ff; *Süddeutsche Zeitung*, 30 Dec. 1992: 10). Among the indicators of a continuing broad reform consensus is the fact that, even under Franco, 88 per cent of the members of parliament favoured the privatization of state enterprises (*Veja* 13 Jan. 1993: 27). After 1994 Fernando Henrique Cardoso continued the carefully liberalizing course, first as finance minister and, after the beginning of 1995, as president. In substance, his policy carried on from Collor's measures. Cardoso's style differed from that of Collor in so far as he made an effort to include important political groups. With his Plano Real, Cardoso achieved an enduring stabilization through low inflation (Fritz 1996: 84–100). Privatization, deregulation, a further reduction of the state sector and opening up of foreign trade rounded off Cardoso's programme.

The liberalizing focus of the MERCOSUR founding treaty of 1991 was seen by the Collor government (and later by Cardoso) as a consistent continuation of the reform programme. MERCOSUR served, on the one hand, as a mechanism to discipline domestic policy vis-à-vis negatively affected sectors[31] and, on the other hand, as an economically more efficient means of implementing liberalization as a 'springboard to better competitiveness in the world economy' (Lima 1996: 150). President Collor (1991a: 193–4) explained his government's preference for MERCOSUR at the signing of the treaty:

> We have undertaken courageous internal reforms to redefine the role of the state... stimulate market forces, open up and modernize the economy... This is the path of integration, which must consolidate the already achieved successes and make room for other, equally creative and consistent efforts for our societies.... To the regional integration mechanisms we owe the assurance of advantageously opening up to third parties, to capital flows and to technological renewal.

According to statements by the former secretary-general of the foreign ministry, Itamaraty, MERCOSUR chief negotiator and Brazil's ambassador to Argentina (1995), Marcos Castrioto de Azambuja, the contractual obligations to the partner countries facilitated the domestic explanation of measures that were intended anyway and made attempts to reverse them less likely to succeed (Azambuja 1995). The reforms, which in part encountered internal opposition, could be legitimized as irreversible through the multilateral obligations. At the same time, transnational actors (banks, investors) were reassured as to the continuity of the new course, and furthermore, an improved competitiveness on the world market was to be expected. In the political discourse, further liberalization was said to be unavoidable because of MERCOSUR: 'Common markets are incompatible with the practice of successive economic shocks. Market economies require free competition with the elimination of government controls' (Cortès 1991).

If the arguments of the proponents of MERCOSUR and liberalization are seen in connection with one another, their circular nature becomes clear: the necessity of liberalization is – not only, but also – justified by MERCOSUR; that of MERCOSUR, on the other hand, is based on securing the reforms. The third element in this circle is the necessity of using MERCOSUR and the reforms to adjust to global competition.[32] This triangular argumentation corresponds to the economic interdependencies: the integration of national economies into global markets essentially triggered the liberal reforms, as a consequence of which competition-oriented regional cooperation became instrumentally attractive (Lima 1996: 156). The Brazilian diplomat Almeida (1994: 16) summarizes the causal logic of 'MERCOSUL's historic mission' from the government's perspective (in a foreign office publication): 'No other alternative, whether unlimited multilateralism or a too early accession... to NAFTA, could give Brazil the political room to maneuver and the amount of economic discipline that it needs... in order to adapt successfully to the new demands of the world economy.'

President Cardoso also used MERCOSUR to justify internal reforms and sees regional cooperation as the only way to 'get ahead in the age of global competition' (quoted from Escobar 1996). MERCOSUR's function as an instrument for the internal implementation of liberalizing efforts could be observed repeatedly: for example, both foreign companies producing in Brazil and national firms had often succeeded in reintroducing customs restrictions (especially in the car industry) in order to protect their *rent-seeking* profits. Following Argentina's protests against these abuses of the treaty, the Brazilian administration partially reduced the new tariffs again, pointing to the external obligations in MERCOSUR (see Escobar 1996). But MERCOSUR also functioned as an instrument for a more acceptable adjustment of import substituting industries: before they were exposed to global competition on 'their' domestic market, they were able to realize the adjustment process in a less rigid form at the regional level (Lima 1996: 153). A further indication that MERCOSUR was instrumentalized for the implementation of liberalizations was the changing of the constitution of 1988, which had discriminated against foreign investment in certain areas. The conversion of the MERCOSUR founding Treaty of Asuncíon (1991) and the protocol on the support for and protection of foreign investment of 1994 (see Republica Argentina, Republica Federativa do Brasil, Republica do Paraguai and Republica Oriental do Uruguai 1994c) into national law had made an amendment of the constitution necessary where it discriminated against foreign capital, such as in the areas of energy and telecommunications. Thus, external obligations provided the government with a justification for measures that corresponded to its strategy.

In view of the economic function of MERCOSUR, first results indicated that Brazil's goals were successfully realized. In addition to the considerable expansion of the volume of trade, the country was able to chalk up new loans and a large influx of foreign investment, following quasi-isolation from global financial markets. After China and Mexico, Brazil received the largest influx of capital of all developing countries between 1994 and 1996: $12.2 billion (1994), $19.1 billion (1995) and $14.7 billion (1996) (*Neue Züricher Zeitung*, 24 Mar. 1997: 5). Brazil's exports to the MERCOSUR states grew from $1.3 billion (1990) to $5.9 billion (1994) (WTO 1995: 50). It is difficult to quantify how much MERCOSUR contributed to the inflow of investment, since the stability-oriented liberalization at the national level and the privatization already represent motivating factors for investment. The statements of transnational companies (such as Ford, General Motors, Melitta and Volkswagen) indicate a causal relevance of MERCOSUR for the sudden growth of investment. They usually referred to MERCOSUR as the explanatory factor: following the MERCOSUR agreement, it became possible to serve a larger market and to assume with greater security that the liberalizing course would be continued.[33]

The election of Cardoso to the presidency because of the liberal reforms he initiated as finance minister, the constitutional amendment permitting him to stand for office again in 1998 and his re-election were indications of the domestic acceptance of the change of course in economic policy. Of course, it is difficult to assess precisely MERCOSUR's contribution to this acceptance. The central role of the connection between the reforms and regional cooperation in the political discourse as described above makes it plausible that MERCOSUR had a positive function in the domestic political legitimation of liberal policy. This interpretation is supported by the broad approval for a deepening of the MERCOSUR process expressed by political parties, media, enterprises and trade unions (Barbosa and César 1994: 295).

4.4   Conclusion

The empirical study of the developments in Argentina and Brazil has shown that the effects of global markets on national economies contributed decisively to the governments' preference for competition-oriented cooperation. As in the case of the European countries, global markets stimulated the replacement of an inward-looking interventionist economic model by a liberalizing and competition-focused policy. However, in contrast to Europe, the indebtedness to global financial markets was the decisive catalyst for Argentina and Brazil.

Global markets' influence on the change of economic policy

In both Argentina and Brazil the three pathways affected by global markets – crises, interests and instruments – were closely intertwined and have mutually reinforced each other. The definitive point of departure was both countries' use of global markets in the form of massive indebtedness to transnationally active private-sector banks. Thus, both economies were integrated into global markets to a much greater extent than before. Taking out foreign loans served to finance the inward-looking development model, but in the last analysis it led to a crisis of this model and finally to a change of paradigm – that is, to relinquishing the very policy that the loans were originally thought to support. As a result of the inward-looking ISI, which lasted into the 1980s, both countries found it hard to earn the currency they needed to a service their debts by pushing exports on to the world market. This precarious situation escalated into a crisis as the creditor banks globalized the US high interest rates and passed them on to Argentina and Brazil. This raised interest obligations at the beginning of the 1980s considerably.

Since both countries, because of their lack of competitiveness and world market orientation, were unable to earn the necessary hard currency, the global financial markets withheld from them the means to continue their inward orientation. Private banks stopped the flow of funds and investors declined to advance capital because of the unattractive investment conditions. The creditor banks sanctioned new loans only with attached conditions and only for the purpose of meeting outstanding debt service payments. In order to ensure that the debtors would focus on earning exchange for servicing their debts (export orientation, stability, austerity), the banks used the IMF, making new loans dependent upon debtors' agreements with the fund. These agreements contained conditions that obliged the debtor to restore its solvency by instituting liberalizing reforms and adjusting to the requirements of the world market.

Consequently, Argentina and Brazil had a choice between isolation from the world economy and a reorientation of their economic policy according to the expectations of global financial markets. Since the first option would have deepened the crisis by disconnecting them from the global economy and would increasingly have run counter to the interests of important national groups (exporters), while the

second option contradicted long-standing economic policy preferences, both states attempted to find an acceptable median between
1982 and 1990. Towards the end of the 1980s, it became clear that this
median was insufficient to secure growth. Global markets also contributed substantially to the failure of this policy: every attempt to use
inward-looking mechanisms to steer economic policy carried a price,
especially in the form of smaller influxes of capital (loans, investment),
but also in the form of higher inflation (reduced purchasing power).
On the other hand, considerable incentives were offered for policies
that conformed to world markets, such as new loans (from banks, the
IMF and the US government) as well as the prospect of increased FDI
(from TNCs) and of better competitiveness – that is, better chances of
earning foreign exchange.

Because of the foreign debt, two groups interested in world market
and stability-oriented liberalization gained importance in both Argentina and Brazil. First, the indebtedness to global financial markets
caused the 'internationalized' part of the national financial sector to
grow. In Argentina, in particular, this included those who profited
from financial speculation (*Patria Financiera*). Second, after 1982, the
export sector became economically and politically more important,
since the governments were more dependent on it for earning the
foreign exchange necessary to service the debt. In addition to this
heightened political standing, the export sector also grew quantitatively as a share of GDP. In the course of the increasing indebtedness
to global financial markets, the *tradables* sector, especially in Brazil,
became more important, and it was more interested in an economic
policy focused on the competitive requirements of the world market
than in an inward-looking state intervention.

At the same time, the political and economic significance of the
protected import substitution industries declined, as they were unable
to contribute to an amelioration of the debt crisis. Furthermore, this
sector was especially hard hit by the recession (unlike the *tradables*
branches) because it found it difficult to compensate for the shrinking
domestic market by stepping up its exports. Given the drastic economic crisis, encompassing hyperinflation and diminished purchasing
power, the majority of consumers experienced a growing interest
in stability-oriented, anti-inflationary policies, the prerequisites for
which included a limitation of state expenditures by cutting budgets
and privatization, a lowering of prices through admitting more
competition and a complementing of national savings with foreign
capital.

In sum, the financial means and the political support for interventionist inward orientation had dissipated under the influence of global markets. These effects of global markets were a result of the indebtedness of the 1970s and thus became possible only through states' decisions to access global financial markets.

Economic efficiency and political acceptability through regional cooperation

As in the case of the three European states, in Argentina and Brazil global markets also stimulated the preference for competition-oriented regional cooperation in two ways.

Indirect causality   The change in the economic policy paradigm in the two countries was the prerequisite for the preference for competition-oriented cooperation. If Argentina and Brazil had continued to pursue their protectionist course, an economic opening (as in MERCOSUR) would have run counter to the national economic policy and therefore would not have been in the governments' interest. Possibly, the sectoral and highly regulated cooperation begun in PICAB in 1986 would have been continued. It would not have aimed at the world market and competition and would very probably have failed because of protectionism and interventionism, like the Latin American efforts at integration in the 1950s and 1960s ('first generation'). Only after the decision in favour of a fundamental economic opening and a reorientation of economic policy towards global competitiveness was the option of a general liberalization towards neighbouring countries compatible with national priorities. Moreover, only as a result of this change of national objectives did the advantages of regional cooperation vis-à-vis the world market become interesting. Thus, reforms at the national level were a *conditio sine qua non* for the preference for MERCOSUR as a springboard for the world market.

Part of the indirect chain of causalities was that the advantages of liberal cooperation could be, and were, only seen as beneficial *after* the national change in paradigms had altered the national order of preferences: lowering inflation through competition, using economies of scale for more competitiveness on the world market (etc.) as the central economic functions of a liberal regional market could work as incentives only after the protectionist model had been relinquished. There is clear evidence that the governments wanted to use MERCOSUR to raise the economic effectiveness of the national reforms – that is, they justified their preference for cooperation with an improvement of the economic efficiency of national policy. MERCOSUR was declared a decisive step for both attracting investment and promoting global competitiveness. In both case studies, however, it was possible to demonstrate, by means of decision-makers' statements, that MERCOSUR was not seen solely as an instrument for an economically more efficient continuation of national reforms with new measures, but also as an instrument for politically securing national reforms: the multilateral agreement made it possible to strengthen the global markets' impression of the national reforms' sustainability. The limiting (the 'disciplining') of the national opposition's effectiveness against the course of liberalization through regional obligations was emphasized. Thus, as the implementation of liberal economic policies created new necessities for policy legitimation, the regional cooperation became more interesting.

Direct causality   Global markets' direct influence on the preference for MERCOSUR manifested itself primarily in the altered perception of the cost–benefit relation of fragmented markets as opposed to a common market. Although the modification of national perceptions was surely also a consequence of those factors that had led to national reforms, government representatives' statements showed an immediate link between global markets and regional cooperation. For example, the priority of the preference for MERCOSUR was justified by higher competitive requirements because of the development of global markets. These requirements demanded a regional solution, since they could not be met to the same extent by individual national efforts. Representatives of both countries emphasized this function of MERCOSUR as a direct response to global markets. After all, the development of global markets also quantitatively altered the opportunity costs of national individualism. As was shown in the case studies, transnationally mobile investment and credit avoid those states that in the investor's opinion do not offer adequate conditions. The consequences of the neoliberal reforms and MERCOSUR confirm this cost–benefit relationship in so far as TNCs explained their sudden increase in investment after 1991 with reference to the enlarged market and the multilaterally secured conditions in MERCOSUR. Finally, it should be recalled that MERCOSUR's liberal and competition-oriented strategy is a dominant tendency but not a concept covering all aspects of economic policy. In order to complete a 'common market' open to the world market, a number of steps still have to be taken to dismantle remaining protectionism. Moreover, apart from the decisive influence of global markets, other factors were also important in forming governments' preferences, such as the opportunity to enhance the MERCOSUR members' negotiating power against the USA and the EU by acting in unison (Schirm 1997a: 84, 104).

Appendix: Transnational Banks and the International Monetary Fund

The IMF[34] gives stand-by loans to states that suffer from short-term balance of payments problems and makes them conditional on the recipient country's promise to adjust its economic policy such that it can solve these problems using its own resources in the future. Consequently, IMF conditions are intended to further the earning of export surpluses by strengthening competitiveness and to attract foreign capital by improving the investment climate. From the IMF's point of view, both these possibilities of solving the balance of payments problem require priority to be given to reducing inflation (lowering budget deficits, domestic demand, debt accumulation, etc.), deregulating the economy (privatization, reduction of state intervention) and opening up to foreign trade (dismantling tariffs and other barriers to trade) in order to enhance competitiveness. Thus, the IMF pursues an essentially neoliberal strategy, like the one dominant in the political discourse of its most important member state, the USA.[35] The IMF is not primarily concerned with the developmental considerations that concern its sister organization, the World Bank. The IMF's exclusive objective is to restore the solvency of the recipients of its loans and conditions.

In order to receive the IMF's support, the recipient states must commit themselves to an economic policy along the above-mentioned lines in a *letter of intent*. If the recipient fails to achieve the detailed 'intentions' (i.e. the rate of inflation or the size of the budget deficit), the IMF blocks payment of the remaining tranches of the stand-by loan. In comparison to the volume of credit given by private banks, the IMF's stand-by loans were small in the 1980s. The IMF's significance in the debt crises of Argentina, Brazil and Mexico (and other debtors) was due to the fact that private creditors of existing debts made the granting of new loans and the rescheduling of old debts dependent on the successful negotiation of agreements with the IMF – that is, on the acceptance of monitored conditions. In this way, private actors in the global financial system instrumentalized an international organization to secure their interests. Some authors conclude from the similar economic policy interests of the IMF and the banks that there is a common attitude of a supposedly homogeneous industrialized world towards the debtor nations of the third world (e.g. Körner et al. 1984: 60–71). On a number of points this interpretation is not in accordance with the facts. First, politically and economically important sectors in the industrialized nations had interests that were diametrically opposed to the requirements of the IMF and the banks. The export industries of the North were among the obvious losers of a restriction of domestic demand and the pressure on debtor nations to produce export surpluses. Second, the IMF has been pursuing its programmes for the improvement of balance of payment problems since its inception as part of the Bretton Woods System and has applied them to the industrial nations as well (for example, to the UK in 1976). Third, it should be kept in mind that the debtor nations knew when they took out loans from private banks that they would be obliged to pay interest rates and to repay their debts. Although the transnational banks lacked caution and were even insistent in granting loans because of their overliquidity in the 1970s (petro-dollars), a minimum of economic comprehension on the part of the debtor should have shown that it would be necessary to pay interest rates and to amortize the debts – after all, they had signed loan contracts. The necessity of orienting their economic policy towards solvency on global financial markets could have been foreseen.

The developing nations could not, however, foresee the external events that triggered the debt crisis, such as the high interest rate policy of the USA, the deterioration of the terms of trade and the recession in the industrialized countries. Nonetheless, these influences do not explain why many states (among them Mexico and Argentina, to a lesser extent Brazil) ran up debts of magnitudes that, even without external factors, would have precipitated critical debt situations and made the orientation of economic policy towards servicing the debt necessary, if in a less drastic way. External factors are also unable to explain why many debtors did not invest or only marginally invested productively and thus were not at all interested in creating an ability to repay the debt (nor in the productive development of their countries). The Argentinian 'enrichment model' (Simon 1988: 159) of state-guaranteed financial speculation and expensive defence programmes as well as the massive capital flight in most of the debtor nations illustrate the irresponsible use of foreign loans by the elites. In the last analysis, there is no 'conspiracy of the industrialized countries' against the indebted developing world, but there is a distinct limitation of the latter's autonomy of action. If the debtor was not prepared to risk economic isolation and exclusion from the world markets, its room to manoeuvre in the face of the contractual demands of private creditor banks and the IMF as their advance guard was very narrow.

GLOBAL MARKETS AND NAFTA

5.1 Liberalization Strategies in the North American Free Trade Agreement

NAFTA[1] represents a substantial change in Mexico's economic and political attitude and less a change in the preferences of the USA. Until the 1980s, Mexico had been one of the driving forces of the various attempts at 'first-generation' Latin American integration (see section 4.1). An intensive economic cooperation with the USA was hindered by a contradictory economic model (industrialization for the substitution of imports), a political distancing from the larger neighbour and a correspondingly narrow ideological orientation towards Latin America. In view of the conflict-laden history of US–Mexican relations, Mexico's suggestion in 1990 to form NAFTA symbolizes a distinct shift in the country's attitude because, since the loss of half its territory to the USA in 1848, Mexico has been concerned to preserve its autonomy from the United States. The military defeat at that time and the traditional strong economic dependency on the USA had contributed to the anti-American orientation of the revolution that began in 1910. With it came a phase of political disharmony in the bilateral relationship that continued into the 1980s (Mols 1992: 453–60). After the revolution, a rejection of Washington's policy towards Latin America and support for revolutionary movements on the southern continent were major pillars of Mexican foreign policy, and were supposed to hide the continued strength of the economic ties. As late as 1980, the then president, Lopez Portillo, vehemently rejected presidential candidate Ronald Reagan's suggestion of a free trade zone as incompatible with Mexican sovereignty (Bagley 1988: 224).

Thus, NAFTA *politically* cements a new chapter in US–Mexican relations. Economically, the Latin American country has long been integrated into the US economic area. This 'silent integration', which was not formally settled, manifested itself primarily in the close trade relations: for decades, Mexico has carried out the greater part of its foreign trade with the USA. This integration also encompasses the dominant position of the USA in FDI in Mexico and among the Maquiladoras. The latter take advantage of low Mexican wages to do the labour-intensive part of production, using parts previously produced in the USA and sending the produced segments back across the border for ultimate assembly. The societal melting pot, the development of *Mexamerica* on both sides of the border through migration and cultural exchange, was part of the two countries' integration prior to NAFTA as well (*TIME*, 11 July 1988: 30ff). Intensive economic and cultural networks had also marked the US–Canadian relationship long before the contractual ties of the US–Canada Free Trade Agreement (CUSFTA) in 1988. NAFTA extended CUSFTA to Mexico as well as expanding and deepening it. More than in the case of the *larger* EC/EU and MERCOSUR states, NAFTA is characterized by a considerable asymmetry in the economic size and strength of its members: in 1995, the USA earned almost 88 per cent of NAFTA's gross domestic product, Mexico contributed 5 per cent and Canada 7 per cent (World Bank 1996: 188, 210). Given this relationship, NAFTA – i.e. the US market – is much more relevant to Canada and Mexico than its neighbouring markets are to the USA.

NAFTA symbolizes not only Mexico's change of foreign policy course towards the USA, but also a definite shift in its economic policy orientation. Into the 1980s, the ruling Partido Revolucionario Institucional (PRI; Party of the Institutionalized Revolution) had pursued a development model of ISI. As in Brazil and in many other developing countries, since the 1950s, the government had pushed the build-up of a domestic industry protected by high tariffs, and, because of a lack of competition, it hardly participated in the global technological development. A central element of Mexican economic policy was the interventionist allocation of resources, a high state quota, a strongly regulated economy and an inward-looking economic policy. In the mid-1980s, liberalizing reforms were introduced and the earlier development model was dropped. Within the framework of NAFTA, Mexico increasingly opened up and pledged to continue a competition-oriented neoliberal policy. In the last analysis, NAFTA and the preceding reforms represented the Latin American country's adjustment to the US American economic model. Thus, NAFTA culminated in a twofold change of Mexico's course. The political rapprochement to the USA ended the ideological distance, and free market rules replaced the traditional development model.

Regulations

The contractually agreed goals of NAFTA were the creation of a free trade zone in compliance with GATT, the dismantling of customs barriers, the encouraging of fair competition and the furthering of investment opportunities. NAFTA takes precedence over other agreements where these are in contradiction to its statutes. Its most important regulations include the following:[2]

1   *Tariffs and market entry.* The signatories provide each other with domestic status for goods. The tariff barriers must either be dismantled immediately or successively reduced within five or ten years, depending on the goods. Certain goods are to have a transition period of fifteen years. This affects primarily agricultural products. Moreover, the signatories agree on a protective clause according to which tariffs can be reintroduced if imports from another NAFTA country are particularly damaging to a domestic economic sector.

2   *Rules of origin.* In order to qualify for tariff-free trade, goods must be produced within the area of NAFTA – a rule similar to those of the MERCOSUR. A 'local-content' share of 62.5 per cent was laid down for the especially sensitive car industry. This means that only those cars that are 62.5 per cent produced in the three members benefit from NAFTA.

3   *Investment.* The treaty members are also given domestic status with regard to the treatment of investment, which liberalizes the innerregional flow of investment. Rules against expropriation and distortion of competition in investment as well as for the protection of intellectual property rights offer the investor additional security.

4   *Services.* Domestic status for treaty members in the tertiary sector should have been achieved by the year 2000. In particular, this meant that the previously rather closed Mexican market would be opened up to US and Canadian banks and insurance companies. As of 1996, they were allowed to open 100 per cent subsidiaries in Mexico, and as of 1998 were also allowed to buy a majority stake in Mexican enterprises (see T. Porter 1997: 177–80).

5   *Government contracts.* Companies from NAFTA countries are to be treated as domestic suppliers in the awarding of government contracts.
6   *Energy.* Mexico was able to prevent a liberalization of its state-owned mineral oil sector, a symbol of Mexican autonomy. However, foreign shares in exploiting and marketing the oil are possible.
7   *Mediation.* Detailed procedures and the corresponding bodies were created for dispute resolution. These include a trade commission and a secretariat, which oversees the adherence to the regulations and decides on violations.
8   *Standardization of norms.* To facilitate trade and investment, rules on technical and sanitary standards were set. They form a first step towards harmonization of norms, which is supposed to improve the compatibility of production processes and the exchange of goods. These directives make it clear that NAFTA extends beyond a free trade agreement and ultimately strives to align economic conditions.
9   *Free market rules.* In most of the specific articles (financial services, investment, government contracts, etc.) and in a separate article on competition policy, the parties pledge to uphold or create rules for free competition within and between the member states. Thus, Mexico – in setting forth its reforms – continues to adjust to the US economic model.

Whereas the free movement of goods, services and capital was written into the treaty, both the free movement of labour[3] and direct financial transfers for the support of adjustment measures in Mexico were excluded. A common external tariff and common institutions are not part of the treaty. This clearly differentiates NAFTA from the European single market, whose basic element – the 'four freedoms' – includes the mobility of 'labour'. Moreover, in contrast to NAFTA, European integration undertakes financial transfers to member states with adjustment needs (structural and cohesion funds) and sets a common external tariff. Because of US environmental groups' and trade unions' criticism of the treaty presented in August 1992, the then presidential candidate Clinton felt obliged to demand improvements, which were implemented in parallel agreements on labour and environmental standards after his election. The criticism of US interest groups was directed primarily at the environmental and social dumping they feared would follow from the low Mexican requirements for companies in this area. The parallel agreements established common 'North American' standards. Mexico rejected the idea of a renegotiation of the original treaty.

Goals

Like the European single market and MERCOSUR, NAFTA's primary objective was to encourage economic growth by freeing market forces. Lowering tariffs was to stimulate the exchange of goods, more competition was to improve the allocation of resources through division of labour and enhanced efficiency, and economy of scale advantages were to lower the costs of production, raise investment and heighten the global competitiveness of the member states' goods (see Haggard 1995: 93ff; Malpass 1992; Zoellick 1992: 1–6). Besides the preference for goods from member states, the agreement also aimed to improve the members' competitiveness globally as a site for production and investment. Attracting investment from third countries was a central goal, especially for Mexico, since, because of NAFTA, it qualified as a production site with free access to the largest national market of the world (USA). NAFTA also anchored free market rules in the North American economic area. The preamble of the agreement clearly states its two central objectives – market economy and global competitiveness:

> The preamble...emphasizes the three countries' obligation to encourage job creation and economic growth in each country through an expansion of trade and investment opportunities in the free trade area and by improving the competitiveness of Canadian, Mexican and US-American companies on the global markets.... The goals of the treaty are the dismantling of trade barriers, the encouragement of conditions for fair competition, and the enhancement of investment opportunities.... (Governments of Canada, the United Mexican States, and the United States of America 1992: Preamble, 1)

Thus, NAFTA joins the European single market and MERCOSUR in forming a new world market and competition-oriented type of regional economic cooperation: they not only aim to take advantage of tariff-free access to the members' markets but also plan to raise the quality of their production for global markets. Unlike those of MERCOSUR and the European single market, however, NAFTA's objectives include neither the creation of a common market nor the construction of common steering mechanisms or institutions, such as the European Commission. Although NAFTA is more than a free trade agreement, it does not aspire to the same depth of regional integration as the other two comparable regions. Whereas NAFTA did not require the USA and Canada substantially to alter their economic policies, Mexico used NAFTA to stabilize the change in paradigm of the 1980s and expand it by obligating itself to further reforms. Furthermore, through NAFTA, Mexico opened up to considerable competitive pressure from the USA, which forced Mexican firms and state regulations to take further steps towards adjustment.

A first accounting of NAFTA shows signs of success. From the start of negotiations in 1991 and especially from the presentation of the treaty in August 1992, the private sector had anticipated its implementation on 1 January 1994. Substantial flows of investment to Mexico and an increase in the exchange of goods in this time period can be observed. In 1994, the first year of NAFTA, the bilateral trade between Mexico and the USA grew from $84.7 billion (1993) to $102.6 billion (Mexican exports came to $51.8 billion). In 1995, trade increased to $112 billion and Mexico's exports to the USA amounted to $66.7 billion.[4] The influx of direct investment to Mexico rose from $2.6 billion (average p.a. 1985–90) via $4.4 billion (1992) to $10.9 billion (1994).[5] Even though these improved trade and investment figures are certainly also due to Mexico's economic reforms before NAFTA and to cyclical and exchange rate effects, it can be assumed that NAFTA made a decisive causal contribution to this outcome (Hornbeck 1995: 8). It should be emphasized that NAFTA, irrespective of its name as a free trade agreement, focuses as much on new investment flows as it does on a greater exchange of goods.

In the case of NAFTA, the examination of the causes for the member states' preference for world-market-oriented regional cooperation can concentrate on the USA and Mexico. They initiated NAFTA and carried out the negotiations. Canada's participation in the process of constructing NAFTA was marginal and its preference for NAFTA was to a large extent defensive in nature (Hufbauer and Schott 1992: 19–22; Schirm 1997a: 71; Storrs 1992; Wonnacott 1995: 140).

5.2 Mexico

The effects of global markets on Mexico demonstrate clear similarities to the developments in Argentina and Brazil, since in all three countries the foreign debt and the crises thereof after 1982 brought similar pressures and options with them and functioned as catalysts for changes in the economic policy paradigm.

The debt crisis and pressure to reform

Mexico also used loans from foreign banks as a means of financing its development strategy. In the mid-1970s, this method seemed particularly attractive for two reasons: because of negative real interest rates, taking out loans was cheap and was not attached to any sort of political dependency because the creditors were not governments but rather private transnational banks. The massive indebtedness was made possible by the expansion of global financial markets in part because of deregulation in industrialized countries and petro-dollar savings. The incentives for greater foreign indebtedness led to an intensive use of this instrument to further Mexico's goals at the time: ISI and political autonomy from the USA. The loans allowed Mexico to postpone the collapse of its development strategy by supplementing its economic model with inexpensive borrowed capital (Rojas 1988: 208). In addition, the discovery of oil reserves in the mid- and late 1970s threw Mexico into an oil bonanza. The expectation of higher revenues due to oil exports caused it to take out larger foreign loans: its indebtedness rose from $14.4 billion (1974) to $80.3 billion (1982) (Aspe Armella 1988: 34; Schubert 1985: 176). Trusting to future oil profits, the country wanted to spend the money immediately, without considering the possibility of a decline in oil prices, which began in 1980, and the concomitant explosion in interest rates.

It became a debt *crisis* in 1982 when Mexico had to declare its insolvency, since it was not able to earn the exchange necessary to service its debt. The causes of this insolvency lay in both the structural weaknesses of the Mexican development model and in the external shocks. For one thing, because of mismanagement and the inward-looking, tariff-protected production, the country was unable to export enough goods competitively to earn the foreign currency necessary for servicing the debt. Moreover, the government's demand-stimulating expenditures ran up a high budget deficit, which, together with the trade deficit and the overvalued peso, led to speculative capital flight from Mexico (Kaufman 1990: 97). For another, the world market price of its most important export good (mineral oil) had dropped and demand in the industrial nations for other Mexican goods had also declined as a result of the recession there. However, the actual trigger for the crisis was the sudden leap in the level of global interest rates, which drastically increased Mexico's debt service bill. As in the case of Argentina and Brazil, integration into global financial markets by means of massive loans also made Mexico dependent on flexible interest rates, which were set by private transnational banks.

The global key interest rate LIBOR, to which a large percentage of the outstanding debt was indexed and adjusted semi-annually, doubled nominally between 1978 and 1982 and in real terms rose even more (Buria 1990: 164ff). In view of its already precarious competitive situation, Mexico was unable to cope with this sudden and strong increase in the expense of its debt service and had to declare insolvency. The worldwide interest rate hike was in part caused by the US Federal Reserve Bank raising the USA's prime interest rate. The 'Fed' intended and achieved a substantial influx of capital into the USA in this way. The portfolio capital came from Europeans and Japanese, but also from the elites in the 'Third World', who wanted to profit from the higher interest rates in the USA. The purpose of the 'Fed's' measure was to balance the USA's budget and trade deficits ('twin deficits') by means of a capital influx (see Cline 1984: 12; Schubert 1985: 93ff; see also sections 2.1 and 5.3). In order to avoid losing too much of their own investment capital, the central banks and the private banks in other industrial nations also raised their interest rates and thus globalized the Federal Reserve Bank's measure.

In declaring its moratorium, the Mexican government triggered not only its own but also a worldwide debt crisis, because, as a result of the Mexican insolvency, the creditor banks almost completely stopped lending not only to Mexico, but also to other countries – new loans that were needed for the payment of interest and amortization of the old debts. Thereafter, the creditor banks made new loans dependent upon Mexico reaching an agreement with the IMF. For the transnational banks' instrumentalization of the IMF, see appendix to chapter 4. The US administration was more interested in a relaxation of Mexico's situation than that of other crisis-ridden debtors, but nonetheless made its offer of assistance contingent upon an agreement with the IMF. Some large American banks were very exposed to the crisis in Mexico, which could have led to the collapse of individual institutions. It would have sent shock waves through the US financial system had Mexico's moratorium continued.[6] For this reason and because of Mexico's relevance for US national security considerations, the USA was prepared to help Mexico reschedule its debt. The interest on old loans was to be financed with new loans, which re-established solvency in the short term but raised the total level of Mexican debt further.

The deficiencies of the ISI model, the consequences of the foreign debt and the exclusion from global financial markets because of the debt crisis caused a deep recession in Mexico, the grave extent of which made a radical change of course seem necessary to the Mexican leadership. To maintain its power, the ruling PRI had to demonstrate some economic success, at least in the mid-term. Continuing the inward-looking ISI model would have invoked the costs of permanent external insolvency and, correspondingly, further renunciation of new inflows of resources. Fulfilling the conditions of the private creditor banks and the IMF through reforms, on the other hand, offered the incentive of new and lasting inflows of capital. In the mid-1980s, especially after 1988, Mexico introduced free market reforms and fulfilled the IMF's conditions, to which it had obligated itself in various 'letters of intent'. By the end of the 1980s, Mexico had become a 'model debtor' – that is, the Latin American debtor that best implemented the measures demanded by the IMF, the USA and the creditor banks (Kaufman 1989: 109–26; Weintraub 1990: 142). Thus, Mexico relinquished its traditional policy of inward-oriented import substitution.

The deterioration of many Mexicans' standard of living because of the recession (real wage losses of 30 per cent (1982–6) – see Kaufman 1990: 102) manifested itself in a poor electoral result for the ruling PRI in 1988, when Salinas de Gortari won by a narrow margin accompanied by widespread speculation of ballot manipulation (Reding 1991: 275). The sinking domestic support led to more stringent reforms with the goal of reaching an economic upswing in the mid-term. This actually occurred in the early 1990s and contributed to the PRI's undisputed electoral victory in the local elections of 1991 (Purcell 1992: 56). The early, radical liberalization and austerity policies and its relevance to US national security made it possible for Mexico to negotiate more favourable conditions for an extension of its liabilities and for new loans than other Latin American debtors. Mexico's role as a 'model debtor' became clear in the country's privileged treatment under the two debt strategies of the US Secretaries of the Treasury, Baker (1985) and Brady (1989).[7] Their plans offered debtor nations financial and organizational support if they reformed their economic policies according to neoliberal principles and thus improved their solvency towards the private creditor banks. Since Mexico was de facto the only (Baker) and the primary (Brady) beneficiary of these programmes, it can be concluded that these measures were created essentially to rescue very exposed American banks. A solution to the debt problem for the entire continent was apparently neither the primary intention nor considered possible.[8]

The *Baker Plan* basically considered the solution to the crisis to be a revival of growth – 'growth-cum-debt' – which was supposed to permit the debtor to earn the service payments for the old debts. To this end, the debtor had to implement structural reforms under the aegis of the IMF, while private banks were supposed to advance new loans. However, given the desolate situation in the debtor nations, few banks were at first prepared to do so. The Baker Plan's problems, which were due to the initial refusal of the private sector to issue funds, are an indication of global financial markets' relative autonomy from the requests of even the most powerful national government, that of the USA. Only in the case of Mexico was the US administration successful in mobilizing hundreds of private creditors to make seven-digit loans. The export-oriented 'growth-cum-debt' strategy implied that the Mexican economy would focus more on global competitiveness and therefore many companies would adjust their output to meet the requirements of the world market. Thus, the country's predicament resulting from its integration into global financial markets was carried over into the real economy: the financial pressure was followed by adjustments in the productive sector. Integration into global financial markets led Mexico to relinquish an inward orientation in the production of goods.

By granting some Latin American debtor nations special conditions, Washington, the IMF and the creditor banks prevented those debtors gathered together in the 'Group of Eight' from proceeding collectively. A concerted effort in the form of a debtor-cartel might have given these states a greater negotiating power than the individual nations could muster. In view of the advantages of cooperating with the banks, Mexico opted against confrontation as part of a debtor-cartel. As a result of neoliberal reforms, the reduction of the debt burden and the trade policy cooperation with the USA, Mexico found a way out of the 'lost decade' to new growth earlier than the other highly indebted nations of Latin America – such as Brazil, Venezuela and Argentina – as early as the beginning of the 1990s. In 1990, Mexico was hailed by the business press as a 'jaguar with new strength' (*Wirtschaftswoche*, 30 Nov. 1990: 58) in analogy to the Asian 'tigers'. However, Mexico achieved an end to the debt crisis and economic success only by turning away from the traditional economic policy maxims and from the goal of autonomy from the USA it had pursued in the 1970s and by playing by the rules set by the trans-national banks, the IMF and the US government.

Liberalization and the path to NAFTA

The 1982 recession, accompanied by negative growth rates, mass un-employment, real wage losses and an impoverishment of low-income segments of the population, had reached such a grave level that even the standard of living of Mexico's upper class and the political sur-vival of the PRI seemed threatened. In view of these costs, a consen-sus developed regarding the failure of the traditional strategy (Lustig 1992: 231ff). It seemed that a stronger concentration on competitive exports and a necessary liberalization were unavoidable in order to achieve growth (Ramirez de la O 1989: 13). The failure of the inward-oriented strategy, triggered by the debt crisis, and the pressures (plus incentives) from creditor banks to undertake economic reforms con-tributed to the prevailing of the proponents of a neoliberal course during President de la Madrid's administration (1982–8) and to their dominance after 1988. The ideas of this group, which until the mid-1980s was losing the inner-party power struggle, corresponded to those of the IMF, the US government and the creditor banks.

Decisive reformers such as the former economics and budget minis-ter and later president, Salinas de Gortari (1988–94), and the former high finance ministry official and later finance minister, Aspe Armella, had been educated in the USA: Salinas de Gortari did a doctorate at the JFK School of Government at Harvard University, Aspe Armella received his PhD in economics at the Massachusetts Institute of Tech-nology (Brookings, IAD and ODC 1992: 7; Feldstein 1992: 43–9). This new generation of Mexican politicians was familiar with eco-nomic liberalism, believed in its tenets and did not share Mexico's traditional political establishment's resentment towards its big neigh-bour. Although the importance of this cultural-ideological factor for the orientation of the reforms cannot be definitively proven, it seems to have had a strong influence according to the statements of leading representatives of the government, the PRI and academia (Casar 1992; Provencio 1992; Torres 1992). One consequence of the Mexican government's free market convictions was that it not only fulfilled the requirements of the banks and the IMF, but actually surpassed them (Provencio 1992), and that the decisive step towards opening up to the world economy was as much its own initiative as was the suggestion for NAFTA. Salinas de Gortari (1992: 19) coined the name of social liberalism – *Liberalismo Social* – for the new economic policy. After Salinas took office in 1988, the intensified neoliberal course essentially contained the following measures:

- opening the economy to the outside and stimulating exports by dismantling import duties in order to raise the global competitiveness of its own production;
- privatizing state companies to reduce public deficits and to raise productivity;
- lowering the budget deficits by cutting subsidies;
- privatizing agricultural *ejido*-companies (cooperatives) to raise productivity in the agricultural sector;
- facilitating direct investment to attract foreign capital; tax reductions, protection from expropriation, and the possibility of obtaining majority shares in joint ventures lowered the barriers for foreign investment that had previously flanked Mexico's nationalistic course.[9]

The reversal of earlier tenets necessitated a domestic and party-internal justification, since traditional support for the legitimacy of the PRI's rule was based on both its economic success and its ideological principles. In order to justify the new economic policy, the government redefined the revolutionary principles of 'nationalism' and 'sovereignty'. The government explained that, while until the early 1980s these terms had referred to autonomy from the USA and an inward-oriented development model (Meyer 1992: 8), the Mexican sovereignty would now be best secured by 'national strength', which in turn could be guaranteed only by an efficient integration into the world market. To meet the competitive requirements of global markets, Mexico would have to ensure that the utilization of its resources was compatible with the world market. In 1989, President Salinas de Gortari stated: 'Exercising sovereignty in a modern way requires a country to fit efficiently into international markets. This expands, to our advantage, the ability to act by providing access to new technological, commercial and financial possibilities' (Salinas Gortari 1989: 8).[10]

The Under-Secretary of the Mexican Foreign Ministry, Javier Valero (1990: 16), clarified the government's view of how the global markets altered its ability to act: 'Every attempt at isolationism is undoubtedly doomed to failure. It is vital to realize that a nation's viability in this new era depends on the knowledge and the ability to act independently and to pay attention [atendiendo] to the rules of the global game.'

The domestic implementation of the new policy was facilitated by two factors: the crisis caused the majority of the population to see the traditional tenets as failed, and the semi-authoritarian political system partially shielded the government from a growing opposition (Roett 1991: 13). This system offered the government a double advantage in implementing the change of paradigm. On the one hand, part of the potential opposition – that is, the adherents of the previous inward-oriented autonomy project – was located within the PRI apparatus. They had profited for decades from their affiliation to the political elite (to the 'revolutionary family') and from the PRI's traditional ruling strategy of silencing controversy by means of co-option and privileges. On the other hand, important societal groups were tied to the state through the corporativist organization of the political system and were financially dependent upon it. In view of the societal opposition to the neoliberal reforms, support from the Mexican trade union federation (Confederación de Trabajadores Mexicanos, CTM), was especially relevant for the new course – the labour organization also redefined previous positions.[11] The CTM's role (slogan: 'For Mexico's emancipation') cannot be described as subordinate to the government; rather, it was a part of the PRI establishment *like the government*.

Since Mexico's integration into global financial markets via its indebtedness contributed decisively to the end of the inward-oriented import substitution policy and steered it in the direction of free market reforms as well as export-oriented competitiveness, the preference for an economically efficient and politically acceptable implementation of these new maxims grew. The 'national development plan' of 1989 declared that, in view of economic 'globalization', regional cooperation should be made a primary goal for economic and geographical reasons (proximity to the US market) (SRE 1989: 17). The closer ties to Japan and Europe, which the foreign ministry wanted, proved to be economically impracticable, and the deepening and securing of the relationship with the USA gained priority. NAFTA was the central element of President Salinas de Gortari's economic strategy. In 1993, Salinas de Gortari declared: 'Thus, we are approaching an agreement with which we will establish clear and lasting rules for trade and investment and which will bring our country jobs and opportunities. In view of this fact, I would like to repeat that this contract is a further instrument for the Mexican strategy of opening . . .' (Salinas de Gortari 1994: D 61).

The following goals were to be reached:

- securing the economic reforms and codifying the neoliberal strategy;
- assuring access to the most important market as an 'insurance policy' against US protectionism and anchoring a privileged status compared to third states; the new strategy of 'export-led-growth' required a lasting openness of the most important markets;
- enhancing Mexico's attractiveness as a *Standort* (location) for global capital markets (especially for foreign investment) by stabilizing and guaranteeing the economic fundamentals with a multilateral contract (Castañeda 1993: 73);
- qualifying for support from the USA in the form of loans, help with rescheduling, guarantees, etc.[12]

NAFTA was to attract global investment capital first by offering the possibility of servicing the US market through investment in Mexico, second by supporting a greater economic policy stability in Mexico and third by multilaterally securing investment conditions (Pastor 1994: 165ff). In the 1980s, transnational investors had complained about the lack of legal security in the investment conditions and demanded assured conditions (Mexico–US Business Committee [1987/8]: 9). NAFTA's 'lock-in' function was of central importance in enticing investors: by signing the agreement, the country was multilaterally obliged to implement investment friendly regulations. Thus, NAFTA was an instrument for cementing neoliberal reforms – they were to be intensified and made irreversible for future governments. President Salinas declared the free trade agreement to be a *conditio sine qua non* for the continuation of the reforms (US Government Printing Office 1991: 30) One of the chief negotiators of the NAFTA treaty, Minister for Trade and Industry Jaime Serra Puche, explicitly justified NAFTA on the causal connection between the goal of global competitiveness and the advantages offered by liberal regional cooperation: 'The constant search for higher levels of competition is the motor of the current economic dynamics. In order to reach these levels, countries enter into alliances with one another, with the goal of making better use of their capacities and resources' (Puche 1992: 8).

From the beginning of the 1990s, it was possible to observe an extensive domestic consensus on the economic reforms and the closer ties to the USA, even outside the PRI. The most obvious indication was the statement by the leader of the opposition party, Partido de la

Revolución Democrática (PRD; Party of the Democratic Revolution), Cuauhtémoc Cardenas. Whereas in the election campaign of 1988 he had sharply criticized the economic reforms and the rapprochement to the USA, in 1993 he approved of the stronger ties within the framework of NAFTA and stated that, in the case of his victory, he would only undertake certain 'improvements'. As late as 1990, Cardenas (1990: 113) had considered Salinas de Gortari's policy to be an 'unprecedented subordination of Mexico's national interests to American preferences'. Although in 1988 Cardenas's party was kept from gaining victories in some states only by fraudulent means, it was clearly defeated in the local elections of 1991, underlining the societal support for Salinas de Gortari's policy, and this may have moved Cardenas to change his anti-NAFTA stance.

In setting the neoliberal tendency of the reforms, the government could also rely on a shift in Mexican entrepreneurs' interests. Whereas, until the early 1980s, large segments of the private sector had been beneficiaries of the protectionist economic model, the extent of the debt-induced recession made the traditional strategy's failure clear and strengthened market-oriented entrepreneurs.[13] Moreover, the decline in the influx of foreign loans had reduced the state's ability to support the inward-oriented sector, while companies that focused on exports gained clout because they were able to earn revenue abroad and had direct access to external sources of credit. As in Argentina and Brazil, the political weight of the *tradables* sector had grown because, as opposed to the import substituting industry, by exporting it was able to contribute to earning the foreign exchange necessary for servicing the debt. In quantitative terms, the importance of the export sector doubled – its share of GDP rose from 7 per cent (1980) to 14 per cent (1990) (*The Economist*, 5 July 1997: 17). The *tradables* sector was also strengthened by the fact that – unlike the inward-oriented branches – it could compensate for the collapse of domestic demand due to the recession by increasing its sales abroad.

The private sector's encompassing of neoliberal concepts in the 1980s was also supported by transnational networks, especially between Mexican and US companies. One example for such networks is the 'Americas Society' in New York, to which influential US entrepreneurs like David Rockefeller and John Reed (Citibank) and Mexicans such as Miguel Alemán and the media czar Emilio Azcarraga (Televisa) belonged.[14] Furthermore, in the 1980s, the Mexican companies had already begun to concentrate on world market compatibility in production for export, because of the government's 'export-led-growth' strategy, the collapse of domestic demand and the liberalization following the outbreak of the debt crisis. Thus, integration into global financial markets via the effects of the debt crisis contributed to a shift in many companies' strategic orientation, and not only raised the acceptance of NAFTA, but also caused parts of the business sector to become proponents of world market orientation and regional free trade.

To what extent the intended goals could be reached within NAFTA can, as in the other case studies, be determined only on the grounds of plausibility. According to statements of the investing companies, a large part of the sudden increase in direct investment in Mexico was due to NAFTA's multilaterally secured investment and production conditions, freer competition and economies of scale. The latter refers to the improved opportunities of serving the US market with goods produced in Mexico – that is, using the Latin American country as a 'work bench' or 'service entrance' to the USA.[15] However, the influx of direct investment would have grown just on the basis of the improved conditions resulting from economic reforms – although not to the same extent. As was mentioned in section 5.1, there was a distinct increase in both the Mexican exports to the USA (from $32.4 billion in 1990 to $66.7 billion in 1995) and the direct investment to Mexico (from $2.6 billion p.a. in 1985–90 to $10.9 billion in 1994).

NAFTA also seems to have paid off politically: Salinas's high popularity following the presentation of the NAFTA idea in 1990 was also attributed to the expectations associated with the free trade agreement, such as economic growth[16] and investment. In 1991, 64 per cent of Mexicans endorsed the NAFTA negotiations, 68 per cent supported the neoliberal economic policy and 85 per cent approved of the president's policy ('agree to performance of the president' – Consejo Nacional de la Publicidad and Gallup Mexico 1992). The peso crisis of 1994–5 is an indication of the successful consolidation of a market economic course. For reasons of campaign tactics, the government declined to gradually adjust the strongly overvalued currency to market expectations, and, after private investors' massive withdrawal of portfolio capital in December 1994, it was forced to accept a devaluation of 70 per cent (Hornbeck 1995: 6–10). But even the subsequent severe recession (from which the country did not recover until 1996) and the corresponding political pressure for state compensation was unable to achieve a change in the economic policy's orientation.

However, it should be taken into account that, of all the countries examined, Mexico had the least democratic regime. That means that both the question of maintaining power and the domestic acceptance of economic reforms must be seen in the light of a semi-authoritarian political system. Following the indications discussed, it can be presumed that NAFTA stimulated economic success and took on a legitimizing function for economic adjustment to global markets in the political discourse. Both factors will have contributed to the political survival of the coalition of interests that has predominated since the mid-1980s – both domestically and within the PRI. After the early 1990s, the government carried out a cautious democratization of the political system, which President Zedillo (PRI), elected in 1994, strongly accelerated. The PRI departed from power with the election of Vincente Fox (Partido Acción Nacional, PAN; Party of National Action) in 2000, who promised to continue the economic strategy and the close ties with the USA in NAFTA. It is fundamental to note that NAFTA is as little capable as MERCOSUR or the European single market of securing maintenance of power and economic growth *by itself* – regional cooperation as an instrument of international relations is only one instrument among many.

5.3   The United States

The case of the USA differs from that of the other states examined in two ways. First, the US economy was more strongly oriented towards competition and less towards state regulation, even prior to the 1970s. Thus, the effects of global markets and the pressure to reform a neo-Keynesian, inward-looking model identified in the other case studies did not occur or were weaker in this case. Second, the USA – both its state and private-sector actors – was an important driving force behind the development of global markets from the 1970s (see chapter 2). The analytical differentiation between 'global markets' and 'national markets and regulations' is more difficult to draw in this case. Moreover, it is quite possible that the influence of global markets on the US economy is not greater than the converse, or, rather, it is difficult to separate them.

Before starting to analyse the US case study, it should be said that the US preference for a free trade agreement with Mexico was not new. In the previous decades, the USA had repeatedly suggested a contractual anchoring of its economic relations to Mexico – under market conditions that Mexico did not wish to accept. In his electoral campaign of 1980, Ronald Reagan made an attempt to persuade Mexico to sign a free trade agreement. However, Mexico rejected this suggestion vehemently – as it had earlier efforts by the USA. Thus, the creation of NAFTA is based primarily on a shift in Mexico's attitude, as examined in the previous chapter. NAFTA's economic strategy demonstrated more continuity than change on the US side. Essentially, the USA regionalized its traditional economic policy ideas. Despite a certain latitude in trade policy ('fair trade' instead of 'free trade'), the economic philosophy and policy of the USA were and are traditionally oriented towards free market, competition and free trade. Unlike the cases in Europe and Latin America, for the USA the world market and competition-oriented elements of the new cooperation agreement were not a manifestation of a change of course in economic policy.

In order to answer the question on the causes of the new preference for competition-oriented cooperation, it would not, therefore, strictly speaking, be necessary to examine developments in the USA. The USA has already demonstrated this preference in a more or less distinct form for quite a while. However, the developments in the USA will be analysed anyway for the following reasons. First, testing the book's hypotheses on a relatively exceptional – 'hard' – case can deliver results that will contribute to a more precise formulation of the theoretical approach and to a further classification of the empirical results in chapter 6. Second, because of the way that politics and the economy influence each other, analysing the most important state in the world economy could illuminate aspects of the relationship between 'state and market' that had not previously been given priority. Third, since the US preference for economic cooperation with Mexico has in principle existed for a longer period of time, the case study can possibly point out other causes than the political-economic factors given centrality here and thus present a broader picture of those elements that stimulate regional cooperation.

Exchange rates, problems of competition and Reaganomics

In the two decades prior to the start of NAFTA negotiations in 1991, the development of the US economy and economic policy was marked by various fluctuations and influences. Thus, generalizations cannot be avoided. The need to neglect individual factors in concentrating on the more sweeping developments applies more strongly to the USA than to the other countries examined, as the USA was not subject to a decisive and clear change of course such as occurred in France (1983), the UK (Thatcherism), Argentina and Mexico (neoliberal reforms). The Reaganomics of the 1980s conjoined neo-Keynesian elements with neoliberal reforms. The economics and economic policies of the USA in the 1970s and 1980s were influenced primarily by two crises, to which the global markets contributed substantially: (1) the exchange rate fluctuations and (2) the sinking competitiveness.

(1) The US dollar came under massive pressure to devalue as early as the 1960s because the global financial markets no longer considered the fixed exchange rate to be realistic. In part because of the rising public debt and the expansion of the supply of dollars in circulation (also a result of the cost of the Vietnam War), the Bretton Woods System's guarantee to exchange 'gold for dollars' had become less than credible. Investors diversified into other currencies or demanded the guaranteed exchange into gold. This pressure contributed vitally to President Nixon's decision in 1971 to cancel the Gold Standard. Throughout the 1970s, speculative attacks were launched against the dollar and led to massive fluctuations and a declining exchange rate. The global investors' loss of trust in the dollar was furthered by the economic recovery of Western Europe and Japan as well as the development of some of the 'Third World' countries into NICs, especially in Asia. The global financial markets, which had gained a great deal of space and volume in the 1970s, increasingly saw the (financial) world as multipolar and sought to adapt their investment decisions to this new situation. This was done mostly at the expense of the dollar's dominance – it remained the most important investment and reserve currency but not to the same extent as before.

The dollar's loss of value against other currencies contributed to inflationary pressure in the USA, in part because imports became more expensive in dollars. The sudden leaps in the price of oil in 1973–4 and 1979 further stimulated this development. In particular during the Carter Administration (1977–81), the American economy was caught up in an inflationary wage–price spiral, which had as bad an effect on the financial markets' trust in the dollar as the further worsening of the country's balance of payments (OECD 1988: 25–34). The global financial markets' lack of trust induced a wide fluctuation and general decline of the dollar, which raised inflation and thus encouraged further speculation. In 1979, the inflation rate reached 13 per cent. As early as 1979, Carter adopted an anti-inflationary course in order to contain this escalation and the domestic economic consequences of inflation, which his successor Reagan then intensified. In addition to the administration's measures, the Federal Reserve Bank's restrictive monetary policy was vital. After 1979, its new head, Paul Volker, drastically raised the interest rates. As in the other states examined here, the goal of monetary stability was made a central pillar of economic policy. The financial markets globalized the US policy of high interest rates and transferred it to debtor nations such as Argentina, Brazil and Mexico. The dollar recovered and its value rose, for example, against the Western European currencies joined together in the European Currency Unit (ECU), from a value of $1.37 : 1 ECU (1979) to $0.76 : 1 ECU (1985) (IMF 1996b: 786ff). The USA was able to reduce inflation, and the speculation on the financial markets, which tended to be directed against the dollar, was reversed. However, the rising course of the dollar exacerbated the US economy's second problem, the growing trade deficit. As imports became cheaper, exports became more expensive on the target markets.

(2) The second critical development was the loss of competitiveness. This phenomenon occupies a central position in the debate over the 'declining hegemony' of the USA (Herz 1989: 41–57; Nye 1990a; Schirm 1994a; 11–13). According to this argument, the USA experienced a loss of its global economic hegemony, because of deteriorating economic strength (productivity, technological innovation) relative to other states. Quantitative indicators were often presented as proof of the American 'decline', such as the share of world trade and world product. These figures were compared to those of the 1950s and 1960s. Joseph Nye argued against this hypothesis that the development was not a 'deterioration', but rather the result of a process of recovery – encouraged by the USA – of the countries destroyed by the Second World War, namely Western Europe and Japan (Nye 1990b: 422ff). In fact, the US share of the world domestic product sank from 30 per cent (1960) to 25 per cent (1980) (Bergsten 1997: 24). Its share of world exports declined more sharply, especially in technology-intensive products: from 27 per cent (1970) to 20.9 per cent (1986) (National Science Foundation's Statistics, quoted from Nye 1990a: 77). The USA faced increasing difficulties in remaining competitive, particularly against the Asian NICs, since, from the 1970s on, these countries were able to combine low wages with growing technological competence (University of Texas 1986: 56ff).

The NICs' successes in industrializing were in turn essentially made possible by the new opportunities to take out loans that resulted from the expansion and mobility of the global financial markets and the enlargement of the transnational corporations' activities – developments in which private and state US actors had played an outstanding role (see chapter 2). The decisive factor for the US position in terms of production site in global competition was the narrowing of its technological head start and productivity in the 1970s and 1980s (Ostry and Nelson 1995: 2–10). The disadvantages of the USA, such as relatively high wages and restrictive regulations (i.e. in environmental protection), were highlighted by the fact that enterprises shifted production to countries in Southeast Asia or to Mexico (S. Cohen, 1991). Overall, the US position in global competitiveness deteriorated in the 1970s and this raised the costs of continuing the previous policy. Although these symptoms of crisis in the US economy were less dramatic than those in the Western European states, they nevertheless made it clear that the USA was also subject to adjustment pressure as a result of the expansion of global markets.[17]

However, American companies' competitive problems had grown not only on the world market, but also on the domestic market. Trade liberalization, Europe's and Japan's recovery and the Asian NICs' industrialization had led to a leap in imports since the 1970s. Whereas in the 1960s the competition with foreign producers on the American market was only a 'marginal phenomenon', by the end of the 1980s, 70 per cent of all US products were competing with the goods from foreign producers (S. Cohen 1991: 80ff). The growing pressure manifested itself in the imports' rising share of GDP, especially in the 1970s. It grew from 6 per cent (1970) to 11 per cent (1980) and remained at this level (11 per cent) in 1990, while at the same time exports' share of GDP also rose from 6 per cent (1970) to 10 per cent (1980) (1990: 10 per cent) (UNCTAD 1997b: 294). In the 1960s, the share of imports had only amounted to 3.1 per cent (1963–67) (Ostry and Nelson 1995: 9). In conjunction with the strong rise of the dollar as of 1980, the growing presence of foreign (especially Japanese) producers on the US market was the cause of the high trade deficit of the 1980s. Despite a certain improvement of US companies' competitiveness through deregulation and tax cuts under Reagan, the trade deficit remained a problem, in part because of the high exchange rate of the dollar.

The high interest rate policy of 1979–85 allowed the USA to avoid the balance of payments and investment problems that, for example, the European states experienced as a result of competitiveness problems. Because of its high interest rates, the USA received a massive influx of foreign portfolio capital and was thus able to compensate for the growing trade deficit in its balance of payments as well as to improve domestic saving.[18] The restrictive monetary policy in the form of high interest rates was one of the central strategies of President Reagan's (1981–9) economic policy, or rather that of the Federal Reserve Bank (Gourevitch 1987: 208–14; Bierling 1995). Another strategic instrument of 'Reaganomics' was the expansive fiscal policy in the form of substantial state expenditures, especially for the defence industry. Coupled with sinking tax revenues (because of tax cuts primarily for businesses and the higher income brackets), this expenditure hike resulted in a sudden leap in the budget deficit. Together with the trade deficit, they formed the 'twin deficits' of the 1980s. Given the improvement of the competitiveness by means of neoliberal reforms such as tax cuts and deregulation, the rapidly rising state expenditures led to an economic boom.

Thus, the American response to recession was to accept the effects of global financial markets and to solve the problem of competitiveness with a mixture of neo-Keynesian deficit spending and neoliberal measures of deregulation and tax relief. In the mid-1980s, this recipe helped the USA achieve a temporary economic upswing, creating jobs and lowering inflation. Reagan's policy mix also included a slight change in the traditional free trade policy: the 'Omnibus Trade and Competitiveness Act' of 1988 replaced the original maxim of 'free trade' with 'fair trade' and increased the punitive measures against allegedly 'unfair competition'.[19] This refers, for example, to 'Section 301', according to which punitive tariffs can be raised against countries that subsidize their exports or use other measures to distort 'fair' competition, such as import limits for US goods. The US government decided what was 'unfair', often in response to lobbying interests (Higashi and Lauter 1992: 66ff).[20] However, because of the increasing global production processes, the punitive measures against states often failed to address the increasingly transnational forms of production.

If one compares the course taken in 1979, intensified and expanded after 1981 under Reagan, with the economic policy of the 1960s and 1970s, a certain change can be seen – as can an original influence of global markets on this transition. However, this process differed substantially from the developments in the Latin American and

European countries. While a clear change of course took place in the latter, the USA carried out more of a rearrangement of old and new economic instruments. The changes in the USA were also different in so far as it had no import substituting policy (Latin America), and the neo-Keynesian inward orientation (France, Germany) prior to the transition was comparatively weak. Moreover, the new policy's growth-stimulating deficit spending demonstrated neo-Keynesian contours, which were not among the reform measures in Europe and Latin America. The same is true of the protectionist tendencies of 'Fair Trade'. Apart from other causes, the European and Latin American countries lacked the resources to carry out a similar mixture of policies, while the USA was able to attract these resources by trading on its high interest rates.

Parallels can be drawn between the developments in the previously examined countries and those in the USA in so far as the – slight – change of course can also be attributed to economic problems and the altered interests of economic actors due to the effects of global markets (Gourevitch 1987: 208–14; S. Cohen 1991: 77):

- the increased global competition reduced US companies' ability to pass the relatively high wage costs (i.e. compared to NICs) on to consumers through the price and increased their interest in better domestic conditions for national and global competitiveness (for tax cuts and deregulation) as an alternative to shifting production abroad;
- fluctuations (currencies, stocks, interest rates) on the global financial markets had a stronger effect on the US domestic economy because of both the expansion of the volume and the mobility of financial transactions, and the rise of the USA to the geographic centre of the world financial system (New York replaced London in the 1970s); state regulations contradicted the transnational financial actors' interest in further mobility and freedom from government restrictions;
- exchange rate fluctuations and global competitive difficulties had a stronger effect on the domestic economy because the foreign trade's share of GDP almost doubled between 1970 and 1980.

Because of these developments, groups interested in global competitiveness gained importance from the end of the 1970s – especially the transnationally active banks and enterprises. The interests of these sectors differed increasingly from those of inward-looking banks and producers (Gourevitch 1987: 212ff). Globally active producers considered favourable conditions for competition more important than rising purchasing power on the domestic market – if necessary, they preferred either real wage cuts and deregulation in the USA or shifting production abroad. For globally active (US) banks, the creditworthiness of debtor nations, such as those of Latin America, was in part more important than the solvency of national US producers. Thus, it was in their interest that Mexico increase its exports to the USA, in order to receive foreign exchange with which to service its debt. Inward-looking actors, on the other hand, sought to protect themselves from the negative effects of global competition. At the political level, Reagan's policy mix reflected these diverging interests in partly deregulating, partly protectionist measures. Overall, however, globally oriented groups carried more weight.

At the end of the 1980s, the US business cycle collapsed and after 1990 the US economy suffered a recession, which only began to be overcome in 1992 (the last year of the Bush Administration), but was mostly overcome under President Clinton. The crisis of 1990–2 demonstrates that some of the fundamental economic problems had not changed, even after a decade of Republican presidents (Bierling 1992). Paul Krugman (1994: 108, 118) argues that the policy mix of Reaganomics had as little influence on the economy as Bush's more moderate approach – other factors were decisive, especially the Federal Reserve Bank's measures. The 'declining hegemony' debate was revived at the beginning of the 1990s and this time focused on the competition between the economic blocs: 'The Coming Economic Battle among Japan, Europe, and America' (Thurow 1992). However, the thesis of a competition between national economies or regional economic blocs was already acknowledged as too narrow and anachronistic in the age of globalization (*Newsweek*, 26 Oct. 1992: 50–2). To that extent, the 'declining hegemony' debate is a contended indicator of the US actual situation and should thus be given consideration only in so far as it influenced the perception of the public and the political decision-makers.

The preference for creating NAFTA

In 1990, the Mexican suggestion for creating NAFTA encountered a government in Washington that after almost ten years of Republican rule and the implementation of numerous recipes needed new economic policy impetus.[21] It was primarily that part of the private sector most interested in global competitiveness that exerted pressure for a further improvement of the production conditions (US Council of the Mexico–US Business Council 1992: 1). The export industry interested in better access to the Mexican market also lobbied in favour. Thus, one can argue that President Bush's choice to accept the Mexican suggestion for NAFTA was also connected to the pressures of global competition. This argument was defended by proponents of NAFTA, which included not only the Bush and Clinton administrations, but also large segments of the private sector. A stronger and most importantly contractually secured integration of Mexico into the US economic area was justified with the following advantages:

- better access to Mexico as a low-wage workbench would improve the global competitiveness of US products, since the stages of production done in Mexico would be cheaper;[22]
- new jobs in the USA could be created and old ones retained by increased exports to Mexico and the mentioned improvement of the global competitiveness (Hornbeck 1995: 15; USTR 1992: 1);
- increased competition with Mexican suppliers, who would focus more on the American market, would force segments of the US economy to specialize – also to produce more competitively; expanding the US market to encompass Mexican consumers could lead to economies of scale, which would make US production more profitable and investment more attractive (Hufbauer and Schott 1992: 336–8);
- with a legal agreement, the existing economic opportunities for US companies in Mexico (Maquiladoras, market access) would not only improve, but would also be secured against change ('locked in'); President Bush (12 Aug. 1992: 1) had made this expectation explicit: 'In the last five years, as President Salinas has dismantled many long-standing Mexican trade and investment restrictions, our exports to Mexico have nearly tripled – that's more than one-quarter of a million new American jobs. This agreement helps us lock in these gains and build on them';
- in addition to the expectation of concrete economic advantages, the US government also saw NAFTA as a fundamental contribution to maintaining or regaining its global economic primacy, as a strategy against the 'hegemonic decline' and as a vital element of an economic 'New World Order' after the end of the East–West conflict.[23]

The expectation of a stronger *global* competitiveness stood at the forefront of the official justification of NAFTA – as expressed by Carla Hills, chief negotiator and US Trade Representative (USTR), at the conclusion of the negotiations (Hills 1992: 1). Although better access to the Mexican market was not (in view of widespread poverty there) as important to the USA as access to the US market was for Mexico, it did play a role given the long-term potential demand of ninety million inhabitants. The expectation of higher exports was based on the prognosis of an upswing in Mexico due to NAFTA. According to the State Department's estimates of 1991, 15 per cent of the growth in Mexican income would be spent on American products, which would create an additional 22,000 jobs in the USA for every billion dollars more of US exports (IRELA 1991: 3). The US government expected an increase in the jobs dependent on exports to Mexico from 600,000 (1992) to one million by 1995 as a result of NAFTA (USTR 1992: 1). In the official announcement that negotiations had been concluded in August 1992, President Bush made it clear that NAFTA would focus primarily on global markets: 'The Cold War is over. The principal challenge now facing the United States is to compete in a rapidly changing and expanding global marketplace .... By sweeping aside barriers and expanding trade, NAFTA will make our companies more competitive everywhere in the world' (Bush 1992: 1).

At the signing of the NAFTA Treaty in 1993, President Clinton explained the function of regional cooperation as an instrument for adjusting to global competition even more clearly:

> We cannot stop global change. We cannot repeal the international economic competition that is everywhere. We can only harness the energy to our benefit. Now we must recognize that the only way for a wealthy nation to grow richer is to export, to simply find new customers for the products and services it makes. That, my fellow Americans, is the decision the Congress made when they voted to ratify NAFTA. (Clinton 1993: 383)

With regard to interest groups, NAFTA was strongly pushed by the export industries. This applies not only to sectors that wanted to supply to Mexico, but also to those that wanted to improve their standing on the world market by investing and partially producing in Mexico.[24] The US Council of the Mexico–US Business Committee, which was also influential in the negotiations, wrote as early as 1990:

We believe a bilateral FTA with Mexico will have a strong stimulating impact on the US economy and will contribute in several important areas to US global competitiveness.... In particular, the benefits which will be gained from efficient North American production, which capitalizes on the complementarity of our two economies, will allow US firms to compete more strongly in Asian and European markets.... In addition, access to the rapidly growing Mexican market will boost US exports.   (Morton 1990: 1)

The US export sector's interest in NAFTA also resulted from the considerable losses of the 1980s, when Mexico experienced a recession and a corresponding decline in imports. Moreover, at that time Mexico aimed to achieve a surplus of exports (to service its debt) in part through a planned reduction of imports.[25] American creditor banks were also among the proponents of NAFTA, as they could expect a higher rate for Mexican obligations on the secondary market because of Mexico's improved economic position through NAFTA. In this case, the shift of interests in the USA can be seen clearly. Whereas in the mid-1980s the US banks' overwhelming interest in Mexico's ability to service its debt (through a surplus of trade) dominated at the cost of American exporters, later the interests of the producing (and exporting) branches prevailed, and the government's goal of reducing the US trade deficit gained influence. Since the banks had partially amortized their outstanding debts and the impact of the debt crisis had been cushioned by the end of the 1980s, a US trade surplus now advanced to a primary goal, which was also achieved until the peso crisis (see below). In addition to the economic lobbying groups, another dimension of transnationality evidently also stimulated the US government's preference for NAFTA: millions of Hispanic voters were supposed to be persuaded to help re-elect President Bush in 1992 (COHA 1992: 5).

During the NAFTA negotiations, opposition stemmed mainly from three camps: (1) trade unions, which represented labour in economic sectors threatened by a stronger Mexican competition or that might, for reasons of lower wage costs, be shifted to Mexico; (2) entrepreneurs from these sectors (especially textile industries and some agricultural branches) and (3) environmental groups, which worried that US companies would migrate to Mexico because of the fewer environmental regulations and their lack of enforcement (Lustig 1991: 16ff). In order to avoid domestic problems with these interest groups, both governments treated the employment and environmental aspects separately from the economic consultations. Moreover, President Bush had Congress grant him a 'fast-track authority', which means that the parliament – and thus the representatives of the interest groups – can only accept or refuse the NAFTA treaty as a whole – that is, they cannot make amendments to it.[26]

A first accounting of NAFTA definitely indicates some success. As was explained in section 5.1, the bilateral trade rose considerably both in anticipation as well as after implementation of the agreement. However, it should be noted that trade probably also increased as a result of Mexico's previous unilateral tariff reduction and would have risen further, although not to the level made possible by NAFTA. A large part of the flow of investment to Mexico can probably be attributed to the better legal security of the multilateral agreement. The US goal of exporting more goods to Mexico was reached by 1994, but experienced a downturn in 1995–6 during the peso crisis. Because of the depreciation of the Mexican currency, American products became rather more expensive and Mexican supplies to the USA considerably cheaper. However, NAFTA prevented the reintroduction of tariffs against US products.[27] The peso crisis will also have contributed to the fact that the US goal of creating new jobs by increasing its exports to Mexico could not be realized to the extent desired. The above-mentioned estimate of an increase from 600,000 to one million was only partially fulfilled: in 1996, an estimated 90,000–160,000 new jobs depended on exports to Mexico that came about through NAFTA (*New York Times*, 11 July 1997: D1/4; Baer 1997: 138–50). In 1994 alone, the loss of jobs through NAFTA was estimated at 10,000 (US Government Printing Office 1993: 96). The course of the peso crisis is an indication that a different US goal was more successfully achieved. Because of NAFTA regulations, the Mexican government was unable to return to a protectionist, dirigistic course to cushion the impact on negatively affected sectors – the reforms were secured against opposition ('locked in'). Treasury Secretary Robert Rubin (1997) was able to present the achievement of this US goal as a success at the third anniversary of NAFTA: 'NAFTA, by eliminating the option of raising tariffs, provided a strong incentive for the government [of Mexico] to choose this reform path rather than turning inward, and NAFTA also provided confidence about Mexico to investors.'

With regard to an improvement of global competitiveness, it is not possible to present clear quantitative results. This is due in part to the short period of time since the agreement came into power, but particularly to the methodological difficulties of substantiation. The US economy did actually grow a great deal under Clinton and gained in global competitiveness – but how can one measure the share of the more cost-effective stages of production done in Mexico? Moreover, the fact that the Mexican economy is very small in comparison to that of the USA should be taken into account. Specialization and economy of scale effects will at best have been marginal and will have influenced the overall economic data of the USA only slightly (ITC 1997: 32; *Neue Züricher Zeitung*, 14 July 1997: 5). The director of the Institute for International Economics (IIE) came to a more positive analysis: according to C. Fred Bergsten's estimate (1997: 28), NAFTA will have provided the US economy with growth of 4 per cent. In view of the small size of the Mexican economy and the limited effects (+ 1.5 per cent growth) of the European single market despite its comparably higher importance for its members, this estimate is possibly somewhat exaggerated.

Restrictions in explaining the US preference

If one considers the economic development of the USA and the political justification for NAFTA, the explanatory approach of this book seems to be confirmed in the case of the USA as well. For a number of reasons, however, this result is subject to caveats, since the empirical plausibility of the causalities proposed by the hypotheses is not as evident as in the other case studies. This concerns (1) the connection between global markets and national economies and (2) the link between economic policy reforms and their economically more efficient as well as political more acceptable implementation through regional cooperation.

Restriction I   Although the negative effects of global markets on inward-looking, neo-Keynesian economies did not entirely bypass the USA, they were relatively mild by comparison to those in the Western European countries studied here. Neither the US attractiveness as a production site nor as an investment site for global financial markets came under the same pressure that the other states experienced. This was partly due to the fact that the USA had a less assertive type of inward-looking neo-Keynesian policy and a traditionally less regulated economy. Both the costs of an inward-looking policy and the incentives for neoliberal reforms conforming to the world market were therefore less intrusive than in Europe. Moreover, the USA possessed an instrument for cushioning the adjustment pressure that the other countries could not exploit to the same extent. The USA was able to attract foreign capital by means of its high interest rate policy and thus avoid other adjustment measures, such as more stringent economic reforms. But, most importantly, the inflow of capital provided the USA with the resources for its new neo-Keynesian deficit spending, which other countries lost to the extent that the global markets judged them unattractive. Why was the USA able to use the interest rate instrument, while other states could not?

- as the world's largest and relatively liberal internal market with traditionally more business-friendly conditions than Europe, the USA played an exceptional role and had a special attractiveness for investors;
- since the 1970s, the New York Stock Exchange had developed into the world's most important financial site and was thus the most attractive (and the most expansive) place to invest portfolio capital;
- in the 1980s, the USA still had the world's leading currency – despite the declining role of the dollar compared to the 1960s; the US currency was still supported by the largest economy in the world;
- the dollar continued to be the world's most important reserve currency: most central banks held large dollar reserves and approved of its appreciation;
- finally, the USA was prepared to accept an unusual risk in conjunction with its high interest rate policy: as a result of the capital inflows, it became the world's largest debtor and became more vulnerable to external influences than before.

This short illustration of the exceptional US role should make it evident that quite possibly no other country in the world would have received the resources from a high interest rate policy in the way the USA did. Overall, the effects of the global markets were weaker on the USA than anywhere else. First, because of the milder form of inward-looking neo-Keynesian policy, and, second, because of the exceptional role of the USA as the largest economy, the most important financial site of the world and the originator of the world's leading currency, the dollar. Global markets did not lead to an economic crisis to the same extent, nor did they alter the instruments and interests as much. As a consequence, the US government was not subject to the same change of the economic cost–benefit relations as others were, which could have stimulated a change in their economic policy course like that in other states. However, the differences are of a *gradual* nature. As was made clear previously, the effects of global markets on the pathways 'crises' and 'interests' could be made plausible. Global markets contributed to changes in the economic situation and within interest groups. A restriction of state 'instruments' for steering the economy, on the other hand, could not be observed. The USA did not have, or was making no (or at least much less) use of, those instruments that were affected by global markets in the European and Latin American countries. In other words, since the USA was not using a comparable set of inward-looking, neo-Keynesian instruments, no equivalent effect could occur. The exceptional role of the USA in using the instrument of high interest rates to finance *deficit spending* has already been discussed.

Restriction II Although this case study showed that the effects of global markets were weaker in the USA than in the other countries examined, nevertheless they existed and contributed to the preference for regional economic cooperation, as the statements of decision-makers have shown. However, the plausibility of the approach to be tested here also depends on a higher 'economic efficiency' and 'political acceptance' (of market economic reforms as well as the adjustment to global markets) that regional cooperation would offer in contrast to national efforts. This point is less plausible in the case of the USA than in that of the other cases. NAFTA certainly improves the US competitiveness, but only marginally. In contrast to the situation with the EC and MERCOSUR, the USA has joined with such a small partner that specialization and economy of scale effects will be slight. When Mexico suggested NAFTA in 1990, it had a GDP of $237 billion, the USA one of $5,392 billion (Canada: $570 billion).[28] Economies of scale and competition effects on the larger partner remain very small when the economic output of the smaller member is only 4 per cent of the larger partner's. For comparison, the GDP of Argentina came to 23 per cent of the Brazilian, and France's economic strength was 80 per cent of the GDP of the FRG.

Regional cooperation's second function – namely, raising 'domestic acceptance' through multilateral ties and gaining legitimacy for national reforms – is not very plausible for two reasons. First, there were no fundamental reforms in the USA that would or could have been given more legitimacy by NAFTA. Second, it would have been rather counterproductive to attempt to gain domestic legitimacy for policies in an industrial country by signing a contract with a developing country. The NAFTA debate in the USA showed plainly that the ties to Mexico that were marked by corruption and underdevelopment did the measures associated with NAFTA more harm than good – 'NAFTA has in fact become a dirty word in Washington' lamented one of the strongest proponents of the agreement, C. Fred Bergsten (1997: 28).

Since in the US case the effects of global markets and the assumed advantages of regional cooperation can only partially explain the preference for NAFTA, other factors could have been decisive. This does not mean that the preferences for the European single market and for MERCOSUR can be explained exclusively using the approach developed here. In the American case, however, other explanations could be of special relevance. Foreign and security policy aspects were evidently among the most important causes of Washington's preferences. The Bush government and later the Clinton Administration aimed to use NAFTA to stabilize the neighbouring country and to strengthen the new, pro-American and market economic attitude that the Mexican leadership had shown since the 1980s (US Department of State 1991: 5ff; 1992). They wanted to stabilize a neighbour whose attitude had recently become friendly and support the success of the politicians responsible for the political and economic change of course. Paul Krugman (1993: 19) considers this foreign policy justification to be the most important factor: 'For the United States, this agreement is not about jobs. It is not even about economic efficiency and growth. It is about doing what we can to help a friendly government succeed.'

Besides the support of Mexican policy, the USA also saw NAFTA as an instrument for solving specific bilateral problems of a wider security agenda, such as environmental degradation and migration – by means of Mexico's success in achieving growth, the USA's new potential for influence through NAFTA and the Mexican government's obligation to implement corresponding measures (see Baer 1991; US Department of State 1992; Schirm 1994a: 103–10). Furthermore, the USA used NAFTA as a bargaining chip to improve its position in economic negotiations vis-à-vis Europe and Japan. The threat of creating its own bloc including a withdrawal to its own region through regionalism – by definition discriminatory against third parties – could now credibly be used against other states and regions. The NAFTA Treaty influenced the EU's and Japan's stances in the last phase of the Uruguay Round of GATT and persuaded these states to show more willingness to compromise with regard to global trade reform (Doran 1995: 100). These foreign policy considerations in the US preference for NAFTA highlight factors other than global markets that can stimulate an interest in regional cooperation. Although the relevance of global markets for the preference for liberal regionalism can be found in the case of the USA as well, it is only *one* explanatory factor. In comparison to the European single market, to MERCOSUR and to Mexico, the US preference for regional cooperation becomes rather more plausible in the light of foreign policy reasons, since the GMA must take the above-mentioned restrictions into account.

5.4   Conclusion

The results of the analysis of the developments in Mexico and the USA diverge more strongly than those in other regions. Thus, the conclusions regarding the two case studies are less unequivocal than in the country studies on the European single market and MERCOSUR. As an overall impression it should be noted that, with respect to the effects of global markets, Mexico demonstrates very obvious parallels to Argentina and Brazil, while the corresponding effects on the USA differ substantially from the three Latin American case studies and even show divergencies in comparison to the three European industrial nations. In summary, it was possible to demonstrate the plausibility of a decisive influence of global markets on the economic situation (*crises*), on domestic interest coalitions (*interests*) and on state instruments (*instruments*) in the case of Mexico – equally the perception of regional cooperation as a means for a more *politically acceptable* and *economically efficient* adjustment to the effects of global markets. As for the case of the USA, this book's approach can explain the developments only by taking into account certain restrictions. For this reason, the two cases will be discussed separately in the following sections.

Global markets' influence on the change of economic policy

Mexico   In the case of Mexico, global markets were a decisive catalyst in the economic crisis of 1982. Because of the Mexican government's decision in the 1970s thoroughly to integrate into global financial markets by taking out large foreign loans, the creditor banks' policy of passing the high interest rates on to their customers while simultaneously reducing the level of new loans led to Mexico's insolvency. Since the inward-looking protectionist model of development was unable to help prevent or defuse the crisis, a change of course was perceived as unavoidable. In the last analysis, the integration into global financial markets affected Mexico in such a way that the costs of continuing the old course rose dramatically by implying Mexico's lasting foreign economic isolation.

In 1982, the global financial markets denied Mexico the means to pursue its inward orientation when it became evident that the previous policy had little chance of improving the country's solvency – that is, of servicing its debt. The effects of global financial markets carried over into the goods sector to the extent that the latter was directed towards earning foreign exchange for servicing the debt and thus had to orient itself towards the requirements of competition on the world market (and not on the domestic market). The recession after 1982 was so severe that the political survival of the ruling PRI was threatened, which implied political costs for the government. The offer of substantial incentives (new loans, rescheduling, etc.) by private creditors and international (IMF) as well as national (US) actors supporting banking interests completed the change in the decision-making parameters with positive stimuli for a change in economic policy.

Domestic interest constellations also changed as a result of the economic crisis. For one thing, the severity of the recession helped to discredit the former inward orientation. For another, the *tradables* sector (as in Argentina and Brazil) was clearly strengthened because the foreign exchange it earned from exports could contribute to servicing the debt. In this way, it was able to aid in avoiding further costs (financial disconnection) and in using incentives (new loans). The import substituting sector was unable to assist in a positive use of externally set cost–benefit relations and was additionally weakened by the decline in demand during the recession. In the case of Mexico, domestic interest groups were less relevant than in the democratized states of Argentina and Brazil, as the Mexican political system was semi-authoritarian.

Regarding the restriction of economic policy instruments through global markets, the most relevant effect was also highlighted by the debt crisis. By stopping further lending to Mexico in 1982, the creditors took away an instrument that the Mexican government had used extensively – that of supplementing domestic savings with external inflows of capital in order to finance the ISI. A further limitation of economic policy instruments followed from the conditionality of the incentives offered: if Mexico wanted to avoid the costs of a continued inward orientation and use the advantages of a neoliberal 'export-led growth', it had to accept extensive dictates regarding the formulation of its economic policy.

The USA   In the examined period of time, the USA experienced less dramatic crises than Mexico or the European states. Global markets had contributed to these relatively moderate crises in so far as they were involved in both the dollar's exchange rate problems (which raised inflation) and the increase in world economic competition. However, in comparison to other states examined, not only were the economic crises less severe, but also the global markets' contribution to the crises could be made plausible only to a limited extent. Finally, the perception of a 'declining hegemony' was based largely on the recovery of states destroyed by the Second World War– a development for which the global markets were not responsible. With regard to the criterion 'crises', the result is less conclusive than in the other case studies: since the USA had pursued a less inward-looking, protectionist policy, the effects of global markets seem to have produced fewer costs and offered fewer incentives for a fundamental reform.

In terms of the internal interest groups, it was possible to observe an expansion of the sectors involved in foreign trade but not a shift of political weight comparable to that in the other countries. The only 'new approach' to economic policy during the time examined, *Reaganomics*, reflected the ambivalent nature of the economic development and interests. Stability-oriented monetarism and deregulation on the one side were combined with neo-Keynesian deficit spending on the other. In summary, it was possible to observe that a stronger orientation of economic policy towards the requirements of competition on the world market was stimulated by interest groups. However, there was no fundamental change in the paradigm.

The state expenditure policy and the ambivalent course were made possible primarily by using the instrument of the high interest rates, which would probably not have functioned to the same extent without the development of global financial markets. Without their deregulation since the 1970s and the expansion of the volume of globally transferable investment funds, the USA would not have received the amount of funds to which it could recur in the 1980s in order to maintain an equilibrium in its balance of payments. Thus, in this case, the mobility and volume of global financial markets contributed to the neo-Keynesian expenditure policy. This *strengthening* of the effectiveness of state instruments by global markets was evident only in the case of the USA. In this aspect, the USA should be considered an exception to the rule. It can satisfy requirements that other states cannot, or not to the same extent.

Economic efficiency and political acceptability through regional cooperation

Mexico and the USA also differ in terms of their preference formation, which indicates that a separate treatment is also appropriate at this point. In both cases indirect and direct causalities can be observed.

Mexico: indirect causality   As in Argentina and Brazil, a liberalizing regional cooperation became a priority for Mexico only after a national change of course. Only after this change of paradigm had altered the government's preference were the advantages of market-oriented cooperation perceived as such. While the protectionist model dominated, Mexico still vehemently refused corresponding suggestions from the USA. Thus, the change of course primarily caused by global markets was a precondition for its willingness to engage in liberalizing cooperation with the USA. It was possible to substantiate the perception that NAFTA was a means towards the economically efficient continuation of the Mexican government's national reforms. NAFTA was considered a prerequisite for the continuity of the neoliberal course. The instrumentalization of NAFTA for securing national reforms through a multilateral treaty played an outstanding role at this point. The 'lock-in' function was seen as necessary for attracting investment, which in turn played a central role in the new economic strategy. Finally, the *de facto* restriction of Mexico's economic sovereignty due to the effects of the debt crisis made it easier to accept the *de jure* restrictions of its sovereignty in NAFTA.

Mexico: direct causality   This last connection also functioned directly: as the Mexican government's redefinition of national sovereignty clearly showed, the external opening and the external contractual obligations were justified with a change in sovereignty due to the development of global markets. In Mexican decision-makers' view, the cost–benefit relation for national solo flights had developed negatively as a result of global markets and global competition, while that of liberal regional cooperation had developed positively. In addition to the indirect causality (via domestic reforms), global markets also contributed directly to the preference for regional co-operation: according to statements from government officials, the search for more competitiveness as the motor of global economic dynamics made regional cooperation necessary. For Mexico, the option of more efficiently attracting global investment through regional cooperation was made especially effective by the economies of scale that the integration with the world's largest national market (USA) could offer.

The USA: indirect causality Since the effects of global markets on the USA were not as extensive as in other countries and the USA had access to exceptional instruments, it was not subject to the same adjustment pressure and did not implement reforms to the same degree. Therefore, the preference for an instrument that would structure such reforms in an economically more efficient and politically more acceptable way was not stimulated to the same degree. Given these restrictions, however, a causality could be observed similar to that seen in the case of the European countries: global competition problems, especially towards the NICs and the growing importance of globally oriented branches, instigated a preference for measures that could help improve the position of US firms in the world economy. NAFTA was also interpreted as an instrument of this type by the government and the private sector. Thus, one can conclude that the preference for NAFTA was stimulated by its perception as an instrument for an economically more efficient adjustment to global competition.

The USA: direct causality The growing global pressures played a central role in the direct causes of the US government's preference for NAFTA: it was possible to demonstrate that NAFTA was perceived as an answer to competitive problems by facilitating and securing access to the production site of Mexico for US firms. Thus, the US preference was also caused by the perception of the need to adapt to the global markets' demands. All in all, NAFTA offered the USA less in the way of economically more efficient and politically more acceptable adjustment to the effects of global markets than regional cooperation did for the other countries examined. The criterion of economic efficiency is still applicable, but much weaker: the connection to the Mexican economy provided only small efficiency gains. The criterion of political acceptance does not seem to apply in the case of the USA: first, no clear reforms were undertaken that could have been made more acceptable with the help of regional cooperation. Second, legitimizing such reforms by integrating with a developing country would have been rather counterproductive. In the case of the USA, factors that contributed to the preference for regional cooperation and that had no connection to global markets could be identified more clearly than in the other case studies. The government's preference formation can be attributed more strongly to foreign and security policy factors than in the other states.

6

COMPARATIVE CONCLUSIONS, EMPIRICAL AND THEORETICAL RESULTS

6.1 Empirical Results: Preferences and the Global Markets Approach

Crises, interests and instruments – impact of global markets

The case studies have shown that global markets had substantial effects – to differing extents and in diverse forms – on rather inward-looking, interventionist economic policies and national economies. Global markets triggered the crisis of neo-Keynesian (Europe) and protectionist (Latin America) policies, strengthened market-oriented interests and limited the efficiency of governmental instruments by modifying states' autonomy of action through a change of the costs and benefits of economic policy options. It became apparent that the pathways 'crises, interests and instruments', differentiated for purposes of analytical clarity, were closely tied to one another in various ways, overlapped and in part even gave rise to one another in the empirical development of the countries studied. The impact of global markets (with the relative exception of the USA) led to a change in the course of economic policy via their influence on these three areas. Inward orientation and interventionism were weakened; liberalizing and competition-oriented policy as well as a focus on the world market were strengthened. Thus, it has been possible to confirm the hypothesis on the effects of global markets put forward in section 1.3.

Hypothesis I: If global markets influence several states by triggering a crisis of inward-looking interventionist policy, by strengthening transnational interest groups, and by weakening the governments' regulatory instruments, then a simultaneous preference for liberal, global competitiveness-enhancing policies will be stimulated.

In this section, the results of the case studies will be aggregated to form a typology of causal connections between the impact of global markets on national economies and the shift in national economic policy.

How were inward-looking, interventionist policies weakened? The case studies have shown that the pathway 'crises' forms a more comprehensive category than the other two areas and that it was strongly influenced by them: the shift in interests and the restriction of instruments contributed to the crisis of inward orientation, but were in turn also results of crises. However, it was also possible to identify effects of global markets, which directly contributed to crises. The most relevant factors were global financial markets and transnational investment flows. They raised the costs of policies that were not oriented towards the global economy and the incentives for liberalizing reforms most noticeably. This cost–benefit relation was transmitted by means of (1) interest rates, (2) exchange rates and (3) portfolio capital.

(1) The interest rates on the global financial markets became more important the more thoroughly a national economy was integrated into them. In the case of the Latin American countries, taking out loans from transnational banks was the means of integration. The European states were connected to the global financial markets by the convertibility of their currencies and private investors' relatively free access to the financial markets. Increases in the global interest rates (because transnational banks had globalized the US high interest rate policy) had substantial effects on national economies: for example, within a short period of time, Latin American debtors had to meet considerably higher interest payments – a task that they were unable to fulfil with the then dominant inward-looking model. In European countries, the increase in the global interest rate – combined with a more effective access to global markets – played a decisive role in so far as it raised the opportunity costs for domestic investment in production. The more attractive conditions on global financial markets contributed to the crisis of the neo-Keynesian politics by strengthening an alternative that competed with domestic productive activity: transnational capital investment. In order to prevent capital outflows, the government, or rather the central banks,

had to raise national interest rates and thus themselves added to the crisis of the neo-Keynesian politics by making investment in the productive sector as well as government borrowing more expensive and by narrowing demand.

(2) Exchange rates were also a relevant means of transmitting the effects of global markets. Transnational private actors' speculative considerations and estimates of a country's attractiveness for production and investment were carried over onto the exchange rate. In this way, global markets could influence the economic situation by increasing the demand for a currency (pressure to appreciate, capital influx, increase in the cost of exports) or by lowering the demand for a currency (pressure to depreciate, capital outflow, increase in the cost of imports). This dimension became relevant for government decisions, particularly in France in 1981–3, but also in Germany and the UK. In the Latin American countries, this mechanism manifested itself primarily on the black market as a consequence of governments' maintaining official – mostly overvalued – exchange rates. This discrepancy between the financial markets' evaluation of a currency and the official exchange rate contributed to crises, particularly in Argentina, but also in the UK (mid-1970s) and France (1981–2).

(3) Finally, portfolio capital developed into a central indicator of global markets' evaluation of a country's attractiveness. In the course of the growing mobility of transnational investment and stock market capital, the importance of this factor had grown. Inward-looking interventionism, state regulations and unattractive conditions for transnational enterprise became associated with costs because such a country either lost investment or could not attract it (at least not to the same extent as it would have done given a course oriented towards the expectations of global portfolio capital). Capital movements that followed this logic could be observed in all seven case studies and thus formed a clear cost–benefit structure for the governments. The higher volume of transnational mobile investment capital raised the opportunity costs of an economic policy that did not offer these resources attractive conditions. This connection's relevance for decisions has been made plausible through governments' perceptions, through statements of transnational investors and by a distinct increase in investment inflows *after* liberal reforms and the corresponding regional cooperation agreements.

How did interests change?   The global markets' influence on domestic interests was primarily a result of the discrediting of the inward-looking interventionist model because of economic crises – that is, this model's inability to contribute to the government's task of securing growth to a degree perceived as sufficient. Moreover, the strategic focus and political importance of the interest groups changed: in all the countries studied, the GDP share of globally operating economic activity grew and with it the weight of those groups (both on the entrepreneurial and labour sides) that were interested in seeing economic policy focus on the requirements of the world market. Their larger share of the national product was also due to the economic crisis, which reduced the sales of inwardly oriented firms, while world market-oriented production could, in principle, make up for decreasing domestic demand through exports. In addition, in the Latin American countries the *tradables* sector not only grew quantitatively, measured as a share of GDP, but also gained further relevance because of the new pressures of the foreign debt crisis – only this sector was able to earn the hard currencies urgently needed to service the debt.

Stronger competition on the world market and on the domestic market from imported goods due to trade liberalization strengthened the producers' interest in globally competitive production conditions in the European states and the USA. If they did not want to accept a loss of revenues on the world or domestic markets, they had to push their governments to implement more cost-effective conditions – that is, to orient policies towards global competition.

How were governmental instruments restricted?   The case studies have shown that restrictions mostly did not imply a 'technical' removal of possibilities. Instead, global markets contributed to a process in which certain options and instruments were connected with growing costs or had their effectiveness reduced. Instruments and the freedom to continue an inward-oriented, interventionist policy were limited by both the withdrawal of resources and the reduction of this policy's effectiveness. The withdrawal of financial means took the form of transnational banks' refusals to continue lending unless a government changed its economic policy to meet the banks' interests (Latin America). Unsatisfactory national investment quotas by the private sector due to more attractive opportunities abroad or on global markets can also be seen as a withdrawal of means that are necessary for securing 'prosperity', or at least growth (Europe). Here, too, it became obvious that, although governments still had the option of implementing 'inward-looking intervention', this would be connected with higher

178 CONCLUSIONS AND RESULTS

economic costs and political risks (in preserving power), which in the last analysis restricted the autonomy of decision making.

A reduced effectiveness of instruments for inward-oriented steering, which also implies a restriction in the state's autonomy to act, could be observed in a number of areas. For example, because of France's foreign trade relations, a large part of its demand stimulation through higher state expenditures (1981–2) flowed into imports and was thus unable to boost national production and create jobs to the extent desired. In the USA, Reaganomics deficit spending offered only a disproportionately low contribution to a lasting increase in production, as the rise of the trade deficit and the economic crisis of 1989–91 showed. The previously explained connection between the global actors' investment decisions and their evaluation of a country's attractiveness also limited the states' autonomy in pursuing inward-oriented policies. As could be observed frequently, governments were unable to achieve the desired effect with measures that did not take into account the expectations of global actors, as the mobile means were increasingly withdrawn. It should not be forgotten that the phrase 'global actors' refers to both foreign *and domestic* producers and investors, who, in contrast to strictly domestic market actors, operate transnationally.

In the case of the USA the hypothesis was confirmed that the effects of global markets, conceptualized and tested in this book, arise when they encounter inward-looking interventionist economic policy. Since the USA had not pursued this policy to the same extent as the European and Latin American countries, global markets caused neither the same severity of economic crisis, a change in interests nor a restriction of instruments. In the USA, the neo-Keynesian component of Reaganomics was made possible by global markets' *strengthening* of the effectiveness of a state instrument. Without the deregulation of financial markets since the 1970s and the expansion of the volume of globally transferable investment funds, the US high interest rate policy would probably not have attracted the amount of capital that was transferred to the USA in the 1980s. Thus, in the case of the USA, the mobility and volume of global financial markets contributed to the state's neo-Keynesian spending policy. On this point, the USA can be seen as a singular case in the world economy, as it can meet conditions that other states cannot meet or at least not to the same extent.

As a result, global markets' effects on national economies and economic policies, delineated here in conclusion, raised both the costs for inward-looking interventionist measures and the incentives for a better consideration of transnationally mobile resources and the competitive requirements of the world market. It was possible to demonstrate this causality plausibly in the three European and the three Latin American states. In the time period examined, all six states reformed their economic policies – in conjunction with the discussed costs and incentives – towards liberalization and stability and adjusted to the expectations of global markets. How did this change of course and the effects of global markets stimulate the governments' preferences for new, liberalizing regional cooperation?

Economic efficiency and political acceptability – reasons for regional cooperation

In all seven case studies, it was possible to show that the governments' preferences for competition-oriented regional cooperation were decisively stimulated by the effects of global markets (with the relative exception of the USA). This causal connection worked in two ways. It could be plausibly demonstrated that the preference for the new co-operation agreements resulted, first, from the change in the national economic policy paradigm (indirect causality), and second, as a direct response to global markets (direct causality). Both causalities produced new requirements, which governments believed could be met in an economically more efficient and politically more acceptable way through regional cooperation than by means of individual state initiatives. Thus, the hypothesis on the attractiveness of regional cooperation as a response to the impact of global markets in section 1.3 has been confirmed.

> *Hypothesis II: Regional cooperation gains attractiveness to the degree that it offers a means for an economically more efficient and politically more acceptable adjustment to global markets and competitiveness, giving governments a better chance of staying in power as a result of an enhanced economic performance.*

In analogy to the preceding section, in the following, the results of the case studies will be aggregated to form a summary of the causal connections between the impact of global markets on national economies and the change in national economic policy as well as the formation of a preference for regional cooperation.

Indirect causality   Global markets' indirect contribution to the formation of preferences functioned via their ability to initiate a change in economic policy paradigms on a national level. It could be plausibly demonstrated for all states (again, with the relative exception of the USA) that the advantages of liberalizing cooperation became compatible only with national preferences after global competition and liberal orientation had dominated national economic policies. Even during the period of interventionist inward orientation, regional cooperation would have offered certain advantages (such as economies of scale). Freeing market forces by reducing governmental intervention would, however, have contradicted the dominant economic policy maxims. Thus, national policy's stronger orientation towards liberalization and the expectations of global markets was vital to the preference for competition-oriented cooperation. Global markets' influence on national economies both at the same time and in the same economic policy direction was in turn a prerequisite for the simultaneous *convergence* of preferences of several states necessary for cooperation.

The second fundamental indirect causality pertained to the changed importance of state sovereignty in terms of the power to set conditions: the restrictions of state instruments' effectiveness and autonomy of action had reduced the governments' ability and willingness to intervene into the domestic economy. The impact of global markets had also stimulated the states' withdrawal from economic steering through liberalization. These de facto limitations made it easier for governments to accept the de jure restrictions on their room to manoeuvre set by international (regional) agreements. Thus, by instigating a change in states' ability to intervene, global markets indirectly made the loss of sovereignty through a regional treaty more bearable. In the 1960s, a *liberalizing* cooperation comparable to that of the EC single market, MERCOSUR or even NAFTA would have implied a considerable renunciation of government power. At that time governments had much more autonomy in their ability to steer the domestic economy in terms of lower costs and a higher effectiveness of neo-Keynesian instruments.

In the case of the European and Latin American countries, it was possible to demonstrate that the governments (and in part the companies and trade unions) viewed regional cooperation as a means for a more *economically efficient* implementation of the previously begun reforms. The heightening of competitive effects through free trade and a common market played an outstanding role in this process.

Via scale, specialization and efficiency, regional deregulation and lib-eralization, they expected to achieve even stronger improvements of the various countries' competitiveness in production, innovation and attracting foreign investment. All six governments prominently justified the regional agreements as a means of better achieving the objectives of the national reforms than would be possible at the indi-vidual state level. In particular, globally oriented investment could be better attracted or retained, while the competitiveness of national pro-ducers could be raised by regional competition and economies of scale.

It was also possible to substantiate the perception that regional co-operation served to secure the national reforms in the long term through multilateral contractual ties. This 'lock-in' function of cooper-ation was seen as superior to individual national initiatives, particu-larly vis-à-vis global investors. The perception of 'locking in' national reforms through regional cooperation was demonstrated using state-ments by government representatives, but also corroboration by busi-ness leaders and critical comments from trade unions.

The indirect causality was also effective by means of the second criterion of the GMA, the greater *political acceptability* or implement-ability of national reforms as a result of regional cooperation. In the case of the European and Latin American states, it was shown that the multilateral obligations served both to discipline the opposition to liberalization and to shift political responsibility for social hardships as a result of reforms to the regional level. For example, measures that were in line with the previous course of national reforms were partially presented as consequences of regional cooperation, for which the gov-ernment was no longer directly responsible. Austerity policies and de-regulation were justified as necessary or obligatory in the regional context. Regional liberalization had also been demanded by transna-tionally active business and partially criticized by trade unions as a means of implementing measures that had been blocked by domestic opposition at the national level before. Indications showed a heightened acceptance of the new economic policy as a result of the regional justification and the actual or expected growth spurts as a result of cooperation. The indirect causality between the effects of global markets and regional cooperation could also be seen in the activities of interest groups. For example, representatives of globally oriented firms made stronger competition and economies of scale in the regional market a condition of a successful implementation of liberalizing policies (Europe).

Direct causality For the European and Latin American countries, and in this case also the USA, the change in the costs and benefits of inward-oriented and individual national policies was central to the global markets' direct contribution to the preference for regional co-operation. This refers to both the change in measurable costs and the change in the perception of such costs. Because of the higher mobility of capital and production and the increased integration of national economies into global markets, the global competition for these factors had risen, while the disadvantages of individual national policies and a relatively strong inward orientation had multiplied. At the same time, the volume of those resources that could be attracted or retained with positive conditions, such as the transnationally mobile share of the total economic resources, had grown. A corresponding perception of the incentives for regional cooperation could be found in all the case studies. In the case of the USA, NAFTA was also justified as a means of strengthening the US economy's global competitiveness. All seven governments explained their preference for competition-oriented regionalism as a function of its ability to react more effectively to the requirements of global markets. In contrast, national solo policies were increasingly seen as inadequate.

For the European countries, the perception of 'lagging behind' in global competition had the effect of creating a sense of identity and contributed directly to the development of simultaneous and similarly oriented preferences by their governments. In all three regions, the governments' perceptions and justifications were confirmed (to differing degrees) in so far as the inflow of investment and the trade and portfolio transfers grew substantially after the decision for cooperation was taken – that is, even before the agreements came into force. Regarding the attitudes of interest groups, there was a consensus on the perceived superiority of regional responses in adjusting to pressure from global markets. It was not possible to identify actors and groups that denied the existence of this adjustment pressure. The differences lay in the opinions on the appropriate economic strategy.

Since inward-looking models had been discredited in the political discourse or seen their implementability weakened (essentially because of the effects of global markets), transnationally inclined interest groups were able to lead public opinion. The acceptance of liberalizing cooperation as an adequate option was also supported by the perception of a fundamental change in international relations and state sovereignty as a result of the increasing integration of national economies into global markets. Statements by decision-makers in all three regions showed that this connection, which functioned indirectly via economic reforms, also functioned as a direct causality.

6.2   Theoretical Development of the Global Markets Approach

The case studies confirmed the two hypotheses (Hypotheses I and II), as the results in section 6.1 clearly show. It could be plausibly demonstrated, using quantitative indicators, that shifts in material flows were caused by global markets. The qualitative analyses of relevant actors' statements substantiated that the perception of global markets' effects and the characteristics of regional cooperation decisively stimulated the preference for new cooperation.

The GMA, developed in section 1.3, refers to a specific factor, a specific *driving force* for interpreting the preference for competition-oriented regional cooperation. Its scope was, therefore, clearly delineated from the beginning and its character defined as a complementary approach to integration theory. What implications do the empirical results of the case studies have for the relevance and the further development of the GMA? This question will be answered in three steps: with comments on (1) the character of global markets, (2) the states' ability to act and (3) the function of regional cooperation. In the following section, these implications will be discussed in relation to integration theory.

The character of global markets

The outstanding characteristics of global markets were defined and substantiated as being, first, their private-sector nature and their particular interest in profit, in contrast to the public ('community') character of states. A second formative feature is the transnationality of the growing, potentially global scope of the activities. Third, a defining and both empirically and theoretically exacting characteristic is the inseparability of the development of global markets from other organizing forms of social interaction – that is, from the 'state' and the 'society', in the last analysis even from the 'community', which forms a latent contradiction to the first feature. Global markets cannot act independently of states and societies. On the contrary, they clearly react to changes in the latter. This is not only theoretically consistent given the three characteristics, but could also repeatedly be demonstrated empirically. However, if the functional logic of global markets and state-communal activities react to one another in a mutual and interdependent way, if no side can ignore the other without incurring costs, then this defines not an antagonistic zero-sum game for power and profit, but rather the fundamental necessity of finding a compromise. This does not contradict the fact that 'states' and 'global markets' (separated here according to the first two characteristics named) mutually influence each other's ability to shape their development and can cause changes in preferences and patterns of behaviour.

States' ability to act

Since the 1970s, the economic environment of state activities has been marked by the growth of global transnational business as a share of the entire economic output. It was possible to confirm this development empirically. The conclusion that is drawn from this phenomenon in parts of the literature, according to which there will be a 'debordering of states' (Brock and Albert 1995), a 'retreat of the state' (Strange 1996) or even 'the end of the nation-state' (Ohmae 1995), could not, however, be empirically established. Moreover, this interpretative direction does not correspond to the hypotheses confirmed in this book and the comments on the character of global markets formulated above. Statehood in the sense of territorial integrity and legal sovereignty is neither negated nor restricted by global markets. On the contrary, the ability of states to restructure their economic policy and substantially to change their international relations was also empirically demonstrated. The 'debordering of the economy' is not followed by a 'debordering of states'. States proved themselves able actively to define the conditions for both the inward-looking and the world market-oriented private-sector actors and for international policy. In doing so, they took into account the cost–benefit effects of global markets. The state's behaviour was formed in correlation with the three characteristics of global markets. The state's preferences were modelled according to the increased integration into global markets, which in turn has been actively pursued by governments since the 1970s.

Policy is shaped not by the dissolution or weakening of 'the state' through global markets, but rather by the intertwining of the two. Governments' autonomy[1] of action was, however, decisively influenced by the effects of global markets. Their expectations and influence are expressed in the specific cost–benefit relations for economic policy options and governments' ability to retain power. A growing integration of national economies into global markets implies growing costs for a government policy in so far as the latter does not orient itself towards the features of global markets – that is, does not consider the criteria of (1) private profit interests, (2) transnationality (mobility) and (3) *other* states' integration into global markets (competition). The price of not taking these factors into account is determined essentially by the degree of integration and the alternative sites to which global markets have access – that is, the policies of other governments.

Autonomy of action is restricted by global markets in two further ways. First, they offer considerable incentives for conformity, which can turn into opportunity costs when nonconformist policies are chosen. Second, it should be taken into account that – independent of national economies' degree of integration into global markets – the growth of global markets raises the opportunity costs, even for a country that is (hypothetically) completely cut off from the world economy. The conceptional features of the global markets, the decisive interest in profit and the potentially global expansion of activities, combined with the fundamental logic of reaction to state measures, basically make it possible for any state to utilize the advantages (capital inflow, production, etc.) of participating in the global economy. If the state does not offer the requisite conditions, it loses these advantages, creating opportunity costs. This cost–benefit relation is relevant for the government in terms of retaining power by securing 'prosperity'.

Interests and the relevance of societal groups are also influenced. The integration into global markets and the option of global markets directly influence domestic coalitions and the relative weight of interests, which in turn have 'internal' effects on the governments. This direct connection to domestic politics results from the transnational character of global markets – that is, the definitional inseparability of state, society and global markets. The consequence is that the government sees itself exposed to the costs/incentives of global markets not only directly but also indirectly via the fact that global markets change the interests of politically relevant groups inside the country. Thus, global markets strengthen the domestic policy level in influencing states' international relations, such as new regional cooperation.

The function of liberalizing regional cooperation

Regional cooperation fulfils the task of responding to transnational processes that are also effective in the territorial 'inside' and therefore shape domestic policy articulation. In this way, international relations in the form of regional cooperation are a continuation of national (economic) policy by other means. And, in this sense, global markets are a decisive driving force of international relations: they change the costs and benefits of individual states' options, and those of multilateral strategies. The preference for world market-oriented regional cooperation arises to the extent that global markets stimulate adjustments that states would find economically less efficient and politically less acceptable to implement individually than in a regional form. Thus, regional cooperation fulfils the function of an instrument of national policy.

Liberalizing regional cooperation is an expression of global markets' increased influence on state activity, since it takes the characteristics of global markets into account better than (national and regional) inward orientation: in the global comparison, it provides better conditions for entrepreneurial profit seeking, raises the country's attractiveness for mobile economic resources and advances the implementation of those domestic policies that focus on world market competition. This implies that regional cooperation is neither a special form of state activity, nor a political category to be seen separated from the state. Rather it is an expression of the still extant sovereignty in the sense of territorial integrity and the state's ability to act both nationally and internationally. At the same time, the change in governments' autonomy of action with respect to global markets' expectations is manifested in the preference for world-market-oriented regional cooperation: because of the growing economic and domestic policy costs of interventionism and the resulting selective retreat of the state from intervening in the economy, there is a decline in the 'sovereignty costs' of the restrictions of international treaties.

The justification of regional cooperation as a result of the effect of global markets on state preferences renders it possible to analyse the character of regional cooperation more precisely. According to this interpretation, cooperation arises not with the goal of creating a new state (supranationality), but rather to gain new instruments with which specific state tasks can be managed better than is possible for an individual state. If the members of a regional agreement were to come to the conclusion that they could better handle these tasks individually, then a stagnation or a reduction of the cooperation would be expected. This does not per se contradict the functionalistic-institutionalist hypothesis that common institutions have a certain independence and can form the expectations of the member states.

Such institutions are, however, dependent upon carrying out functions the members consider vital.

6.3   Implications for Theories of Regional
Integration and International Relations

The analysis of theories of regional integration regarding their ability
to explain the timing and the liberalizing strategy of the new regionalism indicated distinct deficits (see section 1.2). The GMA was developed to fit into this interpretative gap. However, it was formulated
not as an alternative, but rather as a necessary complementary approach to the explanation of the simultaneous formation of governments' preferences for (liberalizing) cooperation. To what extent do
the insights gained from testing the approach complement existing
theories or modify their validity?

Neofunctionalist institutionalism

The most relevant deficit of neofunctionalist institutionalism is this
approach's low ability to suggest a specific driving force that would
be able to explain the governments' simultaneous preferences. The
hypotheses of 'functional efficiency', 'spillovers' and 'institutional self-
dynamics' as formative and stimulating factors for regional cooperation do not offer any explanation for the timing and the strategic
orientation of preferences. The GMA fills this gap. Because of the
effect of global markets on national economies and economic policies,
regional cooperation was seen as a *functionally efficient* instrument by
policy-makers. The transfer of simultaneous changes in economic
policy from the national level to international cooperation can be interpreted as *spillover* – just as can the transmission of private economic
ties (global markets) to political cooperation between states. Where
global markets stimulated the national willingness to cooperate, *institutional self-dynamics* were able to advance the efforts for further regional institution building.

Thus, the theoretical and empirical results of this book do not necessarily contradict neofunctionalist institutionalism. However, the
results make it clear that neofunctionalist institutionalism alone
cannot explain regional integration. Theoretically speaking, neofunctionalist institutionalism can offer only an analytical frame; empirically speaking, only the conditions for the process. It does not supply

the conceptionalization of specific driving forces for concrete political developments. One of the conclusions of this book is that the formation of governments' preferences for cooperation in the 1980s and 1990s came about without decisive participation of common regional institutions.[2] Therefore, it seems appropriate to relativize the importance of institutional self-dynamics for international cooperation.

Neorealist liberal intergovernmentalism

In analogy to the deficits of neofunctionalist institutionalism, neorealist intergovernmentalism is also unable to explain – even given its 'liberal' attachment – why the preference for regional cooperation developed at a certain time and with a specific strategy. This theory also proposes a theoretical frame for analysis, without suggesting specific impelling motivations. The neorealist-intergovernmental *driving forces* of 'power', 'security' and 'prosperity' are as little capable as the 'liberal' (domestic politics) hypothesis of theoretically explaining and empirically determining the causes of the *specific* preference formation. By itself, this theory is also unable to explain regional cooperation. The GMA offers a necessary complement in this case as well. Only by taking into account the effects of global markets can it be made plausible that the striving for national prosperity and domestic political interest coalitions can generate a preference for regional cooperation.

Global markets approach

The most important implication of the results of this book for both theories is the necessity of changing the perspective of theory. If, as has been shown, state preferences are influenced essentially by the logic of global private actors and markets, then political science's explanatory approaches must take this non-state, not-national level of social interaction more strongly into account. As expounded above, the interaction between the state and global markets is marked not primarily by structural antagonism, but rather by mutual influence and ties. An antagonism exists only regarding the conditions for action: the private sector's profit orientation and transnational scope, on the one hand (global markets), and the responsibility for society and national scope, on the other (state). Theories of international relations therefore must add to their previous dimensions of the national (governments), the domestic ('liberal', 'second image'), the transnational (cross-border private actors),[3] the international (inter-state) and the institutional (supranational) a further one: the variable 'global markets' is connected to all the dimensions named, influences them, is influenced by them, but also maintains autonomy in terms of a distinct way of functioning with regard to the other dimensions. This gives 'global markets' the characteristics of an impelling political factor with an inherent logic and level of activity. 'global markets' are thus a *sui generis* driving force of international relations.

In summary, for theories of international relations, there is a de-clining relevance of questions on the distribution and perception of sovereignty (in terms of power to shape policy) between states or between states and supranational institutions – with the latter em-bodying only a different form, a different level of state activity. In-stead, questions on the interaction between states and global markets as a driving force of international relations are becoming increasingly important. How does this interaction change preferences and policy options? The mutual effects of these two powerful forces, and each one's influence on the economy and on politics, mark the character of international relations in the twenty-first century. In view of the effects of global markets as conceptionally and empirically covered here, the research on intergovernmental institutions, the distribution of power between states as well as between states and supranational institutions, takes into account an important, but ever smaller spec-trum of international relations. Further political science research into the interaction between global markets and states is necessary.

NOTES

CHAPTER I EMPIRICAL PUZZLE AND THEORETICAL APPROACH

1 Activities comprised by this definition are understood here as 'regional cooperation' and 'integration'.
2 Paraguay and Uruguay are the other founding members of MERCOSUR.
3 NAFTA includes regulations not only on commerce, but also on other areas, such as competition policy, standards, services, etc. Canada and the USA formed a free trade association in 1989 (CUSFTA).
4 For the following analysis, see the discussions of regional integration theories by Anderson 1995; Bellers and Häckel 1990; Cornett and Caporaso 1992; Risse-Kappen 1996; Rosamond 1995; Zimmerling 1991: 61–138.
5 Beck (1997: 18) writes: 'The nation-state is a territorial state, that is, its power is tied to a specific place . . . The world society, which emerged in the wake of globalization in many (not only economic) dimensions, undermines and weakens the nation-state, because a multitude of social circles, communication networks, market relations, and forms of life cross-network the territorial boundaries of the nation-state.' Rosenau and Durfee (1995: 42–56) define transnational actors as 'Sovereignty-Free Actors', whose activities are by definition difficult to regulate by the nation-state as a 'Sovereignty-Bound Actor'.
6 'Autonomy to act' is defined here as the liberty to undertake economic policy decisions independently of external influences: free from costs and benefits. I do not assume that 'autonomy' defined in this way was ever fully attained. The issue is the way and extent to which autonomy is restricted by costs.
7 A process is presumed in which the above-mentioned integration theories consider factors that are situated between the impact on global markets and new regional cooperation and that are able to influence the way global markets affect politics.
8 Obviously, the contrast between the interests and instruments of the nation-state and those of global actors and markets is an analytical one.

'The' national interest does not exist; rather, it is the result of multiple influences – including transnational ones. On the other hand, the reach and logic of the nation-state's regulatory capacity diverge more clearly (territory, international law, etc.) from the range and form of action of transnational / global actors and processes.

9   Transnational actors were defined above as actors not shaped by specific national interests, norms and boundaries. Therefore, this approach diverges e.g. from the definition by Cameron (1995: 41), who treats the German Bundesbank as a transnational actor. As the Bundesbank fulfils a national task, it is a typical state actor according to the definition of the GMA – even though it enjoys a certain independence from the government as the central, but not singular state actor.

10 See chapter 2; also Hirst and Thompson 1996: 1–13; Milner / Keohane 1996: introduction; Schmidt 1995; Zürn 1995: 149–54.

11 The dirigiste version of regional cooperation can also produce economy of scale effects, but not the specialization and efficiency gains that the competition encouraged by a liberalizing cooperation can bring. Therefore, dirigistic cooperation (as practised in Latin America until the 1980s) cannot be seen as the same type of adjustment to the challenges of global markets and does not attract globally mobile resources to the same extent. A liberalizing cooperation is also called 'open regionalism' as restrictions for the exchange of goods, capital and services are reduced not only within the region, but also vis-à-vis third countries – although in most cases not to the same extent as inside the region. 'Dirigiste' and 'liberalizing' cooperation refer to differing strategic tendencies. Policies such as the Common Agricultural Policy (CAP) in the liberal single market are exceptions to the rule. On 'open regionalism', see Fuentes 1994: 81–9.

12 See Proff and Proff 1996: 84–94; Schirm 1997c: 242–7. The basic works were written, e.g., by M. E. Porter 1991 and Viner 1950 / 1961.

13 By comparison with global cooperation among states (GATT / WTO, UNO), regional cooperation offers specific advantages: balancing divergent interests and a coordination of policies is easier among relatively few partners than among 150 states. Common decisions and actions also depend on the number of participating states. Given the protracted Uruguay Round of GATT, a worldwide extension of the far more complex regulations of the European single market or NAFTA would hardly be viable. In addition, regional cooperation is exclusionary: the members of a regional agreement obtain competitive advantages over third states through improved competitiveness and the relative discrimination of non-members. Furthermore, regional cooperation can build upon existing cultural, economic or security ties between neighbours – ties not provided by the global option.

14 Approaches to this question were developed by Jachtenfuchs and Kohler-Koch 1996a (multiple level system); Kratochwil 1993: 443–74 (reflexivism,

communicative rationality); Moravcsik 1991, 1993 (liberal intergovernmentalism); H. Müller 1994 (communicative action); Stein 1990 (game
theory); Wendt 1994 (collective identity).
15 For a discussion of the developmental implications of regional cooperation, see Schirm 1997c: 242–8.

CHAPTER 2   GLOBAL MARKETS: DEVELOPMENT AND
IMPACT ON STATES

1 On the background of the Bretton Woods System, see Gilpin 1987: 131–
4, 140ff, 364–94; Helleiner 1994: 25–50.
2 On this point, see also Walter 1996: 16ff. Walter's 'causes of globalization' are: (1) market-oriented liberalizations, (2) reduction of transport
costs and (3) innovations in information technology.
3 Helleiner also notes (1994: 121) that at any time it would have been
possible to reintroduce restrictions if all states had instituted cooperative
controls at the same time.
4 Epstein (1996: 219) writes: 'The essential problem posed by international
capital mobility is that short-term capital mobility undermines a country's ability to undertake policies that threaten investor confidence in its
economy. Countries which undertake macroeconomic policies, such as
expansionary monetary or fiscal policy, or dramatic changes in tax or
welfare policy, might find that investors react strongly by moving
finance out of the country to invest in short-term assets abroad. When
this occurs, this short-term capital flight can cause a precipitous decline
in the exchange rate as well as a sharp rise in short-term interest rates as
the central bank raises interest rates to try to prevent the depreciation of
the currency.'
5 See 'The Disappearing Taxpayer', the cover story of *The Economist*, 31
May 1997: 17–19.
6 Scharpf (1987: 306) concludes: 'The internationalization of capital
markets and the rise in the international interest rate level led to a shift
in the "Terms of Trade" between capital, labour and the state in favour
of capital.'
7 It is not always possible to differentiate neatly between FDI and portfolio capital, because the latter *can* be invested in productive capacity via
the stock market.
8 Shifting production to low-wage countries did not, as is often assumed,
play a large role in reducing the number of industrial jobs in the industrialized nations. The loss of jobs in industry is primarily due to the
progress in rationalization and increased productivity made necessary by
the level of competition (*The Economist*, 26 Apr. 1997: 88; *Neue Züricher Zeitung*, 3 May 1997). In other words, these jobs would possibly

have been 'lost' even if TNCs had not shifted production out of the country.

9   For example, income disparities grew in the Latin American NICs, whereas in the Asian 'Tigers' (such as Taiwan and South Korea) the middle class grew in both absolute and relative numbers in the 1970s and 1980s.

10 One motivation for corporate alliances was very probably the reduction of competition.

11 TNC interests are generally directed against protectionism for three reasons: (1) trade barriers can elicit countermeasures by other states, which would make the import of primary products and the export of finished goods more expensive; (2) import barriers in the home country make intra-firm trade more expensive and thus worsen the TNCs' global competitive position; (3) protectionism improves the competitiveness of the TNCs' national rivals (see also Busch and Milner 1994: 269). If protectionism profits TNCs directly, as it did in the import substituting countries of Latin America, then lobbying against trade liberalization is possible.

12 Statistics from Fundaçao Comercio Exterior (FUNCEX), cited in Pereira 1993: 15.

13 If no transnationally / globally oriented sector existed, opportunity costs would arise from the non-participation in global markets.

CHAPTER 3   GLOBAL MARKETS AND THE EUROPEAN
SINGLE MARKET

1   Sandholtz and Zysman (1989: 95) judge the SMP as follows: 'This initiative is a disjunction, a dramatic new start, rather than the fulfillment of the original effort to construct Europe.'

2   The exceptions to 'mutual recognition' have been reduced to a minimum and may not be used for discrimination – i.e. to protect domestic producers from foreign suppliers. For example, the FRG had to admit EC beer that was not brewed according to the 'purity rule', but was allowed to uphold the purity rule for German breweries.

3   For the goals and regulations of the single market, see CEC 1988; Jacquemin and Sapir 1989; Pinder 1988: 35–54.

4   The West European states' involvement in foreign trade on concluding the SEA in 1986 had the following values: exports (imports) as a % of GDP 1986: Germany 27.3 (21.5), France 17.7 (18.3), UK 19.6 (23.2), Italy (estimate) 19.2 (19.7), Spain 12.0 (15.5), Netherlands 49.3 (45.5), Belgium / Luxembourg 59.3 (59.1), Denmark 26.4 (28.4), Greece (estimate) 13.9 (28.8), Portugal 24.9 (32.7), Ireland 50.4 (46.3); for comparison: USA 5.2 (9.3), Japan 10.8 (6.5). Statistics from Dresdner Bank 1987: 4.

5   *rigueur* = French for rigour, stringency.

6   This was also meant to make imports more expensive and to improve the competitiveness of its exports through exchange rate manipulation.

7   Before his decision to change course in 1982–3, Mitterrand met business leaders (among them those he had appointed presidents of nationalized companies). Their strong opposition to a continuation of the 'socialist experiment' (with the necessary partial withdrawal from the world market) is supposed to have played a large role in the decision to adopt an economic austerity policy (see Gourevitch 1987: 189).

8   In 1982 the exports' share of GDP came to 33.5% (imports: 31.1%) (OECD 1984: 9).

9   Until 1979–80, the DM gained value against the dollar. Only as a result of the USA's high interest rate policy after 1979–80 did the exchange rate of the DM to the dollar deteriorate. However, the DM retained its tendency to appreciate against other currencies (such as the French franc). In principle, devaluation and revaluation simultaneously have positive and negative effects on different groups of economic actors (exporters, consumers, importers, etc.). A relative stability or calculability is decisive for planning state economic policy and business initiatives, and this aspect was progressively undermined in the course of the development of global financial markets.

10 Schmidt is said to have stated that he would prefer 5% inflation to 5% unemployment (see Piper 1998). This statement by Schmidt was based on the assumption that there was a 'trade-off' between inflation and unemployment.

11 Balance of goods and services as % of GDP: −0.8 (1979), −1.8 (1980) and −0.8 (1981). Statistics from Scharpf 1987: 187.

12 Economic growth as % of GDP: 4.2 (1979); 1.8 (1980); 0.0 (1981); −1.0 (1982). Statistics from Scharpf 1987: 192.

13 Scharpf (1987: 195) concludes: 'Whereas before capital interests and labour interests could only succeed together, despite constant conflicts over distribution, now the growth policy had become less important to the FDP clientele than the distribution and tax policies – which determined the amount of the earned capital income one could keep.' For the FDP's position, see also Deubner 1986: 52.

14 'While he has restored conservative stability, Mr Kohl has not given West Germany the liberal economic shake-up that was promised' (*The Economist*, 6 Dec. 1986: 13).

15 One indicator for the substitution of exports from Germany by production in target markets is the turnover of German TNCs' subsidiaries abroad: they rose more steeply than the turnover of all German companies on foreign markets, which in turn increased three times as quickly as the turnover in the home market (Klodt et al. 1989: 60).

16 According to estimates at the time by economic research institutes (*The Economist*, 25 Oct. 1986: 75ff). The more pessimistic prognoses were

especially attributed to the expected slowing of exports. The causes were believed to be the weaker dollar and the problems of German products' competitiveness on the world market: 'Beyond the election in January lies the prospect of an export slowdown. West Germany needs to become less of a manufacturing machine. Deregulation would help' ('Survey on Germany', *The Economist*, 6 Dec. 1986: 20).

17 In the late 1980s, the BDI had a membership of more than 1.2 million companies, which gave it – alone by size – a larger influence on the German government than its British counterpart the Confederation of British Industry (CBI), with its 200,000 members, had on the UK government, according to Woolcock (1991: 67).

18 At the same time, Geißler promised the farmers new subsidies (see 'Bonn läuft Gefahr, sich zu isolieren', *Handelsblatt*, 7 July 1987: 3).

19 Prior to his position as EC Commissioner, Narjes was a politician in the CDU, the governing party in Germany.

20 For the following explanation of the economic policies of the years 1974–9, see Ball 1985; OECD 1988: 65–73; Overbeek 1990: 173; Scharpf 1987: 97–117.

21 Hall (1993: 288) argues: 'Little noticed but especially important in the 1975–9 period was the pressure that the financial markets, notably for government debt and foreign exchange, placed on the government. Many of the ad hoc adjustments towards monetarism made by the 1974–9 Labour government were forced on it by the behavior of the financial markets, and the popularity of monetarist doctrine in these markets influenced both the Bank of England and the government.'

22 Statistics from Julius 1990: 44. Julius writes (p. 49), 'By contrast with the situation in Germany and France, British policy towards FDI has been a welcoming one since the Thatcher government came to power in 1979.'

23 For the often emphasized ideological dimension as the element directing the Thatcher government's actions, Marsh (1995: 612) writes, 'Given electoral imperatives and unforeseen events, it is hardly surprising that while "New Right" ideology played a role, it was certainly not the driving force behind policy which the analysis of Wolfe and others suggest. In essence, New Right ideology was a tool rather than a blueprint.'

24 According to Woolcock (1991: 66) the 'average labour costs' (whatever that may be) in 1984 were 1,417 ECU in the UK whereas in Germany they were 2,008 ECU.

25 Accession to the EMS is necessary to achieve 'faster growth through greater world-competitiveness', ('Council Presidency: UK Industrialists call for more Action to free the Internal Market – UK Pound to Join EMS Exchange Mechanism', *Agence Europe*, NS 4345, 23 June 1986: 15).

26 In the last analysis, Thatcher was able to achieve her goals in the single market: 'Mrs Thatcher running off with the bits she wanted – deregulation

of transport, freeing of capital movements – while preventing the others from getting some of the things they want: more monetary integration (France), European labour laws and the abolition of frontiers (most of Britain's partners)' (*The Economist*, 24 Sept. 1988: 25).

27 Fligstein (1993) and Garrett and Weingast (1993) studied the influence of common ideas and institutions on the creation of the SMP – without, however, defining the role of global markets.

28 Among the numerous media, *The Economist* is undoubtedly the most relevant: this weekly magazine is most read Europe-wide by political and private economic decision-makers and is considered competent and serious. The magazine declares its liberal tenets openly and discusses them critically.

29 With regard to the primary sources, this section relies on the work of European institutions (EC Council, Commission, Parliament).

30 See Albert and Ball 1983; *The Economist*, 16 July 1983: 63ff; *The Economist*, 14 Jan. 1984: 61; *The Economist*, 24 Nov. 1984: 99–110.

31 Whereas Europe – in part as a result of the completion of the single market – experienced a recovery at the end of the 1980s, by the mid–1990s the divergence from the USA was again visible in the area of job creation (and the related political debate).

32 Philips's activities culminated in the presentation of a plan for the completion of a free European market by the year 1990 (see 'Common Market: Five-Year Plan Proposed by Philips' President to European Institutions', *Agence Europe*, NS 4005, 12 Jan. 1985: 11.

33 See European Parliament Liberal and Democratic Group Seminar (1984) – contributions of Simone Veil (p. 5), Perrin-Pelletier (29ff) and Vever (35ff).

34 From 'Economy: The European Market Economy Organisations Demand a Common Market without Intervention, Subsidies, the CAP or the EMS', *Agence Europe*, NS 4009, 18 Jan. 1985: 17ff. Members of the association were also representatives of: Arbeitsgemeinschaft Soziale Marktwirtschaft (ASM) (D); Institute of Economic Affairs (UK); Institut Economique de Paris (F); Centro Ricerche Economiche Applicate (I); L'Institut Ludwig von Mises (B); Kritische Nederlandse Ondernemers (KNO) (NL). The chairman of the ASM stated, 'the current European crisis is not that of the market economy but rather that of the policy of intervention' (ibid.).

35 Even before the Delors Commission, there were repeated attempts to complete the single market. See e.g. CEC (1982: 1): 'A sufficiently broad base in technological development, in financing and in marketing is vital in order to compete against international rivals.'

36 Scharpf (1987: 305–6) summarizes this connection pointedly: 'As long as the national economic policy of the European states was neither able to determine the international interest rate level nor effectively limit the

capital mobility, in the early 80s it only had a choice of either accepting the loss of jobs in the private sector of the economy or of raising the average return of real investment so high that it would be able to compete with speculative financial portfolios. Thus, the supply-side oriented recommendations had capitalist logic on their side.'

CHAPTER 4   GLOBAL MARKETS AND MERCOSUR

1 In the contract languages the official name is Mercado Común del Sur (MERCOSUR – Spanish) and Mercado Comum do Sul (MERCOSUL – Portuguese). In this book, I will use the internationally common Spanish version. Members are: Argentina, Brazil, Paraguay and Uruguay. Bolivia and Chile have been associated since 1996.

2 Rent-seekers are, e.g., companies/jobs that owe their profit/existence less to their competitiveness than to state protection (monopolies, subsidies, trade barriers).

3 In the second half of the 1980s, the agreement on nuclear cooperation and reciprocal inspection of research facilities institutionalized a détente in the area of security policy (Schirm 1997a: 156ff).

4 See Republica Argentina, Republica Federativa do Brasil, Republica do Paraguai and Republica Oriental do Uruguai 1994a.

5 The following will refer to: COMISEC 1995; Ernst and Young 1994; Figueiras 1994: 15–82; Republica Argentina, Republica Federativa do Brasil, Republica do Paraguai and Republica Oriental do Uruguai 1994b; *Latin American Weekly Report*, 29 Dec. 1994: 589.

6 If the import of a certain product from MERCOSUR partner states has a strongly negative effect on the producers in the importing country, then the latter has the right to limit the import of the respective good – for example, by means of import quotas.

7 By 1 January 1995, the CET applied to 85% of all products. The remaining goods form a list of exceptions with tariffs between 20 and 35%, whose intended reduction by the year 2001 did not succeed completely. These exceptions were primarily in the areas of capital goods, computers and telecommunications (Machado 1995: 19).

8 However, a number of investment areas were exempt indefinitely from equal treatment with domestic actors (Bouzas 1995: 20; Campbell 1994; Figueiras 1994: 79–81).

9 Statistics from the Argentinian central bank, the OECD and the IDB, cited from Schubert 1985: 230. Statistics for 1983 from de la Balze 1995: 52. In the mid-1980s, foreign assets of Argentinians through capital flight were estimated at $30–5 billion – the equivalent of two-thirds of the country's foreign debt (Simon 1988: 155).

10   The inflation rate was to be reduced to 300% and the budget deficit to 7.5% of GDP. If one compares these figures to the convergence criteria of the Maastricht Treaty on the EMU, it becomes clear how far Argentina was from what the industrial nations consider good economic policy. In return for Argentina's willingness to accept the IMF's conditions, 300 creditor banks extended the repayment schedules of $25 billion worth of debts due in 1985 for fifteen years (*Neue Züricher Zeitung* 28 Sept. 1984).

11   For Menem's economic policy, see Bouzas 1991; Cristini and Balzarotti 1993: 35–7; de la Balze 1995: 65–122; Hufy 1996; Messner 1996; Nicolas and Symma 1992; Starr 1997: 83–99.

12   The securing of purchasing power by buying dollars on the black market was widespread. This encouraged the dollarization of the Argentinian economy and contributed to the functionality and acceptance of the law on convertibility.

13   Kaufman (1990: 81–3) writes: 'the weight of orthodox banking sectors within the business community had increased substantially during the era of financial liberalism in the late 1970s. Finally, many large industrial firms had also entered short-term money activities, which weakened their historic opposition to orthodox monetary and trade policies.'

14   Guadagni was later Argentina's Minister for Industry and Trade. Statements in the same vein as Guadagni's were also made at a symposium of Argentinian banks (Serna 1992: 120). See also *Financial Times*, 7 Jan. 1991: 2.

15   'Argentina sees integration as a lifeboat that will save its drowning industry, providing access to the large Brazilian economy' (*Financial Times*, 21 Sept. 1990: 3).

16   See also 'Der Mercosur lockt Investoren an', *Handelsblatt*, 17 Oct. 1994: 9. 'General Motors and Ferrero to Invest', *BBC Summary of World Broadcasts*, 25 Apr. 1995; 'Ford hat große Pläne Südamerika', *Süddeutsche Zeitung*, 28 July 1995; 'Business Gears Up', *The Economist* – A Survey on Mercosur, 12 Oct. 1996: 8–10.

17   While the interest payments in 1973–8 came to a total of $11.9 billion, they swelled to a total of $35.6 billion in 1979–82 and reached an average of 5.5% of the GDP in 1982–5 (Schirm 1990: 87).

18   Whereas the GDP declined from 1981 to 1983 by an average of 2.4% p.a., it rose in the following four years substantially by 5.3%, 7.9%, 7.6% and 3.6%, before it dropped again in 1988 (−0.1%), rose briefly in 1989 (+3.3%), and declined drastically again in 1990 (−4%); see Malan and Bonelli 1992: 57 (for 1981–3) and BID 1992: 55 (for 1984–90).

19   Reed is supposed to have made this threat as early as December 1986 in view of the approaching moratorium (Bandeira 1989: 295).

20   For the Brazilian government's various heterogeneous 'shock therapies' (as opposed to 'orthodox' neoliberalism), see and Dinsmoor (1990: 73–114) Singer (1987).

21 See 'Drunk not Sick – A Survey of Brazil', *The Economist*, 7 Dec. 1991: 10. In the Brady Plan, the USA offered to act as a mediator for selected – reformist – debtors in their rescheduling negotiations with private creditor banks. In order to benefit from the Brady Plan, debtors had to implement liberal reforms similar to those of the IMF. Thus, in this case, the USA functions as an intermediate authority for improving the debtor's solvency. Unlike IMF policy, the Brady Plan also intends to reduce the burden of debt, that is, aims at the creditor banks' willingness to compromise. See the case study on Mexico in section 5.2.

22 'Era of Free Trade to Begin in Brazil', *New York Times*, 5 July 1990; *Euromoney*, suppl. Aug. 1991: 1–18; Sangmeister 1994: 322–7.

23 For example, private banks, the IMF and the World Bank partially withheld already negotiated loans: 'Brazil's failure to implement appropriate macroeconomic policies has cost it dearly in terms of forgone official and private financial support. Creditor banks withheld the last $600 million tranche of their $5.2 billion new money facility. . . . The World Bank has suspended its policy-based sector lending to Brazil in the absence of appropriate macroeconomic policies' (US Government Printing Office 1990a: 120).

24 In 1990, Washington obstructed loans from the World Bank and the IDB totalling $2.2 billion in order to persuade Brazil to meet its interest payments to private banks (see 'US Wants Brazil Loans Delayed because of Worry over Arrears', *Financial Times*, 16 Nov. 1990). In early 1991, project funds from the IDB were delayed specifically because of US pressure (*The Economist*, 13 Apr. 1991: 90).

25 See 'O Eximbank suspende empréstimos', *Gazeta Mercantil*, 19 June 1990.

26 Brazil's exports rose by 70% between 1980 and 1992 from $20 billion to $36 billion, while imports only grew from $20 billion to $23.8 billion (BID 1992: 309).

27 On 'indirect power' in the US–Brazilian relations, see Schirm 1994a: 121–99.

28 See 'Bush Praises Visiting Collor, Promises Backing for Debt Renegotiation', *Latin America Regional Report*, 11 July 1991.

29 See 'Brasilien mit Banken über Umschuldung einig', *Süddeutsche Zeitung*, 11 July 1992. Only after long negotiations was Brazil able in 1994 to arrange a settlement with the private banks in the framework of the Brady Plan.

30 Collor had not overcome his outsider position within the political and economic establishment even as president. On the contrary, he had kept many groups, which under previous regimes had enjoyed substantial benefits, from gaining access to state funds. An interest-group-sponsored media campaign (*Veja*, *TV-Globo*) and his own moral claims, functionalized in the campaign, as a 'hunter of the corrupt' (caçador dos marajás)

led to Collor's downfall. Regarding the accusation of corruption, the Brazilian population accepts corruption in proportion to the respective politician's ability to implement his announced course (*roba mas faz*).

31   In particular, the import substituting industries had sharply criticized the lowering of tariffs (*Neue Züricher Zeitung*, 30 June 1990: 14).

32   The Brazilian ambassador to the USA in 1994, Flecha de Lima (1994: 4), explained: 'Brazil is convinced that the regional agreements should not be seen as a substitute for, but a way to, a growing globalization of the world economy.'

33   For MERCOSUR as a motive for new investment by TNCs, see *Handelsblatt*, 17 Oct. 1994: 9; World Bank, *FDI News*, 1/1, Dec. 1995 (from www.worldbank.org./:); 'A Survey on Mercosur', *The Economist*, 12 Oct. 1996: 8–10; Thoele 1996: 8ff; and 'Masivo desembarco de tecnología española en Mercosur', *El Pais*, 28 Oct. 1996: 24ff.

34   For the following exposition, see Biersteker 1992: 116–18; Kahler 1995: 48–65; Pauly 1994; for IMF programme ethos, see Biersteker 1990.

35   The IMF was created in the framework of the Bretton Woods System of 1944 and is overseen by a Board of Governors, in which the member states' share of votes is weighted according to their financial assets at the IMF. Thus, the IMF is essentially run by the G7 industrial nations; in 2001 the USA had the highest number of votes, followed by Japan and Germany.

CHAPTER 5   GLOBAL MARKETS AND NAFTA

1   The Spanish name is Tratado de Libre Comercio (TLC).

2   See the following documents: CEC 1994; Governments of Canada, the United Mexican States and the United States of America 1992; SECOFI 1992a; Schirm 1997a: 50–6; 1997d.

3   The only facilitating measures are those for business travellers temporarily residing in another NAFTA country.

4   In 1990, Mexico's exports to the USA were still only $32.4 billion. Statistics for 1990 and 1994 from WTO 1995: 46; statistics for 1995 from IMF 1996a: 47ff, 139, 211ff.

5   Because of the peso crisis in late 1994, the influx of FDI in 1995 declined to $6.9 billion; figures from UNCTAD 1997a: 305.

6   Some US banks had lent Mexico so much compared to their own capital assets that a complete loss of these outstanding debts could have caused them to go bankrupt. By the mid- or late 1980s, however, the banks had built up enough reserves not to have to worry about this threat any more (Weintraub 1990: 141).

7   Besides these plans, initially conceived for all debtor nations, the US government carried out other aid operations for Mexico. One of these

was the emission of US treasury bonds in 1988 with which Mexico could transfer a portion of its debt into titles with low interest rates and longer maturities. The new aspect of the Brady Plan was that not only was the debtor's ability to repay strengthened (Baker), but also the amount of outstanding debt would be reduced – i.e. the burden would be shared by the creditor banks. Since the creditor banks (like other enterprises) can write off their losses, the taxpayers in the industrialized world bear the costs to the extent of the banks' tax rate.

8   For a comprehensive source on the US–Mexican debt negotiations, see US Government Printing Office 1990a.

9   For the fundamentals of the Mexican economic policy, see Aspe Armella 1990: 6–10; Banco de México 1992; *The Economist*, 16 Nov. 1991: 59; Presidencia de México 1991; SHCP 1992.

10   Salinas de Gortari (1991: 5) stated: 'That which strengthens a nation is nationalistic, not, however, those longings for phrases and characteristics of bygone days, which in the context of the present world are far from strengthening it [the nation] and instead only make it weaker, more vulnerable and less able to survive.'

11   Velazques (1992). See also 'Mas empleos y mejor pagados. Con el TLC creceremos mas rápido y concentraremos nuestra atenci'n en quienes menos tienen: CSG', CTM. *Organo de Orientacion e Informacion de los Trabajadores*, 2062, 14 Aug. 1992: 1.

12   Regarding Mexico's motivations, see Driscoll de Alvarado and Gambrill 1992; IRELA 1991: 1; Poitras and Robinson 1994: 6ff; SECOFI 1992a, b.

13   Companies' resistance to NAFTA was relatively small, not only because of the semi-authoritarian rule of the PRI, but also because within the framework of the neoliberal economic policy the tariffs had already been considerably reduced (in advance of NAFTA and in order to qualify for it) from an average of 100 per cent (1985) to 20 per cent (1992) (Inter-American Dialogue 1993: 6).

14   The economic policy orientation of this US–Latin American association was clarified in a speech by its president Rockefeller (1992:1): 'The people of this hemisphere changed something more important than their government – they changed their minds. They brought into power – into intellectual dominance – a new leadership of ideas. And those ideas all begin with the word "free": free markets, free investment, free trade.' A 'free society' seems not to belong to Rockefeller's ideals associated with the prefix 'free'.

15   See *Business Week*, 27 May 1991: 32–5; *Capital – Das Wirtschaftsmagazin*, Mar. 1992: 209; *El Financiero*, 26 Oct. 1992: 12; *The Economist*, 5 July 1997: 17–19.

16   Because of higher interest rates and an overvalued peso, the economic growth and export increases did not reach the levels that would otherwise have been possible. Mexico's GDP grew by 2.8 per cent (1991–2),

0.4 per cent (1992–3), 3.8 per cent (1993–4); the increase in exports came to 8 per cent (1991–2), 12.5 per cent (1992–3) and 16.7 per cent (1993–4) (statistics from UNCTAD 1997b: 16, 288).

17 The economic crisis manifested itself in 1980 with an inflation rate of almost 10 per cent, an unemployment rate of 7.1 per cent and a decline in GDP of −0.5 per cent (Bierling 1995: 120).

18 The US 'prime rate' rose from 6.8 per cent (1977) to 18.8 per cent (1981), the interest rates for government bonds, medium term, from 6.69 per cent (1977) to 14.4 per cent (1981) (IMF 1996b: 378ff, 788ff).

19 Omnibus Trade and Competitiveness Act of 1988 – Public Law 100–418.

20 The share of US imports affected by tariffs rose from 8 per cent (1975) to 21 per cent (1985) (statistics taken from Nye 1988: 123). These figures mean that either more product categories were affected by tariffs or that the volume of imports also grew in categories of goods that were affected by tariffs.

21 *The Economist* (4 Jan. 1992: 11) writes of the chances of the Bush Administration retaining power: 'George Bush and his administration are frightened because the pre-election boom that would keep them in office has failed to appear.'

22 However, it should be considered that low wage costs are only one factor among many for competitiveness, and that according to Pollan and Stankovsky (1993: 519) no systematic relation between wage costs and competitiveness could be established for the USA. But: 'wage costs can play an important role in choosing the site.'

23 In the words of then Under-Secretary for Economic Affairs of the State Department, Robert Zoellick (1992: 1): 'That is why NAFTA is so important. It is a rare strategic opportunity to secure, strengthen, and develop our continental base, economically and politically, in a way that will promote America's foreign policy agenda, our economic strength and leadership, and US global influence.' Zoellick was 'one of the few genuine strategic thinkers in the Bush administration', writes Kondrake (1991: 38).

24 See the speeches of various representatives of enterprises in American Foreign Service Association 1991: 10–14.

25 During the 1982 crisis, US exports to Mexico fell to $4.9 billion (1983) (by comparison, 1981: $13.9 billion), whereas during the NAFTA negotiations they had already risen to $33.2 billion (1991) (IMF 1988: 283; 1992: 279)

26 See Kondrake 1991: 39ff. Because of the influence of private actors, 'parallel agreements' were negotiated (environment, labour) and ratification of the agreement, originally planned for 1992, was postponed until 1993 by the Bush Administration, which did not want to make NAFTA a topic of the US election campaign of 1992.

27 'NAFTA's tariff provisions protected US exporters from Mexico's decision in 1995 to raise tariffs from 20 to 35 per cent on products...

imported from countries with which Mexico did not have free trade agreements' (US ITC 1997: 31).

28 Statistics for 1990 from World Bank (1992: 223). For GDP comparison: the EC internal market deepened the integration between France ($1190 billion), Germany ($1,488 billion) and the UK ($975 billion); MERCOSUR connected Argentina ($93 billion) and Brazil ($414 billion).

CHAPTER 6   COMPARATIVE CONCLUSIONS, EMPIRICAL AND THEORETICAL RESULTS

1 As defined in section 1.3 as freedom from costs.
2 There were no common regional institutions in the case of NAFTA and MERCOSUR. In Europe, the Commission's initiatives to complete the single market found support only after the governments' preferences had shifted (see section 3.5). *After* national governments had developed a preference for a liberal single market, the European Commission was essentially able to influence the structure and implementation of the co-operation (for example, through directives and the Checchini Report).
3 Global markets are not identical with transnational actors. The latter can be of a non-economic nature (Greenpeace) and are considered transnational if they cross only *one* border. Global markets (and transnational actors in this sense) are marked by interest in economic profit as well as potential global expansion. Actors on global markets are always also transnational.

REFERENCES

PRIMARY SOURCES

Albert, Michel and Ball, James 1983: *Wege für einen dauerhaften Aufschwung der Europäischen Wirtschaft in den achtziger Jahren*. Report to the European Parliament, Brussels, 31 Aug.

Almeida, Paulo Roberto de 1994: O Brasil e o MERCOSUL em face do NAFTA. *Boletim de Integração Latino-Americana, Ministério das Relações Exteriores*, 13: 15–23. Article of the Brazilian diplomat in a publication of the Foreign Ministry, Itamaraty.

American Foreign Service Association 1991: The United States and Mexico: Converging Destinies. A Conference in the Department of State, Washington, 4–5 Apr.

Aspe Armella, Pedro 1988: Mexico: Growth with Structural Change in the Presence of External Shocks. In Thornton F. Bradshaw et al. (eds), *America's New Competitors: The Challenge of the Newly Industrializing Countries*, Cambridge, Mass.: Ballinger, 31–45. Article of the Mexican Finance Minister.

Aspe Armella, Pedro 1990: New Ideas for Progress: From Debt to Renewed Growth. In Inter-American Development Bank and *International Herald Tribune* (eds), *Latin America: How New Administrations Will Meet the Challenges*, London and Washington, 6–10. Speech of the Mexican Finance Minister.

Azambuja, Marcos Castrioto de 1995: Author's interview with the former Secretary General of the Brazilian Foreign Ministry, Itamaraty, negotiation leader of MERCOSUR and Brazilian ambassador to Argentina, Buenos Aires, 22 Mar.

Bacha, Edmar L. 1988: Brazilian-Based Reflections: Debt, Stabilization, and Growth. In Thornton F. Bradshaw et al. (eds), *America's New Competitors: The Challenge of the Newly Industrializing Countries*, Cambridge, Mass.: Ballinger, 19–29. Article of the President of the Brazilian Central Bank.

Banco de México 1992: *The Mexican Economy 1992*. Mexico.

BDI 1987: Bundesverband der Deutschen Industrie (Federal Association of German Industry), *Memorandum zur Europapolitik*. Cologne, Nov.

BID 1992: Banco Interamericano de Desarrollo (Inter-American Development Bank), *Progreso Economico y Social en America Latina. Informe 1992*. Washington.

Breit, Ernst 1987: Soziale Errungenschaften müssen erhalten bleiben. In *Handelsblatt*, Themenausgabe: 'Den Binnenmarkt vollenden – Den Weltmarkt stärken', no. 251, 31 Dec.: 12. Article of the President of the DGB.

Bush, George 1992: Statement by the President, Office of the Press Secretary, The White House, Washington, 12 Aug.

Campbell, Jorge 1994: Un polo de atracción de inversiones. *La Nación*, 6 Dec.: 12. Article by the head of the Department for International Economic Relations in the Argentinian Foreign Ministry.

Cardenas, Cuauhtémoc 1990: Misunderstanding Mexico. *Foreign Policy*, 78 (Spring): 113–30. Article by the Mexican opposition leader (PRD).

Casar, José 1992: Author's interview with the Director of ILET, Mexico City, 26 Oct.

CEC 1982: Commission of the European Communities, *Mitteilung der Kommission an den Rat über die Wiederbelebung des europäischen Binnenmarktes* (KOM (82) 735 final), Brussels, 12 Nov.

CEC 1988: Commission of the European Communities, Completing the Internal Market. White Paper from the Commission to the European Council (Milan, 28–9 June 1985) (COM (85) 310 final), Brussels, 14 June 1985. In Bieber et al. 1988: 387–441.

CEC 1994: Commission of the European Communities, Vermerk der Kommission der Europäischen Gemeinschaften (KOM (1993) 188), zum Inhalt des Nordamerikanischen Freihandelsabkommens (NAFTA). *Europa Archiv*, 2: D58–D61.

Checchini, Paolo 1988: *The European Challenge 1992. The Benefits of a Single Market, Official Facts and Figures*. Aldershot: Wildwood House, Commission of the European Communities.

Clinton, Bill 1993: President Bill Clinton Proclaims the North American Free Trade Agreement December 8th 1993. In Jim F. Watts, Fred L. Israel (eds), *Presidential Documents*, New York/London: Routledge 2000, pp. 380–5.

Collor de Mello, Fernando 1991a: Speech of the Brazilian President at the signatory ceremony of the Treaty of Asunción, 26 Mar. 1991. In Menem 1991a: 193–4.

Collor de Mello, Fernando 1991b: Speech of the Brazilian President at the official visit to Washington, 18 June. In *Weekly Compilation of Presidential Documents: Administration of George Bush*, 27: 808–9.

COMISEC, Uruguay 1995: Comisión Sectorial para el Mercosur, El MERCOSUR después de la reunión de Ouro Preto. *Enfoques MERCOSUR*, 1/3 (Feb.): 33–8.

Consejo Nacional de la Publicidad and Gallup Mexico 1992: Mexico is on the Right Track. In US Government Printing Office, *Update on Recent Developments in Mexico*. Hearing before the Subcommittee on Western Hemispheric Affairs of the Committee on Foreign Affairs, House of Representatives, Washington, 16 Oct. 1991: 5–17.

Cortès, Glauco José 1991: Remarks of the Director of the Center for Industry of the Brazilian State of Santa Catarina. In Christina Lamb, South America's Mercosul Trade Zone Leaps Ahead, *Financial Times*, 30 Oct.: 6.

Dekker, Wisse 1985: Europa 1990: Ein Maßnahmen-Katalog. Fortschritte und Fortsetzung. Deutsche Gesellschaft für Auswärtige Politik (DGAP), Bonn, 9 Oct. Speech of the CEO of Philips and Head of the REI.

Delors, Jacques 1996: Author's interview with the former (1985–95) President of the European Commission, CES, Harvard University, Cambridge, Mass., 6 May.

Dresdner Bank 1987: *Wirtschaftsberichte*, 39 / 2.

EEA 1986: *Einheitliche Europäische Akte* (the Single European Act) 1986. In Werner Weidenfeld and Wolfgang Wessels (eds), *Jahrbuch der Europäischen Integration 1985*, Bonn: Europa Union Verlag: 431–52.

Ernst and Young 1994: *MERCOSUR*. Sao Paulo, July.

Europäischer Rat / European Council 1986: Schlußfolgerungen des Vorsitzes des Europäischen Rates über die 33. Tagung des Europäischen Rates in Den Haag am 26. und 27. Juni 1986. In *Europa Archiv*, 41 / 17 (10 Sept.): D485–D488.

European Parliament Liberal and Democratic Group Seminar 1984: *The Internal Market*. Brussels, 6–7 Nov.

Flecha de Lima, Paulo Tarso 1994: A importância de ser um global trader. *Carta do Mercosul, ADEBIM*, 6 (Feb.): 4. Article of the Brazilian ambassador to the USA.

Geißler, Heiner 1987: Bonn läuft Gefahr, sich zu isolieren. *Handelsblatt*, 7 July: 3. Remarks of the Secretary General of the German CDU.

Governments of Canada, the United Mexican States and the United States of America 1992: *Description of the Proposed North American Free Trade Agreement*, Washington.

Guadagni, Alieto Aldo 1993: Argentina: Integración en el Mercosur e Inserción en el mundo. In Centro de Economia Internacional (ed.), *Estudos Argentinos para la Integración del MERCOSUR*, Argentinian Foreign Ministry, Buenos Aires, 22–33. Article of the Argentinian ambassador to Brazil (1993) and Argentinian Minister for Industry and Trade (1997).

Hills, Carla A. 1992: Statement by the USTR, Ambassador Carla A. Hills, Washington, 12 Aug.

Howe, Geoffrey 1985: Die Gemeinschaft muß Europas Wettbewerbsfähigkeit stärken. In Britische Botschaft (ed.), *Britische Dokumentation*, D10, 31 May: 3. Speech of the UK Foreign Secretary.

IMF 1988: International Monetary Fund, *Direction of Trade Statistics Yearbook 1988*. Washington.

IMF 1992: International Monetary Fund, *Direction of Trade Statistics Yearbook 1992*. Washington.

IMF 1995a: International Monetary Fund, *Direction of Trade Statistics Yearbook 1995*. Washington.

IMF 1995b: International Monetary Fund, *International Financial Statistics Quarterly*. Washington, June.

IMF 1996a: International Monetary Fund, *Direction of Trade Statistics Quarterly*. Washington, June.

IMF 1996b: International Monetary Fund, *International Financial Statistics Yearbook 1996*. Washington.

IMF 1997: International Monetary Fund, *World Economic Outlook*. Washington, May.

Lambsdorff, Otto Graf 1987: EG-Binnenmarkt rührt an 'Tabus'. *VWD*, 11 Sept.: 4. Remarks of the FDP politician and former German Minister of the Economy.

Madelin, Alain 1988: Creating a Single European Market II: A French View. *World Today*, 44/3 (Mar.): 41–2. Article of the Parti Républicain politician.

Malpass, David R. 1992: Testimony of the Deputy Assistant Secretary for Inter-American Affairs, Department of State, before the Joint Economic Committee, US Congress, Hearing on the Role of Trade in US–Latin American Economic Relations, Washington, 2 Apr.

Marques, Renato L. R. 1994: O MERCOSUL Real. *Boletim de Integração Latino-Americana*, 14 (July–Sept.): 12–15. Article of the Brazilian negotiator of the Treaty of Asunción and Head of the Department for Latin American Integration in the Brazilian Foreign Ministry, Itamaraty.

Menem, Carlos Saúl 1991a: Integración *Americana*. Buenos Aires: Editorial CEYNE.

Menem, Carlos Saúl 1991b: Speech of the Argentinian President at the signatory ceremony of the Treaty of Asunción. In Menem 1991a: 189–92.

Mexico–US Business Committee [1987/8]: *Report of the Advisory Group on Capital Development for Mexico*. Washington, n.d.

Mitterrand, François 1989: Speech of the French President at the European Parliament in Strasbourg. *Frankreich-Info* 27/89, French Embassy, Bonn, 6 Nov.

Monti, Mario 1996: Der Binnenmarkt funktioniert   aber es kann noch besser werden. In Philip Morris Institute for Public Policy Research, *Funktioniert der Binnenmarkt?*, Brussels, Nov.: 54–64. Interview with the then Commissioner for the Single Market.

Morton, Colleen S. 1990: Letter of the Director of the US Council of the Mexico–US Business Committee (Sponsors: Council of the Americas, US Chamber of Commerce) to the US ITC, Washington, 3 Dec.

Murmann, Klaus 1987: Vollbeschäftigung und Strukturwandel sind mit Vollkaskomentalität unvereinbar. *Handelsblatt*, 251, 31 Dec., 13. Article of the President of the German BDA.

Narjes, Karl-Heinz 1987: Kompromißbereitschaft und politischer Mut sind Schlüssel zum Binnenmarkt 1992. *Handelsblatt*, 31 Dec.: 4. Article of the CDU politician and Commissioner at the European Commission.

OECD 1984: Organization for Economic Cooperation and Development, *Wirtschaftsbericht Deutschland*. Paris, June.

OECD 1988: Organization for Economic Cooperation and Development, *Why Economic Policies Change Course: Eleven Case Studies*. Paris.

OECD 1990: Organization for Economic Cooperation and Development, *National Accounts*, ii. *1976–1988*. Paris.

Office of the USTR 1992: *Overview – The NAFTA*. Washington, Aug.

Omnibus Trade and Competitiveness Act of 1988 – Public Law 100–418, in US Government Printing Office, *United States at Large, 100th Congress 1988*, vol. 102, pt 2, Washington 1990: 1121.

Peña, Felix 1992: MERCOSUR y la Inserción Competitiva de Sus Paises Miembros en la Economia Internacional. Paper prepared for the conference 'Latin America's Future in World Trade: Regional vs. World Market Integration', Friedrich-Ebert-Stiftung, Frankfurt / M, 24–5 Mar. Speech of the Argentinian negotiator of the Treaty of Asunción and Adjunct Under-Secretary in the Foreign Ministry.

Perigot, François 1987: Datum 1992: Warten auf das Europa der zweiten Generation. *Handelsblatt*, 31 Dec.: 28. Article of the President of the CNPF.

Presidencia de México 1991 (ed.), *Agenda de México*. Mexico, July. General Directory for Social Communication.

Provencio, Marco 1992: Author's interview with the Director General of the SHCP, Mexico City, 18 Oct. (tape recording).

Puche, Jaime Serra 1992: *Conclusión de la Negociación del Tratado de Libre Comercio entre México V, Canadá y Estados Unidos*. Mexico: SECOFI. Mexican Minister for Industry and Trade.

Republica Argentina, Republica Federativa do Brasil, Republica do Paraguai and Republica Oriental do Uruguai 1994a: Tratado de Assunçao. In Marcos Simao Figueiras, *O MERCOSUL no Contexto Latino-Americano*, Sao Paulo: Editora Atlas, 87–91.

Republica Argentina, Republica Federativa do Brasil, Republica do Paraguai and Republica Oriental do Uruguai 1994b: *Protocolo Adicional ao Tratado de Assunçao sobre a Estrutura Institutcional do Mercosul – Protocolo de Ouro Preto*. Brasilia, Dec.

Republica Argentina, Republica Federativa do Brasil, Republica do Paraguai and Republica Oriental do Uruguai 1994c: Protocolo para a Promoçao e Proteçao Reciproca de Investimentos (Protocolo de Colonia) MERCOSUR. In Marcos Simao Figueiras, *O MERCOSUL no Contexto Latino-Americano*, Sao Paulo: Editora Atlas, 115–21.

Ricupero, Rubens 1992a: Author's interview with the (then) Brazilian ambassador to the USA, Washington, 7 Oct. (tape recording).

Ricupero, Rubens 1992b: Interview with the (then) Brazilian ambassador to the USA. *Revista Brasileira de Comércio Exterior*, 8 (July–Sept.). Taken from a manuscript of the embassy.

Ricupero, Rubens 1992c: Brazil and Latin America in the Context of Political and Economic Transformations Worldwide. Speech at University College Berkeley, Calif., 17 May, mimeo. Brazilian ambassador to the USA.

Rockefeller, David 1992: *A Vision for the Americas*. Washington: Forum of the Americas, Americas Society, 23 Apr. President of the Americas Society.

Rubin, Robert 1997: Statement of the Treasury Secretary on NAFTA Three-Year Anniversary Report. In US Information Agency, *US Information & Texts*, Washington, 16 July: 29.

Salinas de Gortari, Carlos 1989: *El reto de la soberania, Textos de Politica Exterior No. 1*. Mexico: Secretaria de Relaciones Exteriores. Speech of the Mexican President.

Salinas de Gortari, Carlos 1991: 3. Informe del Gobierno, Presidencia de la Republica, Mexico, 1 Nov. Speech of the Mexican President.

Salinas de Gortari, Carlos 1992: Liberalismo social: nuestro camino. *Examen*, 3/35 (Apr.): 19. Speech of the Mexican President on the 63rd Anniversary of the PRI, 4 Mar.

Salinas de Gortari, Carlos 1994: Speech of the Mexican President, 17 Nov. 1993, at the Los Pinos Palace on the occasion of the ratification of the NAFTA Treaty through the US House of Representatives. *Europa-Archiv*, 49/2 (25 Jan.): 61–2.

SECOFI 1992a: Secretaria de Comercio y Formento Industrial, *Tratado de Libre Comercio en América del Norte*. 2 vols. Mexico.

SECOFI 1992b: Secretaría de Comercio y Fomento Industrial, *Tratado de Libre Comercio entre México, Canada y Estatos Unidos*. Mexico.

SHCP 1992: Secretaria de Hacienda y Credito Publico, *El Nuevo Perfil de la Economia Mexicana*. Mexico, Aug.

Serna, Rodolfo Lanús de la 1992: La Internacionalización del Mercado de Capitales Argentino y su Integración en el MERCOSUR. In Asociacion de Bancos de la Republica Argentina (ed.), *El Rediscumrimiento del Mercado. La Nueva America/La Nueva Europa*, Buenos Aires: 119–24.

SRE 1989: Secretaría de Relaciones Exteriores, Objetivos de la acción internacional de México en el Plan Nacional de Desarrollo 1989–1994 (Textos de Politica Exterior, No. 5), Mexico.

Thatcher, Margaret 1993: *The Downing Street Years*. New York: HarperCollins.

Torres, Martin 1992: Author's interview with the Subsecretario de Assuntos Internationales of the PRI, Mexico City, 23 Oct. (tape recording).

UNCTAD 1997a: United Nations Conference on Trade and Development, *World Investment Report 1997*. New York.

UNCTAD 1997b: United Nations Conference on Trade and Development, *Handbook of International Trade and Development Statistics 1995*. New York.

UNCTC 1988: United Nations Center on Transnational Corporations, *Transnational Corporations in World Development: Trends and Prospects*. New York.

US Council of the Mexico–US Business Council 1992: *Talking Points on the Completion of the NAFTA Negotiations*. Washington, 7 Aug.

US Department of State 1991: *Background Notes – Mexico*. Washington, Sept.

US Department of State 1992: *GIST: US–Mexico Relations*, Washington, 31 July.

US Government Printing Office 1990a: *The Mexican Debt Agreement*. Hearing before the Subcommittee on International Development, Finance, Trade, and Monetary Policy, House of Representatives, Washington, 7 Feb.

US Government Printing Office 1990b: *United States at Large, 100th Congress 1988*, vol. 102, pt 2. Washington.

US Government Printing Office 1991: *Trip Report on Congressional Delegation Bentsen*. Committee on Finance, United States Senate, Washington.

US Government Printing Office 1993: *The Impact of the North American Free Trade Agreement on US Jobs and Wages*. Committee on Banking, Housing, and Urban Affairs, US Senate, Washington. Study of the Manufacturing Policy Project.

US ITC 1997: US International Trade Commission, Executive Summary on Effects of NAFTA. In US Information Agency, *US Information and Texts*, Washington, 16 July: 29–34.

USTR 1992: US Trade Representative, *Overview – The NAFTA*. Washington.

Valero, Javier B. 1990: *México – Estados Unidos: seguridad nacional y cooperación* (Textos de Politica Exterior No. 54). Mexico: Secretaria de Relaciones Exteriores. Speech of the Assistant Minister in the Mexican Foreign Ministry, 17 Sept.

Védrine, Hubert 1996: *Les Mondes de François Mitterrand. À l'Élysée 1981–1995*. Paris: Fayard. Memoirs of the former Mitterrand consultant and French Minister of Foreign Affairs (1998).

Vegas, Jorge Hugo Herrera 1994: MERCOSUR. Somos 200 milliones. *Boletín Centro de Economia Internacional*, 4/59 (Aug.): 45–6. Article of the Argentinian Assistant Foreign Minister.

Velazques, Fidel 1992: Author's interview with the (then) President of the Mexican CTM, Mexico City, 20 Oct. (tape recording).

Vogel, Hans-Jochen 1987: Vorteile des Einheitsmarktes nicht kostenlos. *VWD*, 7 July: 11. Remarks of the (then) President of the German SPD.

Walter, Norbert 1996: *Globalisierung – Ende nationaler Wirtschaftspolitik?* (Akademiegespräche im Landtag), Munich, 18 July. Chief Economist of Deutsche Bank AG.

World Bank 1988: *Weltbank: Weltentwicklungsbericht 1988*. Washington.
World Bank 1991: *Trends in Developing Countries*. Washington.
World Bank 1992: *World Development Report 1992*. New York: Oxford University Press.
World Bank 1995: *FDI News*, 1 (Dec.): 1 (taken from: http:// www.worldbank.org.).
World Bank 1996: *World Development Report 1996*. New York: Oxford University Press.
WTO 1995: World Trade Organization, *International Trade: Trends and Statistics*. Geneva.
Young, Lord 1988: Creating a Single European Market I: A British View. *World Today*, 44/3 (Mar.): 38–40. Article of the UK Minister for Industry and Trade.
Zoellick, Robert B. 1992: The North American FTA: The New World Order Takes Shape in the Western Hemisphere, conference of the Columbia Institute. In *Dispatch*, US Department of State, 3/15: 1–6. Speech of the Undersecretary for Economic Affairs of the State Department.

SECONDARY SOURCES

Altvater, Elmar 1994: Operationsfeld Weltmarkt oder: Vom souveränen Nationalstaat zum nationalen Wettbewerbsstaat. *Prokla*, 24/4: 517–47.
Altvater, Elmar and Mahnkopf, Birgit 1996: *Grenzen der Globalisierung. Ökonomie, Ökologie und Politik in der Weltgesellschaft*. Münster: Westfälisches Dampfboot.
Anderson, Jeffrey J. 1995: The State of the (European) Union: From the Single Market to Maastricht, from Singular Events to General Theories. *World Politics*, 47/3: 441–65.
Baer, M. Delal 1991: North American Free Trade. *Foreign Affairs*, 70/4: 95–112.
Baer, M. Delal 1997: Misreading Mexico. *Foreign Policy*, 108 (Fall): 138–50.
Bagley, Bruce 1988: Interdependence and US Policy toward Mexico in the 1980s. In Riordan Roett (ed.), *Mexico and the United States. Managing the Relationship*, Boulder, Colo.: Westview Press, pp. 223–41.
Bairoch, Paul 1996: Globalization. Myths and Realities. One Century of External Trade and Foreign Investment. In Boyer and Drache 1996, pp. 173–92.
Ball, James 1985: Demand Management and Economic Recovery: The United Kingdom Case. *Quarterly Review (National Westminster Bank)* (Aug.): 2–17.
Bandeira, Luiz A. M. 1989: *Brasil – Estados Unidos. A Rivalidade Emergente (1950–1988)*. Rio de Janeiro: Civilização Brasileira.

Baracho, José A. de Oliveira 1989–90: A Constituiçao de 1988 e a Nova Regulamentaçao do Capital Estrangeiro. *Revista Brasileira de Estudos Politicos*, 69–70 (July–Jan.): 105–18.

Barbosa, Rubens Antonio and César, Luis Fernando Panelli 1994: A Integraçao Sub-Regional, Regional e Hemisphérica: O Esforço Brasileiro. In Gélson Fonseca and Sérgio Nabuco de Castro (eds), *Themas de Politica Externa Brasileira II, Sao Paulo: Paz e Terra, pp. 285–304.*

Beck, Ulrich 1997: *Was ist Globalisierung? Irrtümer des Globalismus – Antworten auf Globalisierung.* Frankfurt / M: Suhrkamp.

Bellers, Jürgen and Häckel, Erwin 1990: Theorien internationaler Integration und internationaler Organisationen. In Rittberger 1990, pp. 286–310.

Berger, Suzanne and Dore, Ronald (eds) 1996: *National Diversity and Global Capitalism.* Ithaca, NY: Cornell University Press.

Bergsten, C. Fred 1997: American Politics, Global Trade. *The Economist*, 27 Sept.: 23–8.

Bernard, Mitchell 1994: Post-Fordism, Transnational Production, and the Changing Global Political Economy. In Stubbs and Underhill 1994, pp. 216–29.

Betz, Joachim 1983: Verschuldungskrise der Dritten Welt? In *Jahrbuch Dritte Welt 1983*, Munich: Beck, pp. 30–44.

Bieber, Roland, Dehousse, Renaud, Pinder, John and Weiler, Joseph H. H. (eds) 1988: *1992: One European Market? A Critical Analysis of the Commission's Internal Market Strategy*, Baden-Baden: Nomos.

Bierling, Stephan G. 1992: Zur Lage der US-Wirtschaft. Bestandsaufnahme und Perspektiven am Ende der ersten Amtszeit von George Bush. *Aus Politik und Zeitgeschichte*, B44 23 Oct.: 35–42.

Bierling, Stephan G. 1995: Das Vermächnis der Reaganomics. In Uwe Andersen et al. (eds): *Politik und Wirtschaft am Ende des 20. Jahrhunderts. Festschrift für Dieter Grosser*, Opladen: Leske & Budrich, pp. 119–33.

Biersteker, Thomas J. 1990: Reducing the Role of the State in the Economy: A Conceptual Exploration of IMF and World Bank Prescriptions. *International Studies Quarterly* 34 / 4 (Dec.): 477–92.

Biersteker, Thomas J. 1992: The 'Triumph' of Neoclassical Economics in the Developing World: Policy Convergence and Bases of Governance in the International Economic Order. In James Rosenau and Ernst-Otto Czempiel (eds), *Governance without Government: Order and Change in World Politics*, Cambridge: Cambridge University Press, pp. 102–31.

Bouzas, Roberto 1991: *Beyond Stabilization and Reform: The Argentine Economy in the 1990s* (Documentos e Informes de Investigación, No. 122). Buenos Aires: FLACSO.

Bouzas, Roberto 1995: *Mercosur and Preferential Trade Liberalization in South America. Record Issues, and Prospects* (Documentos e Informes de Investigación. No. 176). Buenos Aires: FLACSO.

Boyer, Robert and Drache, Daniel (eds) 1996: *States against Markets: The Limits of Globalization*. New York: Routledge.

Bressand, Albert 1990: Beyond Interdependence: 1992 as a Global Challenge. *International Affairs*, 66 / 1: 47–65.

Briesemeister, Dietrich, Kohlhepp, Gerd, Mertin, Ray-Gude, Sangmeister, Hartmunt and Schrader, Achim (eds) 1994: *Brasilien heute. Politik, Wirtschaft und Kultur*. Frankfurt / M: Vervuert.

Brock, Lothar and Albert, Mathias 1995: Entgrenzung der Staatenwelt. Zur Analyse weltgesellschaftlicher Entwicklungstendenzen. *Zeitschrift für Internationale Beziehungen*, 2 / 2: 259–85.

Brookings Institution, IAD and ODC (eds) 1992: *The State of Latin American Finance*. Washington.

Buria, Ariel 1990: Evolucion y la Estrategia de la Deuda. In Blanca Torres (ed.), *Interdependencia. Un Enfoque util para el Analisis de las Relaciones México–Estados Unidos?*, Mexico: El Colegio de México, Centro de Estudios Internacionales, pp. 163–75.

Busch, Marc L. and Milner, Helen V. 1994: The Future of the International Trading System: International Firms, Regionalism, and Domestic Politics. In Stubbs and Underhill 1994, pp. 259–76.

Cable, Vincent 1995: The Diminished Nation-State: A Study in the Loss of Economic Power. *Daedalus*, 124: 23–53.

Calcagnotto, Gilberto 1987: Brasiliens Antworten auf die Krise (1982–1985). *Lateinamerika. Analysen-Daten-Dokumentation*, 4: 63–73.

Cameron, David R. 1992: The 1992 Initiative: Causes and Consequences. In Alberta Sbragia (ed.), *Euro-Politics: Institutions and Policymaking in the 'New' European Community*, Washington: Brookings Institution, pp. 23–74.

Cameron, David R. 1995: Transnational Relations and the Development of the European Economic and Monetary Union. In Risse-Kappen 1995, pp. 37–78.

Carnoy, Martin 1993: Multinationals in a Changing World Economy: Whither the Nation-State? In Martin Carnoy, Manuel Castells, Stephen S. Cohen and Fernando Henrique Cardoso, *The New Global Economy in the Information Age*, University Park, Pa.: Pennsylvania State University Press, pp. 45–96.

Castañeda, Jorge G. 1993: Can NAFTA Change Mexico? *Foreign Affairs*, 72 / 4: 66–80.

Clement, Rainer 1988: Liberalization of the Internal Market: Efficiency Advantages and Requirements. *Intereconomics*, 23 / 5: 228–32.

Cline, William 1984: *International Debt: Systemic Risks and Policy Response*. Washington: Institute for International Economics, Cambridge, Mass.: MIT Press.

Cohen, Benjamin J. 1996: Phoenix Risen. The Resurrection of Global Finance. *World Politics*, 48 / 2 (Jan.): 268–96.

214 REFERENCES

Cohen, Stephen S. 1991: Statement and Testimony. In US Government Printing Office, *Globalization of Manufacturing: Implications for U.S. Competitiveness*. Hearing before the Subcommittee on Technology and Competitiveness, US House of Representatives, Washington, 3 Oct., pp. 74–86.

Cornett, Linda and Caporaso, James A. 1992: 'And Still it Moves!' State Interests and Social Forces in the European Community. In James Rosenau and Ernst-Otto Czempiel (eds), *Governance without Government: Order and Change in World Politics*, Cambridge: Cambridge University Press, pp. 219–49.

COHA 1992 Council on Hemispheric Affairs, How important is the Latino vote? *Washington Report on the Hemisphere*, 12/22, 29 Sept.: 5.

Cristini, Marcela and Balzarotti, Nora 1993: *El Arancel Externo Commun del MERCOSUR: Los Conflictos* (Fundación de Investigaciones Económicas Latinoamericanas no. 36). Buenos Aires.

Czempiel, Ernst-Otto 1991: Weltpolitik im Umbruch. Das internationale System nach dem Ende des Ost-West-Konflikts, München: Beck.

de la Balze, Felipe 1995: *Remaking the Argentine Economy* 'A Council on Foreign Relations Book'. New York: Council of Foreign Relations Press.

de Melo, Jaime and Panagariya, Arvind 1995: (eds), *New Dimensions in Regional Integration*. Cambridge: Cambridge University Press.

Deubner, Christian 1984: Change and Internationalization in Industry: Toward a Sectoral Interpretation of West German Politics. *International Organization*, 38/3: 501–35.

Deubner, Christian 1986: Mitterrands Reformpolitik in Westeuropa. Die Relevanz der 'contrainte extérieure', Stiftung Wissenschaft und Politik S 335, Ebenhausen, Dec.

Deubner, Christian 1989: Frankreichs Europapolitik und der europäische Binnenmarkt. In Deutsch-Französisches Institut (ed.), *Frankreich Jahrbuch 1989*, Opladen: Leske & Budrich, pp. 81–94.

Devlin, Robert 1996: In Defense of Mercosur. In *The IDB*, Washington, Dec.: 3.

Dinsmoor, James 1990: *Brazil: Responses to the Debt Crisis. Impact on Savings, Investment, and Growth*. IDB, Washington: Johns Hopkins University Press.

Dombrowski, Peter 1996: *Policy Responses to the Globalization of American Banking*. Pittsburgh: Pittsburgh University Press.

Doran, Charles F. 1995: Building a North American Community. *Current History*, 94/590: 97–101.

Dreher, Sabine 1996: Globalisierung ist nicht *nur* Schicksal. Zur Erweiterung eines Koordinatensystems. *Berliner Debatte INITIAL*, 5: 55–67.

Driscoll de Alvarado, Barbara and Gambrill, Monica C. (eds) 1992: *El Tratado de Libre Comercio: Entre el Viejo y el Nuevo Orden*. Mexico: UNAM.

Dunning, John H. 1990: The Globalization of Firms and the Competitiveness of Countries. In John H. Dunning, Bruce Kogut and Magnus Blomstrom (eds), *Globalization of Firms and the Competitiveness of Nations*, Lund: Lund University Press, pp. 9–58.

Efinger, Manfred, Rittberger, Volker, Wolf, Klaus and Zürn, Michael 1990: Internationale Regime und internationale Politik. In Rittberger 1990, pp. 263–85.

Epstein, Gerald 1996: International Capital Mobility and the Scope for National Economic Management. In Boyer and Drache 1996, pp. 211–24.

Escobar, Gabriel 1996: S. American Trade Bloc Expands and Prospers. *Washington Post*, 3 July.

Evans, Peter B., Jacobson, Harold K. and Putnam, Ronald D. (eds) 1993: *Double-Edged Diplomacy: International Bargaining and Domestic Politics*. Berkeley and Los Angeles: University of California Press.

Fawcett, Louise and Hurrell, Andrew (eds) 1995: *Regionalism in World Politics. Regional Organization and International Order*. New York: Oxford University Press.

Feldstein, Martin and Feldstein, Kathleen 1992: Mexico's Maestro. *Christian Science Monitor Monthly* (July): 43–9.

Figueiras, Marcos Simao 1994: *O MERCOSUL no Contexto Latino-Americano*. Sao Paulo: Editora Atlas.

Fligstein, Neil 1993: The Cultural Construction of Political Action: The Case of the European Community's 1992 Single Market Program, Center for European Studies, Harvard University, WPS 47, Cambridge, Mass.

Frankl, Thomas 1991: *Amerikanische IWF-Politik: Die Reagan-Administration*. Frankfurt/M: Lang.

Frieden, Jeffry A. and Rogowski, Ronald 1996: The Impact of the International Economy on National Policy: An Analytical Overview. In Keohane and Milner 1996, pp. 25–47.

Fritz, Barbara 1996: Die Standortdebatte in Brasilien und der Theorienstreit um den Wechselkursanker. *Lateinamerika. Analysen-Daten-Dokumentation*, 13/32: 84–100.

Fröhlich, Hans-Peter 1986: Die französische Wirtschaftspolitik unter Präsident Mitterrand aus europäischer Perspektive. *Europa-Archiv*, 3: 79–88.

Fuentes, Juan Alberto 1994: Open Regionalism and Economic Integration. *CEPAL Review*, 53: 81–9.

Gamble, Andrew 1988: *The Free Economy and the Strong State: The Politics of Thatcherism*. London: Duke University Press.

Garrett, Geoffrey and Weingast, Barry R. 1993: Ideas, Interests, and Institutions: Constructing the European Community's Internal Market: In Judith Goldstein and Robert O. Keohane (eds), *Ideas and Foreign Policy: Beliefs, Institutions, and Political Change*, Ithaca, NY: Cornell University Press, pp. 173–206.

Gehring, Thomas 1994: Der Beitrag von Institutionen zur Förderung der internationalen Zusammenarbeit. Lehren aus der institutionellen Struktur der Europäischen Gemeinschaft. *Zeitschrift für Internationale Beziehungen*, 1/2: 211–42.

Gereffi, Gary 1995: Global Production Systems and Third World Development. In Barbara Stallings (ed.), *Global Change, Regional Response: The New International Context of Development*, Cambridge: Cambridge University Press, pp. 100–42.

Germann, Harald, Rürup, Bert and Setzer, Martin 1996: Globalisierung der Wirtschaft: Begriff, Bereiche, Indikatoren. In Ulrich Steger (ed.), *Globalisierung der Wirtschaft – Konsequenzen für Arbeit, Technik und Umwelt*, Berlin: Springer, pp. 18–55.

Giersch, Herbert, Paqué, Karl-Heinz and Schmieding, Holger 1992: *The Fading Miracle: Four Decades of Market Economy in Germany*. Cambridge: Cambridge University Press.

Gilpin, Robert 1987: *The Political Economy of International Relations*. Princeton: Princeton University Press.

Goodman, John B. 1989: Monetary Politics in France, Italy, and Germany: 1973–85. In Paolo Guerrieri and Pier Carlo Padoan (eds), *The Political Economy of European Integration: States, Markets, and Institutions*, New York: Harvester Wheatsheaf, pp. 171–201.

Gourevitch, Peter 1987: *Politics in Hard Times: Comparative Responses to International Economic Crises*. Ithaca, NY: Cornell University Press.

Grieco, Joseph M. 1994: Variation in Regional Economic Institutions in Western Europe, East Asia, and the Americas: Magnitude and Sources. Discussion Paper P 94 – 006 Wissenschaftszentrum WZB, Berlin.

Haas, Ernst B. 1958: *The Uniting of Europe*. Stanford, Calif.: Stevens.

Haas, Ernst B. 1975: *The Obsolescence of Regional Integration Theory* (IIS/UC Berkeley Research Series No. 25). Berkeley, Calif.

Haggard, Stephan 1995: *Developing Nations and the Politics of Global Integration*. Washington: Brookings Institution.

Haldenwang, Christian v. 1995: Erfolge und Mißerfolge dezentralisierender Anpassungstrategien in Lateinamerika: Argentinien und Kolumbien. *Politische Vierteljahresschrift*, 36/4: 681–705.

Hall, Peter A. 1987: The Evolution of Economic Policy under Mitterrand. In George Ross, Stanley Hoffmann, and Sylvia Malzacher (eds), *The Mitterrand Experiment: Continuity and Change in Modern France*, New York: Oxford University Press, pp. 54–72.

Hall, Peter A. 1993: Policy Paradigms, Social Learning, and the State: The Case of Economic Policymaking in Britain. *Comparative Politics* 25/3 (Apr.): 275–96.

Helleiner, Eric 1994: *States and the Reemergence of Global Finance: From Bretton Woods to the 1990s*. Ithaca, NY: Cornell University Press.

Helleiner, Eric 1996: Post-Globalization: Is the Financial Liberalization Trend Likely to be Reversed? In Boyer and Drache 1996, pp. 193–210.

Herrmann, Anneliese, Ochel, Wolfgang and Wegner, Manfred 1990: *Bundesrepublik und Binnenmarkt '92. Perspektiven für Wirtschaft und Wirtschaftspolitik*. Berlin: Duncker and Humblot.

Herz, Dietmar 1989: Anmerkungen zur Literatur über den Verfall amerikanischer Macht. *Neue Politische Literatur*, 34/1: 41–57.

Higashi, Chikara and Lauter, G. Peter 1992: *The Internationalization of the Japanese Economy*. 2nd edn. Boston: Kluwer Academic Publishers.

Hinze, Jörg 1989: Voraussichtliche Auswirkungen des EG-Binnenmarktes für den Standort Bundesrepublik. In Otto G. Mayer, Hans-Eckart Scharrer and Hans-Jürgen Schmahl (eds), *Der Europäische Binnenmarkt. Perspektiven und Probleme*, Hamburg: Hamburgisches Welt-Wirtschafts-Archiv, pp. 57–76.

Hirschmann, Albert O. 1970: *Exit, Voice, and Loyalty*. Cambridge, Mass.: Harvard University Press.

Hirschmann, Albert O. 1978: Exit, Voice, and the State. *World Politics*, 31/1 (Oct.): 90–107.

Hirst, Monica 1989: *El Programa de Integración y Cooperación Argentina-Brasil. Los Nuevos Horizontes de Vinculación Economica y Complementación Industrial* (Documents e Informes de Investigación, no. 81). Buenos Aires: FLACSO.

Hirst, Mônica 1993a: *La Dimensión Politica del MERCOSUR: Especificidades Nacionales, Aspectos Institucionales y Actores Sociales* (Documentos e Informes de Investigación, no. 148). Buenos Aires: FLACSO: 27–54.

Hirst, Monica 1993b: *Las Relaciones de América Latina en os Años '90: Nuevos Desafios y Viejos Dilemas* (Documentos e Informes de Investigación, No. 148). Buenos Aires: FLACSO: 1–26.

Hirst, Monica, Russell, Roberto and Segre, Magdalena 1989: *Las Politicas Exteriores de Argentina y Brasil a Fines de la Primera Etapa de Transicion* (Documentos e Informes de Investigación, no. 73. Buenos Aires FLACSO, Feb.

Hirst, Paul and Thompson, Grahame 1996: *Globalization in Question: The International Economy and the Possibilities of Governance*. Cambridge: Polity.

Hoffmann, Lutz 1994–5: Der Standort Deutschland im Vergleich. In Erhard Kantzenbach and Otto G. Mayer (eds), *Deutschland im internationalen Standortwettbewerb*, Baden-Baden: Nomos, pp. 47–76.

Hoffmann, Stanley 1966: Ostinate or Obsolete: The Fate of the Nation-State and the Case of Western Europe. *Daedalus*, 95: 865–85.

Hornbeck, J. F. 1995: United States-Mexico Economic Relations: Has NAFTA Made a Difference? Congressional Research Service CRS, Report for Congress, Washington, 15 Mar.

Hufbauer, Gary and Schott, Jeffrey 1992: *North American Free Trade: Issues and Recommendations*. Washington: Institute for International Economics.

Hufy, Marc 1996: Argentina: The Great Opening Up. In Gordon Mace and Jean-Philippe Thérien (eds), *Foreign Policy and Regionalism in the Americas*, Boulder, Colo.: L. Rienner, pp. 159–79

Inter-American Dialogue 1993: *Convergence and Community: The Americas in 1993*. Washington.

IRELA 1991: Instituto de Relaciones Europeo-Latinoamericanas, Towards a North American Trade Bloc? The NAFTA, Latin America and Europe, IRELA-Dossier no. 35, Madrid, Dec.

Jachtenfuchs, Markus and Kohler-Koch, Beate 1996a: Einleitung: Regieren im Mehrebenensystem. In Jachtenfuchs and Kohler-Koch 1996b, pp. 15–44.

Jachtenfuchs, Markus and Kohler-Koch, Beate (eds) 1996b: *Europäische Integration*. Opladen: Leske and Budrich.

Jacquemin, Alexis and Sapir, André (eds) 1989: *The European Internal Market: Trade and Competition*. Oxford University Press.

Jacquemin, Alexis and Sapir, André 1991: The Internal and External Opening-Up of the Single Community Market: Efficiency Gains, Adjustment Costs and New Community Instruments. *International Spectator*, 26/3: 29–48.

Jaguaribe, Helio 1991: contribution to 'Beyond Debt and Dictators'. A Panel of Latin American Experts foresees a Decade of Painful Economic and Political Problems for the Region's New Democracies.... *TIME*, 138/43 (28 Oct.): 17.

Julius, DeAnne 1990: *Global Companies and Public Policy: The Growing Challenge of Foreign Direct Investment* (Chatham House Paper RIIA). London: Pinter.

Junne, Gerd 1994: Multinational Enterprises as Actors. In Walter Carlsnaes and Steven Smith (eds), *European Foreign Policy*, London: Sage, pp. 84–102.

Junne, Gerd 1996: Integration unter den Bedingungen von Globalisierung und Lokalisierung. In Jachtenfuchs and Kohler-Koch 1996b, pp. 513–30.

Kahler, Miles 1995: *International Institutions and the Political Economy of Integration*. Washington: Brookings Institution.

Kaiser, Karl 1969: Transnationale Politik. Zu einer Theorie der multinationalen Politik. In Ernst-Otto Czempiel (ed.), *Die anachronistische Souveränität. Zum Problem des Verhältnisses von Innen- und Außenpolitik* (PVS Sonderheft 1), Cologne: Westdeutscher Verlag, pp. 80–109.

Katzenstein, Peter 1995: contribution to 'The Role of Theory in Comparative Politics' – A Symposium. *World Politics*, 48/1: 10–15.

Kaufman, Robert R. 1989: Economic Orthodoxy and Political Change in Mexico: The Stabilization and Ajustment Policies of the de la Madrid Administration: In Barbara Stallings and Robert Kaufman (eds), *Debt and Democracy in Latin America*, Boulder, Colo.: Westview Press, pp. 109–26.

Kaufman, Robert R. 1990: Stabilization and Adjustment in Argentina, Brazil, and Mexico. In Loan M. Nelson (ed.), *Economic Crisis and Policy Choice: The Politics of Adjustment in the Third World*, Princeton: Princeton University Press, 63–111.

Keohane, Robert O. (ed.) 1986: *Neorealism and its Critics*. New York: Columbia University Press.

Keohane, Robert O. 1989: *International Institutions and State Power: Essays in International Relations Theory*. Boulder, Colo.: Westview Press.

Keohane, Robert O. and Hoffmann, Stanley 1990: Conclusions: Community Politics and Institutional Change. In William Wallace (ed.), *The Dynamics of European Integration*, London: Pinter, pp. 276–300.

Keohane, Robert O. and Hoffmann, Stanley 1991: Institutional Change in Europe in the 1980s. In Robert O. Keohane and Stanley Hoffmann (eds), *The New European Community*, Boulder, Colo.: Westview Press, pp. 1–39.

Keohane, Robert O. and Milner, Helen V. (eds) 1996: *Internationalization and Domestic Politics*. Cambridge: Cambridge University Press.

Keohane, Robert O. and Nye, Joseph S. 1972: *Transnational Relations and World Politics*. Cambridge, Mass.: Harvard University Press.

Keohane, Robert O. and Nye, Joseph S. 1977: *Power and Interdependence: World Politics in Transition*. Boston: Little, Brown.

Klodt, Henning, Schmidt, Klaus-Dieter et al. 1989: *Weltwirtschaftlicher Strukturwandel und Standortwettbewerb. Die deutsche Wirtschaft auf dem Prüfstand*. Tübingen: J. C. B. Mohr.

Kohler-Koch, Beate 1990: Interdependenz. In Rittberger 1990, pp. 110–29.

Kohler-Koch, Beate 1996: Politische Unverträglichkeiten von Globalisierung. In Ulrich Steger (ed.), *Globalisierung der Wirtschaft – Konsequenzen für Arbeit, Technik und Umwelt*, Berlin: Springer, pp. 83–114.

Kondrake, Morton 1991: Mexico and the Politics of Free Trade. *National Interest*, 25, (Fall): 36–43.

Körner, Peter, Maass, Gero, Siebold, Thomas and Tetzlaff, Rainer (eds) 1984: *Im Teufelskreis der Verschuldung. Der Internationale Währungsfonds und die Dritte Welt*. Hamburg: Julius.

Kratochwil, Friedrich 1993: Norms versus Numbers: Multilateralism and the Rationalist and Reflexivist Approach to Institutions – a Unilateral Plea for Communicative Rationality. In John G. Ruggie (ed.), *Multilateralism Matters: The Theory and Praxis of an Institutional Form*, New York: Columbia University Press, pp. 443–74.

Kreile, Michael (ed.) 1992: *Die Integration Europas* (PVS Sonderheft 23). Opladen: Westdeutscher Verlag.

Krugman, Paul 1993: The Uncomfortable Truth about NAFTA: It's Foreign Policy, Stupid. *Foreign Affairs*, 72/5: 13–19.

Krugman, Paul 1994: *Peddling Prosperity: Economic Sense and Nonsense in the Age of Diminished Expectations*. New York: Norton.

Krupp, Hans-Jürgen 1997: Die Folgen der Globalisierung für die Geld- und Währungspolitik, paper presented at the conference 'Die Globalisierung der Märkte', 18 Jan. 1997, Politische Akademie Tutzing, Hamburg.

Lequesne, Christian 1988: Die Europapolitik in den Mitgliedstaaten der EG: Frankreich. In Werner Weidenfeld and Wolfgang Wessels (eds), *Jahrbuch der Europäischen Integration 1987/1988*, Bonn: Europa Union Verlag, pp. 360–9.

Lerda, Juan Carlos 1996: Globalization and Loss of Autonomy by the Fiscal, Banking and Monetary Authorities. *CEPAL Review*, 58 (Apr.): 65–78.

Lima, Maria Regina Soares de 1996: Brazil's Response to the 'New Regionalism'. In Mace and Thérien 1996: 137–58.

Lindberg, Leon and Scheingold, Stuart A. (eds) 1971: *Regional Integration: Theory and Research.*, Cambridge, Mass.: Harvard University Press.

Link, Werner 1997: Zur internationalen Neuordnung – Merkmale und Perspektiven. *Zeitschrift für Politik*, 44/3: 258–77.

Lustig, Nora 1991: *Bordering on Partnership: The US–Mexico Free Trade Agreement.* Washington: Brookings Institution, 25 Feb.

Lustig, Nora 1992: Equity and Growth in Mexico. In Simón Teitel (ed.), *Towards a New Development Strategy for Latin America*, IDB, Washington: Johns Hopkins University Press, pp. 219–58.

Mace, Gordon and Thérien, Jean-Philippe 1996 (eds), *Foreign Policy and Regionalism in the Americas.* Boulder, Colo.: Lynne Rienner.

Machado, Joao Bosco 1995: MERCOSUL. Entra em Operaçao a Uniao Aduaneira Flexivel. *Revista Brasileira de Comércio Exterior* (FUNCEX), 11/42: 19–20.

Malan, Pedro and Bonelli, Regis 1992: The Success of Growth Policies in Brazil. In Simón Teitel (ed.), *Towards a New Development Strategy for Latin America*, IDB, Washington: Johns Hopkins University Press, pp. 47–101.

Manzetti, Luigi 1993–4: The Political Economy of MERCOSUR. *Journal of Interamerican Studies and World Affairs*, 35/4 (Winter): 101–41.

Marsh, David 1995: Explaining 'Thatcherite' Policies: Beyond Uni-dimensional Explanations. *Political Studies*, 43/4: 595–613.

Mearsheimer, John J. 1990: Back to the Future: Instability in Europe after the Cold War. *International Security*, 15/1: 5–56.

Messner, Dirk 1996: Wirtschaftstrategie im Umbruch. Anmerkungen zu den ökonomischen und politischen Determinanten von Wettbewerbsfähigkeit. In Detlef Nolte and Nikolaus Werz (eds), *Argentinien. Politik, Wirtschaft, Kultur und Außenbeziehungen* (Institut für Iberoamerika-Kunde, vol. 42), Frankfurt/M: Vervuert, pp. 149–76.

Meyer, Lorenzo 1992: México-EU: de Fracaso a Virtud. *El Financiero-Zona Abierta*, 1/5 23 Oct.: 1, 8–9.

Milner, Helen V. and Keohane, Robert O. 1996a: Internationalization and Domestic Politics: An Introduction. In Keohane and Milner 1996, pp. 3–24.

Milner, Helen V. and Keohane, Robert O. 1996b: Internationalization and Domestic Politics: A Conclusion. In Keohane and Milner 1996, pp. 243–58.

Mitrany, David 1943 / 1966: *A Working Peace System*. Chicago: Quadrangle Books.

Mols, Manfred 1992: Mexikos Außenpolitik am Beginn der neunziger Jahre. In *Europa Archiv*, 47 / 15–16 (25 Aug.): 453–60.

Mols, Manfred 1993: The Integration Agenda: A Framework for Comparison. In Peter H. Smith (ed.), *The Challenge of Integration: Europe and the Americas*, New Brunswick: Transaction Publishers, pp. 51–75.

Montoro, Franco 1987: Uma Visao Global da Divida Externa da America Latina. ILAM, manuscript, Sao Paulo.

Moravcsik, Andrew 1991: Negotiating the Single European Act: National Interests and Conventional Statecraft in the European Community. *International Organization*, 45 / 1: 651–88); repr. in Robert O. Keohane and Stanley Hoffmann (eds), *The New European Community*, Boulder, Colo.: Westview Press, 1991, pp. 41–84.

Moravcsik, Andrew 1993: Preferences and Power in the European Community: A Liberal-Intergovernmental Approach. *Journal of Common Market Studies*, 31 / 4: 473–524.

Mucchielli, Jean Louis 1991: Strategic Advantages for European Firms. In Beat Bürgenmeier and Jean Louis Mucchielli (eds), *Multinationals and Europe 1992: Strategies for the Future*, London: Routledge, pp. 36–58.

Müller, Anton P. 1991: Zwischen Schuldenerlaß und Staatsbankrott. Brasilien in der permanenten Zahlungskrise. *Aus Politik und Zeitgeschichte*, B 39, 20 Sept.: 29–38.

Muller, Harald 1994: Internationale Beziehungen als kommunikatives Handeln. Zur Kritik der utilitaristischen Handlungstheorien. *Zeitschrift für Internationale Beziehungen*, 1 / 1: 15 44.

Müller, Harald and Risse-Kappen, Thomas 1990: Internationale Umwelt, gesellschaftliches Umfeld und außenpolitischer Prozeß in liberaldemokratischen Industrienationen. In Rittberger 1990, pp. 375–400.

Narr, Wolf-Dieter and Schubert, Alexander 1994: *Weltökonomie. Die Misere der Politik*. Frankfurt am M: Suhrkamp.

Neyer, Jürgen 1995: Globaler Markt und territorialer Staat. Konturen eines wachsenden Antagonismus. *Zeitschrift für Internationale Beziehungen*, 2 / 2: 287–315.

Nicolas, Alrich and Symma, Britta 1992: Der Plan Cavallo in Argentinien: Stabilisierungspolitik mit konvertibler Währung. *Nord-Süd-Aktuell* 6 / 1: 132–45.

Nye, Joseph S. 1971 / 1987: *Peace in Parts: Integration and Conflict in Regional Organization*. Lanham, Md.: UPA.

Nye, Joseph S. 1988: Understanding US Strength. *Foreign Policy*, 72 (Fall): 105–29.

Nye, Joseph S. 1990a: *Bound to Lead: The Changing Nature of American Power*. New York: Basic Books.

Nye, Joseph 1990b: Die Debatte über den hegemonialen Niedergang der USA. *Europa Archiv*, 13–14, 25 July: 421–7.

Ohmae, Kenichi 1995: *The End of the Nation-State: The Rise of Regional Economies*. New York: Free Press.

Ostry, Sylvia and Nelson, Richard N. 1995: *Techno-Nationalism and Techno-Globalism: Conflict and Cooperation*. Washington: Brookings Institution.

Overbeek, Henk 1990: *Global Capitalism and National Decline: The Thatcher Decade in Perspective*. London: Unwin Hyman.

Pastor, Manuel 1994: Mexican Trade Liberalization and NAFTA. *Latin American Research Review*, 29/3: 153–73.

Pauly, Louis W. 1994: Promoting Global Economy: The Normative Role of the International Monetary Fund. In Stubbs and Underhill 1994, pp. 204–15.

Pereira, Lia Valls 1993: O Projeto Mercosul: Uma resposta aos desafios do novo quadro mundial? In Departamento de Estudos Sócio-Econômicos e Políticos da CUT and Instituto Cajamar (eds), *MERCOSUL. Integração na América Latina e Relaçoes com a Comunidade Européia*, Sao Paulo, pp. 11–40.

Petersmann, Ernst-Ulrich 1994: Why do Governments Need the Uruguay Round Agreements, NAFTA and the EEA?. *Aussenwirtschaft*, 49/1: 31–55.

Petrella, Riccardo 1996: Globalization and Internationalization: The Dynamics of the Emerging World Order. In Boyer and Drache 1996, pp. 62–83.

Philip, Butt 1987: Pressure Group Power in the European Community. *Intereconomics*, 22/6 (Nov.–Dec.): 282–9.

Pierson, Paul 1996: The Path to European Integration: A Historical Institutionalist Analysis. *Comparative Political Studies*, 29/2 (Apr.): 123–63.

Pinder, John 1988: Enhancing the Community's Economic and Political Capacity: Some Consequences of Completing the Common Market. In Bieber et al. 1988, pp. 35–54.

Piper, Nikolaus 1998: Der Traum, wählen zu können. Vor vierzig Jahren wurde die Phillips-Kurve erfunden. *Süddeutsche Zeitung*, 3 Jan.: 23.

Poitras, Guy and Robinson, Raymond 1994: The Politics of NAFTA in Mexico. *Journal of Interamerican Studies and World Affairs*, 36/1: 1–35.

Pollan, Wolfgang and Stankovsky, Jan 1993: Lohnkosten, Wettbewerbsfähigkeit und Integration am Beispiel der USA. *Monatberichte* 66/10: 516–20.

Porter, Michael E. 1991: *Nationale Wettbewerbsvorteile. Erfolgreich konkurrieren auf dem Weltmarkt*. Munich: Droemer Knauer.

Porter, Tony 1997: NAFTA, North American Financial Integration and Regulatory Cooperation in Banking and Securities. In Geoffrey R. D. Underhill (ed.), *The New World Order in International Finance*, Houndmills: St Martin's Press, pp. 174–92.

Proff, Heike and Proff, Harald V. 1996: Effects of World Market Oriented Regional Integration on Developing Countries. *Intereconomics*, 31 / 2: 84–94.

Purcell, Susan Kaufman 1992: Mexico's New Economic Vitality. *Current History*, 91 / 562 (Feb.): 54–8.

Ramirez de la O, Rogelio 1989: Economic Outlook of Mexico in the 1990s and Economic Policy. Paper presented to the conference on US–Mexico Industrial Integration, The Woodlands, Texas, 7–10 Dec.

Reding, Andrew 1991: Mexico: The Crumbling of the 'Perfect Dictatorship'. *World Policy Journal*, 8 / 2: 255–84.

Reich, Robert B. 1990: Who Is Us? *Harvard Business Review*, 68 / 1 (Jan.–Feb.): 53–64.

Rieger, Elmar 1995: Politik supranationaler Integration. Die Europäische Gemeinschaft in institutionentheoretischer Perspektive. In Birgitta Nedelmann (ed.), *Politische Institutionen im Wandel*. Opladen: Westdeutscher Verlag, pp. 349–67.

Risse-Kappen, Thomas (ed.) 1995: *Bringing Transnational Relations Back In: Non-State Actors, Domestic Structures and International Institutions*. Cambridge: Cambridge University Press.

Risse-Kappen, Thomas 1996: Exploring the Nature of the Beast: International Relations Theory and Comparative Policy Analysis Meet the European Union. *Journal of Common Market Studies*, 34 / 1: 53–80.

Rittberger, Volker (ed.) 1990: *Theorien der Internationalen Beziehungen. Bestandsaufnahme und Forschungsperspektiven* (PVS 21). Opladen: Westdeutscher Verlag.

Rittberger, Volker (ed.) 1993: *Regime Theory and International Relations*. Oxford: Clarendon Press.

Roett, Riordan 1991: Das Wiedererwachen von Demokratie und Marktwirtschaft in Lateinamerika. *Europa-Archiv*, 1: 7–16.

Rogowski, Ronald 1989: *Commerce and Coalitions: How Trade Affects Domestic Political Alignments*. Princeton: Princeton University Press.

Rojas, Raul 1988: Fünf Jahre Verschuldungskrise. In Elmar Altvater, Kurt Hübner, Jochen Lorentzen, and Raul Rojas (eds), *Die Armut der Nationen*, (2nd edn), Berlin: Rotbuch Verlag, pp. 204–19.

Rosamond, Ben 1995: Mapping the European Condition: The Theory of Integration and the Integration of Theory. *European Journal of International Relations*, 1 / 3: 391–408.

Rosenau, James N. and Durfee, Mary 1995: *Thinking Theory Thoroughly: Coherent Approaches to an Incoherent World*. Boulder, Colo.: Westview Press.

Ruggie, John Gerard 1982: International Regimes, Transactions, and Change: Embedded Liberalism in the Postwar Economic Order. *International Organization*, 36 / 2: 379–415.

Ruggie, John Gerard 1993: Territoriality and Beyond: Problematizing Modernity in International Relations. *International Organization*, 47 / 1: 139–74.

Sandholtz, Wayne and Zysman, John 1989: 1992: Recasting the European Bargain. *World Politics*, 42/1 (Oct.): 95–128.

Sangmeister, Hartmut 1994: Der schwierige Weg in den Weltmarkt: Brasiliens außenwirtschaftliche Beziehungen. In Briesemeister et al. 1994, pp. 318–31.

Scharpf, Fritz W. 1987: *Sozialdemokratische Krisenpolitik in Europa*. Frankfurt am M: Campus.

Scharpf, Fritz W. 1991: Die Handlungsfähigkeit des Staates am Ende des zwanzigsten Jahrhunderts. *Politische Vierteljahresschrift*, 32/4: 621–34.

Scharpf, Fritz W. 1996: Negative and Positive Integration in the Political Economy of European Welfare States. In Gary Marks, Fritz W. Scharpf, Philippe C. Schmitter, and Wolfgang Streeck, *Governance in the European Union*, London: Sage, pp. 15–39.

Schirm, Stefan A. 1990: *Brasilien – Regionalmacht zwischen Autonomie und Dependenz. Außenpolitik, Wirtschaft und Sicherheit im internationalen und lateinamerikanischen Kontext* (Institut für Iberoamerika-Kunde, vol. 32). Münster: LIT-Verlag.

Schirm, Stefan A. 1994a: *Macht und Wandel. Die Beziehungen der USA zu Mexiko und Brasilien. Außenpolitik, Wirtschaft und Sicherheit*. Opladen: Leske and Budrich.

Schirm, Stefan A. 1994b: Argentinien und Brasilien: Von Rivalität zu Kooperation. In Wilfrid von Bredow and Thomas Jäger (eds), *Regionale Großmächte. Das internationale System zwischen Globalisierung und Zersplitterung*, Opladen: Leske & Budrich, pp. 121–35.

Schirm, Stefan A. 1996: Transnational Globalization and Regional Governance: On the Reasons for Regional Cooperation in Europe and the Americas, Center for European Studies, Harvard University, WPS 6.2, Cambridge, Mass.

Schirm, Stefan A. 1997a: *Kooperation in den Amerikas. NAFTA, MERCOSUR und die neue Dynamik regionaler Zusammenarbeit* (Stiftung Wissenschaft und Politik vol. 46). Baden-Baden: Nomos.

Schirm, Stefan A. 1997b: Transnationale Globalisierung und regionale Kooperation. Ein politikökonomischer Ansatz zur Erklärung internationaler Zusammenarbeit in Europa und den Amerikas. *Zeitschrift für Internationale Beziehungen*, 4/1: 69–106.

Schirm, Stefan A. 1997c: Entwicklung durch Freihandel? Zur politischen Ökonomie regionaler Kooperation. In Peter J. Opitz (ed.), *Grundprobleme der Entwicklungsregionen. Der Süden an der Schwelle zum 21. Jahrhundert*, Munich: Beck, pp. 240–58.

Schirm, Stefan A. 1997d: The Political and Economic Impact of NAFTA. *Aussenpolitik – German Foreign Affairs Review* (English edn), 48/1: 68–78.

Schirm, Stefan A. 1998: Europe's Common Foreign and Security Policy: The Politics of Necessity, Viability, and Adequacy. In Carolyn Rhodes (ed.), *The European Union in the World Community*, Boulder, Colo.: Lynne Rienner Publishers, pp. 65–81.

Schirm, Stefan A. 1999a: *Globale Märkte, nationale Politik und regionale Kooperation in Europa und den Amerikas*, Baden-Baden: Nomos.

Schirm, Stefan A. 1999b: Krisen, Interessen und Instrumente. Zur Konzeption der Wirkungen globaler Märkte auf Staaten. *Zeitschrift für Politikwissenschaft*, 9/2: 479–98.

Schmidt, Vivien A. 1995: The New World Order, Incorporated: The Rise of Business and the Decline of the Nation-State. *Daedalus*, 124/2: 75–106.

Schreiber, Kristin and Woolcock, Stephen 1991: Großbritannien, Deutschland und '1992': Grenzen der Deregulierung. *Integration*, 14/1: 21–32.

Schröder, Wolfgang 1988: Die Globalisierung der Finanzmärkte – Folgen für die Geldpolitik. *Wirtschaftsdienst*, 68/7: 378–84.

Schubert, Alexander 1985: *Die internationale Verschuldung. Die Dritte Welt und das transnationale Bankensystem*. Frankfurt am M: Suhrkamp.

Siebert, Horst 1989: The Single European Market – A Schumpeterian Event? Institut für Weltwirtschaft Kiel Discussion Paper 157, Kiel, Nov.

Simon, Gabriela 1988: Argentinien: Das bittere Erbe des 'Süßen Geldes'. In Elmar Altvater, Kurt Hübner, Jochen Lorentzen and Raul Rojas (eds), *Die Armut der Nationen. Handbuch zur Schuldenkrise*, 2nd edn, Berlin: Rotbuchverlag, pp. 155–66.

Singer, Paulo 1987: Lo Crucial del Plano Cruzado. *Nueva Sociedad*, 88 (Mar.–Apr.): 150–65.

Sorensen, Georg 1995: States are not Like Units: Types of State and Forms of Anarchy in the Present International System. Paper prepared for the APSA Meeting Chicago 1995, Aarhus.

Starr, Pamela K. 1997: Government Coalitions and the Viability of Currency Boards: Argentina under the Cavallo Plan. *Journal of Inter-American Studies and World Affairs*, 39/2: 83–133.

Stein, Arthur A. 1990: *Why Nations Cooperate: Circumstance and Choice in International Relations*. Ithaca, NY: Cornell University Press.

Storrs, Larry 1992: *Mexico–US Relations in the Salinas Period (1988–1994): Issues for Congress*. Washington: Congressional Research Service, August.

Strange, Susan 1996: *The Retreat of the State: The Diffusion of Power in the World Economy*. Cambridge: Cambridge University Press.

Streeck, Wolfgang 1996: Public Power beyond the Nation-State: The Case of the European Community. In Boyer and Drache 1996, pp. 299–315.

Stubbs, Richard and Underhill, Geoffrey R. D. (eds) 1994: *Political Economy and the Changing Global Order*. New York: St Martin's Press.

Thiel, Elke 1992: *Die Europäische Gemeinschaft* 4th edn. Munich: Bayrische Landeszentrale für Politische Bildung.

Thierstein, Alain and Langenegger, Thomas 1994: Der Prozess der Internationalisierung: Handlungsspielraum für Regionen? *Aussenwirtschaft*, 49/4: 497–525.

Thoele, Alexander 1996: Com a globalizaçao, apenas as melhores empresas vao sobreviver. *Brasil-Alemanha em Revista*, 4/6 (July) 6–11.

Thompson, Grahame 1992: Economic Autonomy and the Advanced Industrial State. In Anthony McGrew and Paul G. Lewis (eds), *Global Politics: Globalization and the Nation-State*, Cambridge, Mass.: Blackwell, pp. 197–215.

Thurow, Lester 1992: *Head to Head: The Coming Economic Battle among Japan, Europe, and America*. New York: Morrow.

Tsoukalis, Lukas 1992: *The New European Economy: The Politics and Economics of Integration*. 2nd edn. Oxford: Oxford University Press.

University of Texas (1986): *US Trade Policy Research Report: US Trade with Newly Industrializing Countries*. Austin, Tex.

Uterwedde, Henrik 1987: Internationalisierung und politischer Wandel in Frankreich 1974–1986, Stiftung Wissenschaft und Politik S 340, Ebenhausen, June.

Viner, Jakob 1950/1961: *The Customs Union Issue*. New York: Carnegie Endowment for International Peace, 1950 (repr. Washington: Anderson Kramer Associates, 1961).

Volle, Angelika 1989: Großbritannien in der Europäischen Gemeinschaft. Vom zögernden Außenseiter zum widerspenstigen Partner. In Gustav Schmidt (ed.), *Großbritannien und Europa – Großbritannien in Europa. Sicherheitsbelange und Wirtschaftsfragen in der britischen Europapolitik nach dem Zweiten Weltkrieg* (Annual Conference 1988 of the England Studies Association), Bochum: Studienverl. Brockmeyer, pp. 315–46.

Wade, Robert 1996: Globalization and its Limits: Reports of the Death of the National Economy are Greatly Exaggerated. In Berger and Dore 1996, pp. 60–88.

Waldmann, Peter 1985: Argentinien: Ein 'Schwellenland' auf Dauer? In Franz Nuscheler (ed.), *Dritte Welt-Forschung. Entwicklungstheorie und Entwicklungspolitik* (PVS Sonderheft 16), Opladen: Westdeutscher Verlag, pp. 113–34.

Wallace, Helen 1990: Britain and Europe. In Patrick Dunleavy, Andrew Gamble and Gillian Peele (eds), *Developments in British Politics 3*, London: Macmillan, pp. 150–72.

Wallace, William 1994: *Regional Integration: The West European Experience*. Washington: Brookings Institution.

Weidenfeld, Werner and Turek, Jürgen 1993: *Technopoly – Europa im globalen Wettbewerb*: Gütersloh: Verlag Bertelsmann Stiftung.

Weidenfeld, Werner and Wessels, Wolfgang (eds) 1986: *Jahrbuch der Europäischen Integration 1985*. Bonn: Europa Union Verlag.

Weintraub, Sidney 1990: *A Marriage of Convenience: Relations between Mexico and the United States*. New York: Oxford University Press.

Welz, Christian and Engel, Christian 1993: Traditionsbestände politikwissenschaftlicher Integrationstheorien: Die Europäische Gemeinschaft im Spannungsfeld von Integration und Kooperation. In Armin von Bogdandy (ed.), *Die Europäische Option*, Baden-Baden: Nomos, pp. 129–69.

Wendt, Alexander 1994: Collective Identity Formation and the International State. *American Political Science Review*, 88/2 (June): 384–96.

Wessels, Wolfgang 1992: Staat und (westeuropäische) Integration, Die Fusionsthese. In Kreile 1992, pp. 36–61.

Winters, L. Alan 1995: The European Community: A Case of Successful Integration? In De Melo and Panagariya 1995, pp. 202–28.

Wonnacott, Ronald 1995: Canada's Interests and the NAFTA. In Richard S. Belous and Jonathan Lemco (eds), *NAFTA as a Model of Development*, Albany, NY: SUNY Press, pp. 140–4.

Woolcock, Stephen 1991: Großbritannien und der Binnenmarkt. In Michael Kreile (ed.), *Europa 1992 – Konzeptionen, Strategien, Außenwirkungen*, Baden-Baden: Nomos, pp. 57–70.

Wörl, Volker 1994: Die EU wächst in eine globale Verantwortung. *Süddeutsche Zeitung*, 14 June: 21.

Zellentin, Gerda 1992: Der Funktionalismus – eine Strategie gesamteuropäischer Integration? In Kreile 1992, pp. 62–77.

Zibura, Gilbert 1989: Frankreich: Umrisse eines neuen Wachstumsmodells? In *Aus Politik und Zeitgeschichte*, B39 3–13.

Zimmerling, Ruth 1991: *Externe Einflüsse auf die Integration von Staaten. Zur politikwissenschaftlichen Theorie regionaler Zusammenschlüsse*. Freiburg: Alber.

Zürn, Michael 1993: Bringing the Second Image (Back) In. In Rittberger 1993, pp. 282–311.

Zürn, Michael 1995: The Challenge of Globalization and Individualization: A View from Europe. In Hans-Hendrik Holm and Georg Sorensen (eds), *Whose World Order? Uneven Globalization and the End of the Cold War*, Boulder, Colo.: Westview Press, pp. 137–63.

NEWSPAPERS AND MAGAZINES

Agence Europe, Brussels
BBC, Summary of World Broadcasts, London
Business Week, New York
Capital – Das Wirtschaftsmagazin, Frankfurt / Main
CTM Organo de Orientación e Inform. de los Trabajadores, Mexico DF
The Economist, London
El Financiero, Mexico DF
El Pais, Madrid
Euromoney Supplement, London
Examen, Mexico DF
Financial Times, London
Frankfurter Allgemeine Zeitung, Frankfurt / Main
Gazeta Mercantil, Sao Paulo

Handelsblatt, Düsseldorf
La Nación, Buenos Aires
Latin America Regional Report, London
Latin American Weekly Report, London
Neue Züricher Zeitung, Zurich
New York Times, New York
Newsweek, New York
Süddeutsche Zeitung, Munich
TIME, New York
Veja, Sao Paulo
Vereinigter Wirtschaftsdienst (VWD), Eschborn
Washington Post, Washington DC
Wirtschaftswoche, Düsseldorf

INDEX